The Socialist Myth

THE
SOCIALIST
MYTH

Peregrine Worsthorne

WEYBRIGHT AND TALLEY
New York

THE SOCIALIST MYTH

First Published in England, 1971

First American Edition, 1971

Published by Weybright and Talley
750 Third Avenue
New York, New York 10017

LIBRARY OF CONGRESS CATALOG CARD NUMBER: 71-165092

MANUFACTURED IN THE UNITED STATES OF AMERICA

To Claudia

Acknowledgements

I am deeply grateful to the editor of the *Sunday Telegraph* for allowing me to draw on themes which were originally outlined in that newspaper over the years, and in particular for permission to quote from an article that appeared on 11 October 1964.

My thanks are also due to the editor of *Foreign Affairs*, that invaluable American quarterly, in whose pages I first developed some of the ideas in Chapter 5, in my article 'Class and Conflict in British Foreign Policy' (1958) and likewise to the editor of *Encounter* for allowing me to draw upon themes initially put forward in my article 'The New Inequality' (November 1956). I should also like to express particular indebtedness, so far as Chapter 7 is concerned, to Irving Kristol's remarkable article in *Foreign Affairs* 'American Intellectuals and Foreign Policy', which influenced me greatly; as in the earlier parts of my book did that seminal work by S. H. Beer, *Modern British Politics*.

I should like to thank the authors and publishers of the following who have given me permission to quote copyright material: Joseph Schumpeter, *Capitalism, Socialism and Democracy* (Allen & Unwin, 1947); Arthur Schlesinger, *The Politics of Hope* (Eyre & Spottiswoode, 1964); S. H. Beer, *Modern British Politics* (Faber, 1967); I. Kristol, 'American Intellectuals and Foreign Policy' in *Foreign Affairs*, Vol. 45; Daniel Bell, 'Notes on the Post-Industrial Society' in *The Public Interest*, No. 6; and Paul Johnson, 'A Sense of Outrage' in Hugh Thomas (ed.), *Conviction* (MacGibbon & Kee, 1958).

Prologue

Because of the high and widespread hopes that accompanied Labour's rise to power in 1964, the subsequent record of relative failure was all the more disillusioning. Naturally enough people want to know what went wrong, and explanations flow from the printing-presses pointing to this, that or the other critical mistake when the wrong turning is supposed to have been taken. Some would have it that Mr Wilson was mad not to devalue immediately on coming to office; others blame Mr Callaghan's first budget, which frightened the city and business with menacing noises about corporation and capital-gains tax; others again put the blame on the Prime Minister's insistence on retaining forces east of Suez out of loyalty to the socialist ally, Lee Kuan Yew of Singapore, or, as others claim, out of subservience to President Johnson.

Needless to say, there is no shortage of explanations, many of them highly plausible, as to why the Wilson Government did so badly, and I hasten to add that it is not my intention to augment their number; at least, not in their normal form. For I am not at all sure that the Labour Government did do badly, if by doing badly is meant doing worse than might reasonably have been expected. Indeed, what fascinates me about the years 1964–70 is not that the Labour Government did so badly but that it avoided doing very much worse. Any political observer of this period must have become increasingly aware of the handicaps under which a Socialist Government labours; of the very special difficulties that affect Labour Governments in this country—difficulties that give to the phrase 'a Labour Government' almost a new meaning: a group of good men and true condemned by fate to labour in a hopeless cause, Sisyphus-like, for ever pushing a great stone uphill, doomed to make no progress.

To my mind there was something tragic about the Wilson Government which puts it beyond the reach of ordinary political criticism. One is not surprised when a man grossly overburdened stumbles by the wayside; nor does one look for explanations, as if it were interesting to know which particular stone or puddle tripped him up. The interesting question is not why he stumbled and fell, but how he came to be overburdened in the first place. The same is true of this Labour Government. What is it about British politics that so overburdens a Labour Government that one is not surprised at its faintness; not surprised that it should have stumbled so often and eventually fallen; surprised rather that it should ever have taken to the road at all?

My intention in this book is to examine the nature of the burden that weighs down a Labour Government. What really is the boulder that fate compels them to push up the mountain? It is an immense subject, so immense that it is difficult to know where to start. After all, how does one start describing a subject that touches on the history, social structure and character of the British people? This is not an exaggeration: I believe that the burden weighing down a Labour Government is nothing less than the history, social structure and character of the British people.

This is a bold claim. But as a professional observer of the political scene I have found it impossible these last six years not to conclude that a Labour Government operates in a political and social context that gives it little chance. There is nothing dramatic or obvious about this. The realization dawns slowly, as problem succeeds problem and one is forced to conclude that in each case it is almost impossible for a Labour Government to do what is required to solve it; impossible because of the composition of the Labour Party, because of the nature of popular prejudice, because of the dictates of the social structure, because, in short, of British history.

Increasingly one has come to feel that day-by-day and week-by-week political analysis is missing the point. One can analyse the measures proposed, say, by Mr Jenkins or by Mrs Castle, or by Harold Wilson himself, and find them sensible or stupid, practical or impractical, or argue endlessly about, say, the virtues or vices of an incomes policy or reform of the trade unions or a wealth tax; but over and over again one comes back to the conclusion that this is all academic: the policy may make sense, but not if it has to be implemented by a Labour Government. Labour supporters must be excused for pretending otherwise. It is obviously much less depressing to blame a failed policy on ministerial inadequacy or on the flaws of the policy itself than to recognize that the truth lies at a deeper and much less easily curable level: in the *inherent* weaknesses of Labour Government itself. Who would not prefer to blame the doctor in charge of a loved one for his or her failure to get better—or if not the doctor, the medicine he has prescribed—rather than to recognize the tragic possibility that the patient may be mortally sick. Tory supporters, on the other hand, are so busy enjoying the sport of pointing to the failure of Labour ministers and socialist policies that they have no time and less inclination to probe for deeper explanations than human incompetence and ideological misguidedness. This is natural enough. A boxer with his opponent up against the ropes or being counted out on the floor cannot be expected to start calling for a medical examination to prove that the poor victim should never have been allowed into the ring in the first place. Both Left and Right, in short, have a vested interest in examining the Labour Government's record on a narrow front: the former so as to avoid a fundamentally depressing diagnosis, and the latter so as not to have to admit that its victory has been won more easily than it likes to imagine. At the risk of annoying both Left and Right, I should like to suggest that the Labour Government was bound to fail in the ordinary sense of that word, and that no great blame should attach to the Government for doing what it was bound to do. Any mature discussion of those six years must start with a clear understanding that a Labour Government has to be judged by a special yardstick; special allowances have to be made. The conclusion may be that Labour Governments are luxuries that this country cannot afford; and would not want even if it could afford them. On the other hand, the conclusion could be that it is worth while having Labour Governments, in spite of the fact that there are built-in reasons why they are bound to fail.

This seems to me the interesting point. Is it more in the national interest to fail under Labour than to succeed, at least comparatively speaking, under the Tories? Does the country gain more from a Labour Government governing against the grain of the national character than from a Tory one governing with it? I do not want to prejudge the issue. All I am seeking to do at this stage is to insist that this is the central dilemma exposed by the experience of these six years. What they have shown is that British politics is not a race between two horses of comparable weight. That view is terribly unfair to a Labour Government. A Labour Government, because of its handicaps, is bound to stumble and fall, and the queston that has to be decided is whether there is something about it so unquestionably virtuous that we should tolerate it in spite of its sorrowful performance, or perhaps because of it. But before this crucial question—which is fundamental to the future of British politics—can be answered, it is essential to get one truth clear. These six years have not shown that this particular Labour Government failed. They have shown something far more significant and profound: that Labour Government itself cannot succeed.

The Socialist Myth

1

What is meant by 'Labour government cannot succeed'? Very broadly, that Labour, while it can arouse electoral enthusiasm —that is to say, win votes—has yet to prove that it can sustain a public response that allows for effective administration once it is in power. It is not enough for a party simply to be able to win elections. It must also be able to produce a Government capable of getting the best, or at any rate something pretty good, out of the country once it is in power. The years 1964-70 suggest that this is precisely what a Labour Government cannot do.

In the first place, it obviously cannot rely on the ardent co-operation of the existing governing class, whose power it is pledged to destroy. In practice, of course, it comes to terms with the capitalist order, but it would be unrealistic not to recognize that the relationship is at best uneasy and distrustful. Industry and the city are obviously not going to give of their best under Labour.

Yet it is equally obvious that, since operating a mixed economy involves Labour in coming to terms with the capitalist order, it cannot adopt policies likely to arouse the enthusiasm of the working class. Indeed, it is pretty well certain to disappoint the working class, since the gap between what it promises at the election and what it can deliver in office is bound to be embarrassingly wide. It has to be assumed, therefore, that a Labour Government will have to operate within a context of a governing class that has been threatened and frightened but not destroyed and replaced and a working class whose expectations have been awakened but not satisfied —within a context, that is, which allows it neither to fall back on the weight of tradition nor to move forward behind the momentum of revolution. Left-wing euphoria and right-wing habit, both these primitive but formidable forces are denied it. So also are the charms of utopianism and nostalgia.

To some extent all Governments in a democracy are caught in a comparable dilemma. Obviously a Tory Government is forced to disappoint its city and industrial supporters, out of respect for the susceptibilities of the trade unions. But the problem is much more acute for Labour than for the Tories. A radical party, dedicated to the transformation of society, clearly requires a stronger head of popular steam behind it than a conservative party committed to the maintenance of the status quo. Living in a society that is in process of rapid change is a frightening experience, particularly for those at the bottom of the social ladder who lack the education to understand what is going on and who fear nothing so much as the unknown and the unfamiliar. Any Government pledged to bring about radical change has, therefore, to assume widespread unease even—indeed, particularly—among those whose interests the changes are meant to favour. A radical Government, in short, requires to be much more positively popular than a conservative one, since it has to overcome not only the opposition of those who stand to lose by change but also, in practice, the unease of those who stand to gain, the gains in many cases being far from obvious or immediate.

Party enthusiasm is much more essential to a Labour Government than it is to a Tory Government. A Tory Government, precisely because it does not want to do a great deal, and because it can rely on the general habits and customs of society, can get along nicely without much passion behind it. Indeed, passion would be a positive disadvantage, since the Tories do not know what to do with it. But for a radical Government to overcome the dead weight of custom and inertia, it has to be able to inspire its supporters to great sacrifices and exertions. Passionate enthusiasm is an absolute necessity. Yet this is precisely what a Labour Government finds it most difficult to arouse, since once in power it is cut off, almost by definition, from its emotional roots. The very act of winning office, of occupying the seats of power, of assuming the mantle of authority, and of doing what is necessary just to administer the country—the very act, that is, of being Her Majesty's Government—deprives Labour of its principal dynamic, which is the freedom to challenge authority and the establishment. It is precisely Labour's tone of cheeky irreverence about the great institutions of State, irresponsible utopianism, euphoric optimism, which accounts for the enthusiasm it can arouse in its supporters. But once it is in office, operating a mixed economy, compelled to appease the city and industry, and to rely on the very establishment it used to mock, its prime source of appeal swiftly drys up. No sooner does it have its hands on the lever of power than the current is broken.

It was always assumed, of course, that Labour in power would be able to arouse passionate support because of all the benefits it would introduce. Working-class attitudes to the State would be transformed, with suspicion turned into gratitude. This has not happened, and each new experience of Labour in power makes it ever more clear that it is never going to happen. If Labour's last six years made anything clear, it was surely that a Labour Government cannot so transform society as to bring about a new working-class attitude to the State, and is forced instead to do many things which actually increase rather than decrease working-class suspicion. It is idle to go on pretending, therefore, that a Labour Government can create a new dynamic, arising from what it *does* in office, to take the place of the old dynamic which arose from what its members *said* in opposition. But this is what the success of British democratic socialism depends on: the ability of Labour in power to create a new social context which would justify the working class in trusting the State, in identifying with it. For Labour to be able to do what it wants to do it has got to create a new kind of State, whose officials the working class would cease to regard as 'them'; a new kind of State which, instead of arousing suspicion and fear, would command trust and devotion; a new kind of State in which the Labour Party would become the party of conservation, the establishment party, able to adopt the mantle of power and the habits of authority quite naturally, without seeming to the working class to have sold out to the enemy.

This is something which only one Labour Government has been able to do, very briefly after 1945. In those post-war halcyon years—for reasons which I shall go into shortly—Labour seemed in the process of creating a new State, the Welfare State, which really looked as if it might transform working-class attitudes. But then in 1951 began the thirteen years in opposition, which were spent by Labour propaganding about the inadequacies of the Welfare State under the Tories. Judging by Labour Party rhetoric, nothing much had changed. No sooner were the Tories back in power than society reverted to a condition which working-class people—according to Labour—ought to distrust. But this is precisely the point: unless one postulates permanent Labour rule and a one-party State nothing ever *is* fundamental or irreversible. So how can working people be expected to adopt a trusting attitude to a State that is always likely to revert into enemy hands? Indeed, while in opposition, Labour finds it necessary actually to exaggerate the iniquities of the State under Tory guidance, since only by pointing out the extent of all the existing—or allegedly existing—social injustices can it hope to win its way back to power. In other words, it can reasonably be assumed that it is almost a condition of Labour's winning an election that it should have been particularly successful in whipping up popular suspicion of the State in the preceding months and years. A Labour Government, therefore, takes office against a background of widespread anti-Establishment feeling, of distrust of State authority, of doubts about existing institutions, all of which it has done its best to engender; in spite of the fact that, once it is in office, these attitudes will be the very opposite of what socialism requires if it is to work effectively. For socialist policies to prove acceptable, trust of the State is a prime necessity. Yet a Labour Government, in practice, can never do as much to create that confidence in office as it has done to undermine it in opposition.

As a result, a Labour Government on taking office finds itself seeking to promote policies that increase the power of the State in a society which has been successfully taught to distrust all the institutions of State. Labour wins power only by successfully exacerbating dissatisfaction with existing society. Yet socialism, in practice, requires a degree of trust and goodwill which the Labour Party has made certain does not exist.

In fact, Labour Governments are really a contradiction in

terms. In so far as they are Labour they are not Governments, and in so far as they are Governments they are not Labour. A Labour Opposition makes perfect sense, since the British working class, or a very sizeable part of it, is still deeply suspicious of the State. In the act of opposing, Labour is doing what comes naturally. But a Labour Government, operating the State machinery, giving the orders, is in a very different position. The more convincingly it behaves like a Government, as to the manner born, the less easy it is for its supporters to trust it. It moves from the category of 'us' into the category of 'them'. But only half-heartedly, and certainly not with enough conviction to win the confidence of those who really are 'them'. So far as most of the middle class is concerned, a Labour Government is never likely to become 'one of us'. So it occupies a kind of limbo position, neither fully 'them', nor fully 'us', distrusted by both.

A strong Government needs a governing class to do its will. This is the trouble with Labour. It has not got one, and the more it makes do with the help and co-operation of the old governing class the less enthusiasm it arouses among those who expected to comprise the new one. But it *has* to make do with the old governing class. There is no one else. Not being a revolutionary party Labour inherits a going concern, an existing society, which it wants to change but not subvert. No new governing class bursts upon the scene when Labour comes to power. This is a source of profound weakness. Labour is committed to a form of socialist rhetoric that arouses the distrust of the old ruling class, without being able to implement socialist policies radical enough to produce a new ruling class; to a form of socialist analysis that weakens respect for the State 'as it was', without being able to create a new State 'as it ought to be'.

Yet the first condition for the success of any measure of State planning, if it is to be voluntary, is that it should have the support—or at any rate avoid having the opposition— of a majority of at least the working class. Democratic socialism clearly depends on the existence of a State which the masses are prepared to trust or identify with. (And this means much more than 'supply votes for'.) If the masses are going to co-operate freely in plans determined by the State, then they must first be persuaded that the State is on their side; that they, the workers, *are* the State.

Socialist literature has always minimized the obstacles in Britain which prevent the achievement of this goal. It was really assumed that the election of a Labour Government would itself do the trick; or at least begin to do it. Once the levers of State power were seen to be in the hands of working-class people then a new era of co-operation would dawn. The socialist, or collectivist, policies pursued would produce a new kind of working man, anxious to serve the community. Once it was realized that society was organized on the principle of fair shares for all, rather than privileges for the few, the masses would voluntarily want to serve the State.

In 1924, Ramsay MacDonald told the Labour Party conference:

> ... the aim of socialism to to get at the hearts of men, because we cannot survive unless we discover how to produce the *willing* workers and not merely the man who toils for reward. We have been too long thinking and speaking as though the spirit of artistic production was different in kind from the spirit required for manual production. Those of us who drank early from the refreshing springs which William Morris made to flow in a dull and deadening generation never held that heresy and never will. Men live by their generosities, by their loyalties, not by their interest, and their self-regarding interests. And until somehow or other, by change of heart and condition, or both, we can put our industry on the footing of the willing gift of service, we shall have nothing but quarrels and the sacrifice of the common weal. It is the aim of getting our industry on that footing, that is the aim of the socialist inspiration that gives us power in our Labour movement.

Mark those words: *we cannot survive unless we discover how to produce the willing workers.* Would any Labour leader wish to commit himself to them today? He would be rash to do so, since if the last fifty years have demonstrated nothing else, they have shown that democratic socialism in Britain has made no progress whatsoever in realizing this essential

6

condition. Can it ever do so? And if it cannot, does this not mean, as Ramsay MacDonald warned, that democratic socialism cannot survive?

This is the critical question facing British democratic socialism. Can it so radically alter the nature of the State as to turn working-class suspicion into trust? George Orwell hinted at the answer in his famous wartime essay 'The Lion and the Unicorn'.

The difference between Socialism and Capitalism is not primarily a difference of technique. One cannot simply change from one system to the other as one might install a new piece of machinery in a factory, and then carry on as before, with the same people in positions of control. Obviously there is also needed a complete shift of power. New blood, new men, new ideas—in the true sense of the word, a revolution.*

But a revolution is the one thing that *democratic* socialism is incapable of bringing about, since its instrument, the Labour Party, believes in parliamentary government, which precludes revolution.

Here, in a nutshell, is the problem. Only a revolution could so transform the nature of the State, the accent in which it speaks, the clothes it wears, the values it enshrines, the associations it arouses in the public mind, as to make it an object of working-class trust. But the Labour Party has rightly concluded that there is no majority in favour of such a revolution.

This is the point which has to be grasped if the difficulties facing a Labour Government are to be fully understood. Its socialist economic goal of a planned economy requires an ever-increasing willingness on the part of the workers to do what the State tells them to do, the assumption being that the socialist State will be in a position to inspire such trust. But the democratic commitment of British socialism has precluded the creation of such a radically altered State. All we have is the old historic State—traditionally an object of suspicion— seeking to promote planning. Of course it is also seeking to promote social justice. But the spread of social justice is far

* George Orwell, *The Lion and the Unicorn* (Secker & Warburg, 1941).

7

too gradual, far too piecemeal, and far too precarious to bring about the radical change in the whole nature of society which socialism requires. Increasingly, therefore, the truth is becoming inescapable: democratic socialism cannot bank on the creation of the willing worker, on the transformation of human nature.

I want to examine this socialist dilemma in some detail since it goes to the heart of the matter. All would agree today that British socialist assumptions about how society was to be 'transformed' need fundamental re-examination. The class structure has proved far more indestructible than anyone had supposed. Labour's bloodless so-called revolution has not brought about that 'complete shift of power' which Orwell sensed to be necessary. If one examines the composition of the Civil Service, of the universities, of industrial management, of the city, banking, and so on, it is scarcely less middle-class now than it was before the war. Careers are admittedly much more open to talent, but the middle class has shown itself to have most of the talent. Barring the imposition of tyrannical handicaps, it is very difficult to see how this could be changed. Unless one postulates social changes of a punitive nature aimed at crippling the middle class, which in turn would require a non-democratic Government to impose them, it being inconceivable that they could ever be acceptable voluntarily, the middle class, in fact, is likely to monopolize power for the foreseeable future.

What is becoming clear is that democratic socialism—which is socialism adapted to fit into the existing social context, or to grow out of it—in practice does very little to strengthen the working class. In theory it provides opportunities for all. But history has given the middle class such overwhelming natural advantages that it has little difficulty in keeping ahead in the race, and in determining the rules by which the race is conducted.

But how does this affect the problem of producing the 'willing worker', without which democratic socialism 'cannot survive'? It will be objected here that socialism has never supposed that society could ever be run by the workers. The aim has always been to organize it around the principle of social justice, with fair shares for all, so that the workers would recognize that although they were not themselves in charge, those who had their interests at heart were. To this end socialism laid primary emphasis on State ownership of the means of production, so that the economy could be run for the good of all.

One can see that in the early twentieth century this approach made political sense. It was possible to concentrate then on those aspects of collectivism which would obviously appeal immensely to the workers, and to talk about the State as if it was a kind of giant Father Christmas. Collectivism meant better wages, free handouts in terms of education and medical services, cheaper housing, a less unequal distribution of the national wealth, and so on. The State could be presented as an instrument which would take away from the rich and give to the poor. It is worth noting, however, that even then the idea was far from popular with working people, such was their deep-seated distrust of State handouts, and their conviction that no good could come from letting the State look too closely at what they were up to. Nevertheless it was possible then to present the State to the working class as the great giver rather than the great taker-away; or at any rate to suggest that it could be, if only control over wealth was taken out of private hands.

In a sense, the failure of capitalism, or rather the early hardships that it caused, encouraged British socialism or collectivism vastly to underestimate the basic problem. So obvious were the abuses of capitalism that, in theory at any rate, it seemed unnecessary to worry about the problem of making the socialist State popular with the workers. This seemed such a distant problem that nobody really got down to studying it. It was simply assumed as axiomatic that State intervention could not fail to benefit the workers, since private ownership so plainly benefited the owners—a view that seemed to be confirmed by the intense opposition to collectivism displayed by the owners. In other words, the central problem of how to make the socialist State popular or authoritative with the workers once it was forced to hurt them, or make them do what they did not want to do, was never squarely faced. It was simply assumed that socialism would consist of putting right the sins of capitalism, to the enthusiastic applause of a grateful working class who would always be the beneficiaries; or that the socialist State's record having done so much for the workers in the past would somehow guarantee it working-class gratitude for all time.

This is what is so fascinating about the last six years of Labour. A Labour Government with a massive majority had to start showing its stern face to the working class; had to start asking *them* to make sacrifices and accept restraints, without being able to offer, as was possible in 1946–51, glittering consolations in the form of massive new social-welfare breakthroughs. In other words, British socialism has come to the end of its bonanza period, when the socialist State could pose to the workers as Father Christmas, and this has forced a new question into British politics: will the workers willingly serve a socialist State when it pursues policies that seem to threaten their interests?

This is a crucially important question. The last six years have clearly underlined the fact that socialism is not some miraculous nostrum which banishes the unpleasant necessity of squeezing and freezing the working class. It does not require much imagination to realize that the socialist State might be forced—in fact, has been forced—into policies aimed at reducing working-class standards of living, which would make it quite as unpopular as was the old capitalist owning class. How does British socialism see the State in these circumstances? What roots will it have in society that will enable it to take this strain?

In seeking to discover the answer one hits upon the incredible flimsiness of British socialist thought. The State called upon to implement socialism is the State as it has always existed, manned by very much the same people, speaking in very much the same accents, creating very much the same impression as it always has done. Working-class people no more identify with it today than they did a hundred years ago, and are probably less impressed by it than they were then because its ceremonial trappings carry less conviction. In what sense has the Labour Party made the State able to take the new strains which are being put upon it?

This is not a quibbling question. It is absolutely central to the feasibility of British democratic socialism. Socialism requires that the State should enjoy the kind of authority that a father does in a family: authority based on voluntary acquiescence rooted in trust. It presupposes a new relationship between State and people anointed by social justice. Such a relationship in Britain, however, could never grow out of the past, since the soil of our social history is totally unsuited to nurture such a plant. As Orwell says, it could only grow out of revolution, which the Labour Party has never sought. The idea that it might arise out of the Welfare State—or out of nationalization, or alongside a mixed economy—was quite excessively naïve. That mystical Robert Blatchford side of socialism—a new society being born based on co-operation and service—was clearly never going to materialize in a Britain which remained as traditional as it does today.

This is the point. The authority of a socialist Government still lies in its constitutional legitimacy; in the fact that it has come to power by traditional methods and operates against the traditional background and through the traditional institutions. It is as much the Queen's Government as a Tory Government is. In a very important sense, of course, this has always been a source of very great strength for the Labour Party, since it has enabled it to borrow from the capital of authority built up in the past. When Mr Wilson, for example, wanted to promote a socialist cause, like reform of the House of Lords, he got the Queen to announce it to Parliament in the speech from the throne; and he himself operated from the same dispatch-box as did Winston Churchill. Unquestionably this emphasis on continuity enormously strengthened the authority of early Labour Governments; without it, indeed, they would never have got elected. It was the price paid by Labour for middle-class trust and acquiescence. So much is obvious. But in inheriting traditional authority, Labour Governments also inherit traditional distrust of authority. They took over the State intact, without revolutionary disruption. But just as this enabled them to rely on all the traditional middle-class inclination to obey the State, so also it guaranteed that they would inherit all the traditional working-class instinct to distrust it. Continuity meant not only the continuation of middle-class obedience—doing what a hated Labour Government said because it was also the Queen's Government

—but also the continuation of working-class distrust and reluctance to do what a Labour Government said, also because it was the Queen's Government. Those early Labour Governments were praised for statesmanship because they had a proper respect for history. But history is indivisible, and the result is that a modern Labour Government enjoys its advantages and its handicaps, the weaknesses as well as the strengths of being rooted in and having grown out of the old order. In a word, it has condemned itself to operate within a context that precludes reliance on what was regarded as an essential condition of successful socialism: a new type of working man born of a new type of society.

Fundamental to the theory of democratic socialism was the assumption that under a Labour Government the workers would be so fired by the prospect of social justice that the economy would be transformed by their idealism. It would not be necessary for a Labour Government to dictate wage levels, because the trade unions would want to co-operate. This new working-class spirit or proletarian patriotism was to be the essential key which would open the gates to the socialist New Jerusalem.

It is not difficult, of course, to explain why the workers showed such a marked disinclination to be transformed. They can point to the fact that Britain today is a mixed economy which is very far from being the kind of workers' utopia which was meant to justify and engender this transformation. So why should they become socialist angels when there are so many capitalist devils around? But in a mixed economy there are always going to be capitalist devils around. Indeed, the experience of the past six years suggests that Labour planning tends to strengthen rather than weaken them.

This is the paradox of democratic socialism trying to operate a mixed economy. The more a socialist Government seeks to intervene in the affairs of Big Business, the more Big Business is in a position to interfere in the affairs of the socialist Government. Or, to put it another way, the more responsibilities for economic management the Government undertakes, the more opportunities this gives Big Business to make its co-operation conditional on the socialist plan's being adapted to its needs. Under socialism, in short, the blackmailing power of business is not broken; it is vastly augmented.

The trade-union leaders are well aware of this. They see how socialist planning in a mixed economy inevitably forges closer links between industry and Government. The idea, therefore, of a noble spirit of working-class restraint and enthusiasm dawning under Labour gets even more chimerical. This raises a new question for the party: how can democratic socialism be made to work without the co-operation of the working class? Business intransigence is no longer seen as the threat to British socialism. Private enterprise, by and large, has shown itself amazingly co-operative. For the first time a dreadful doubt is beginning to grow that the rock on which it may founder is the rock on which it was meant to be built: the working class itself.

The fascinating development in contemporary British politics is the extent to which it is becoming clear that socialism, at any rate in practice, is quite peculiarly unsuited to appeal to the one section of the community for which it was primarily designed. Extension of State intervention in the various fields of national life could only be a popular concept so long as it was interpreted by the workers as State intervention with everybody else but them. The statutory incomes policy killed that illusion stone dead.

It is difficult to exaggerate how this has transformed the nature of socialist debate. For the first time reality is beginning to impinge. Socialist theory had it that in some miraculous way the community would settle these matters in the light of social justice. In fact what is happening is that the bureaucracy—the same bureaucracy that operated in the bad old days—is seeking to settle these matters in the interests of the State.

Yet the State, which the Labour Party is seeking to exalt in this way, has seldom meant less to ordinary people. Its natural authority and prestige have never been so low.

Paradoxically, this is to a large extent the fault of the socialists themselves. They have persistently denigrated the national institutions, derided the concepts of rank and hierarchy on which the State depends, deplored the spirit of national pride from which it draws its strength. The Tory idea

13

of the State, rooted in history and tradition, pomp and circumstance, at least had some popular appeal. But in the language of socialism the State spells bureaucracy and bureaucracy spells all those aspects of the past which the working class find least palatable—bowler-hat-and-rolled-umbrella values, rigid hierarchy, orders from on high that have to be obeyed, impersonal authority. A socialist State, in practice if not in theory, turns out to be the very last kind of State likely to appeal to the British working class.

This is the real problem facing the Labour Party today. All its economic plans require for their fruition a deep surge of working-class faith and enthusiasm which was meant to materialize out of a new vision of social justice. In fact, however, the inevitable limitations of a mixed economy preclude any such radical transformation. Mr Wilson did his best and we shall no doubt hear much more in the future of his plans to soak the rich and so on. But if the experience of the past six years is any guide, such attempts at socialist demagogy will do more to depress business than to impress the workers; weakening capitalist confidence without in any way strengthening trade-union trust. For the time being at any rate, socialism can still appear convincing as a spectre, but has entirely lost its capacity to act as an inspiration.

In the early days of the Wilson administration this tragic failure was disguised by a strange, and for a time successful, attempt at a British version of National Socialism, with the Prime Minister concentrating on the role of world statesman, peacemaker in Vietnam, upholder of justice in Rhodesia, east-of-Suez warrior, grand defender of sterling. Unable to give the workers any cause for rejoicing over a new dawn at home, he did his best to prolong the sunset of empire. It was a masterly performance. No effort was spared to enlist patriotism, even jingoism, in the socialist crusade.

In time, however, even this ploy failed. The socialist engine of state ran out of popular fuel both at home and abroad. What was there left at the end to attract the great mass of ordinary people? Socialism is essentially a crusade, a movement, a promise of corporate regeneration. If the State is to be given the new power and authority which socialist planning requires, it must be able to inspire people with a profound sense of community. This is why a condition of national depression and disillusionment is so infinitely damaging to the socialist cause. Only when a nation is riding high, confident in its own communal future, can the State expect to receive that degree of voluntary assent from individuals without which democratic socialism must inevitably relapse into either compulsion or chaos.

Herein lay Mr Wilson's true dilemma. That essential degree of voluntary assent simply did not exist, and it did not exist pre-eminently where today a Labour Government most needs it—among the working class. When Mr Wilson used to address business conferences he was often able to win their acquiescence by striking a series of particular bargains. But asking the workers to hand over the rights of collective bargaining to a socialist State was a wholly different matter. That required an act of corporate working-class trust, which was the one thing Mr Wilson found himself totally unable to get.

2

We have been considering some of the difficulties faced by the Labour Government in winning the confidence and inspiring the enthusiasm of the working class. The assumption before 1964, of course, was that this problem would solve itself as a result of economic growth; that this would itself come about by virtue of Mr Wilson's technological expertise, and then out of the resulting surplus would spring all the blessings of socialism, of which the poor would be the first beneficiaries. In other words, socialism was seen almost as the child of technology, and technology as the parent of socialism.

But this was putting the cart before the horse. It assumed that the workers would co-operate in all the painful adjustment made necessary by technological change without the industrial climate's first being sweetened by the socialist fruits of that change. The reason for this wholly unjustifiable assumption was, of course, very obvious. If a Labour Government had pressed ahead with socialism too fast it would have frightened the country's capitalist creditors, both at home and abroad, as we saw happening in 1964–5, when even the mildest socialist measures caused grave upsets in the money markets. No Labour Government, in contemporary circumstances, can therefore possibly pretend that socialism itself is to be an instrument for bringing about economic growth, since such a claim would endanger essential business and city co-operation. All it can say, which indeed is all it did say, is that non-ideological technology, as opposed to socialism, will do the economic trick —that is to say, create the surplus wealth—out of which socialism will emerge as a buckshee social perk or luxury.

Thus it was hoped to satisfy both capitalist fears and socialist principles, disarm the rich and placate the poor. Socialism was transformed from the yeast of the economic cake itself into merely the icing on its top, something nice and sweet and decorative to catch the eye once the hard job of baking had been completed.

I have already tried to suggest that this idea of socialism growing out of economic growth was wholly unrealistic since it overlooked the crucial *political* fact that economic growth under a Labour Government can only grow out of socialism. It is axiomatic, with the benefit of hindsight, that if Labour is to overcome the disadvantage of arousing business and city suspicion, from which its party composition precludes it from altogether escaping, at least in the foreseeable future, it is necessary for it to be able to rely on a specially favourable relationship with the unions and with the working class generally. It has to be able to transform the industrial climate. Only in this way can a Labour Government persuade the workers to tolerate technological change which in turn gets the economic growth. But how can it transform the economic climate without introducing socialism; that is to say, without bringing about a radically altered social context in which the workers feel a wholly new relationship with the Government?

Right from the start Mr Wilson begged this question preferring to pretend that technologically orientated planning could be made to work in an industrial climate not yet sweetened by the socialist fruits of that planning. He preferred, or was compelled by circumstances, simply to assume an enthusiastically co-operative and trusting working class— while admitting that very little could be done for the time being to fulfil any of the conditions which are likely to induce that co-operation and trust. Such an attitude was sadly unrealistic in the circumstances of this country. It postulated a highly educated working class well disposed towards the State, which, by socialist definition, does not exist here, it being one of Labour's aims to bring it into being. What the modern Labour Party attitude overlooks is that democratic socialism only becomes practicable politically in a society that does not suffer from the social ills which socialism is meant to cure; only becomes practicable, that is, in circumstances where it is unnecessary.

This is the logical flaw in the socialist argument which has bedevilled the Labour Government at every point. Its economic plans have assumed the existence of the very society they were meant to create, a society based on a spirit of working-class patriotism. It was assumed that the social side of socialism would give the working class that extra fillip which would make its economic planning acceptable, although in fact there was never any doubt that until economic growth was achieved that fillip could not be given. As a result, Mr Wilson had increasingly to fall back on compulsion, which actually only worsens the industrial climate and in so doing worsens the prospect of economic growth.

The more one studies the Labour Government's actual experience in power the less adequate must its basic intellectual preparations appear. It is incredible how little attention it paid to the *political* problems of economic growth. Mr Wilson conned the country into believing that he had a magic wand or formula, technology, which would do the job somehow outside politics. The only political act needed was to elect him. It can now be seen that this was his fundamental error. I am inclined to think that the Tories made a similar error in the last few years before 1964, and are still sadly unprepared to learn the lesson. But it does not matter so crucially for them, since in their case the need for a fundamental political reappraisal is less important. Let us be clear about this. The Tories operated stop–go economic policies with reasonable results, at least until the end of their last thirteen years in power, and would probably have gone on doing so if they had been re-elected in 1964. The rate of economic growth was far too low, but not disastrously low. My guess is that they will do roughly the same this time. There is, of course, no secret about why the Tories can operate this kind of economic policy better than Labour. Not only do they enjoy greater goodwill and confidence in international and domestic financial circles, but also they do not suffer from the political pressures which compel any Labour Government to do things that worry these circles. No Labour Government is ever likely to do less to worry these circles than that of Mr Wilson. He pushed his party to the uttermost limits of its patience in rejecting left-wing pressure for more public expenditure. Even so, if one studies the record, which does not need repeating here, it is clear that the touchiness of business and banking and the touchiness of the Labour Party combine to make it impossible in practice for Labour to walk along the knife-edge of stop–go without falling off balance. If Mr Wilson, that superb balancer, failed, it is reasonable to doubt whether any other Labour leader will ever succeed.

What the years 1964–70 made clear was the absurdity of supposing that Labour could operate the economic system in a conservative manner. If it was to work better than under the Tories, instead of worse, something new had to be introduced. This was what led me to write an article in the *Sunday Telegraph* on the eve of the 1964 election called 'A Man With Fire in his Belly', which was to prove hopelessly wrong in fact, although utterly right in theory. I was looking at the situation facing Labour, which seemed to me to suggest that only a man with fire in his belly could cope. Seven years later I still believe I was right about the need, but wrong to assume that because the need was so obvious Mr Wilson had to be the man to meet it. Here is what I wrote, and may God forgive me, since no one else can be expected to:

By this time next week we shall know who our new rulers are. We may well have Mr Harold Wilson sitting in Downing Street. I seem to be alone in finding this prospect *positively* exciting.

In my view he would prove a formidable Premier, the first passionately radical leader this country has ever experienced in peacetime, Cromwell and Lloyd George being primarily the products of war. Far more than Ramsay MacDonald or Attlee, and immeasurably more than Gaitskell, Harold Wilson despises the existing order with a fierce moral fervour. He is *passionately* for change.

To my mind this is his most important quality, and certainly one which the voters would be wrong to ignore. To some extent Mr Wilson has purposefully played it down, so as not to frighten the cautious. He has allowed the flames to flicker only very occasionally through the smokescreen of verbal moderation. But this is much more than mere tactical opportunism. I suspect that Mr Wilson is the type of man who will find it much easier to do justice to his true feelings in deeds rather than in words. Only the exercise of power, therefore, will give him the opportunity to reveal the depths of his radicalism.

And it is this difference which really goes to the crux of this election. For what Mr Wilson is really offering the country is much more than a different set of practical proposals, much more than a different plan, programme or blueprint. It is a deeply different political attitude. In essence he believes that the only way to modernize Britain is to foment and harness social tensions. Given a large enough majority he would seek to galvanize this country by releasing the archaic passions of the class war, rather as de Gaulle has sought to galvanize France by deliberate incitement to old-fashioned xenophobia.

Just as de Gaulle always made it crystal clear that he would seek to shake France into a new lease of life by naked appeal to nationalism, so Mr Wilson is equally insistent that the only way Britain can break out of its rut is through a crusade for what he calls social justice. By waging a war against profits, privilege, inherited wealth, public schools, expense accounts, etc., he would hope to engender enough political momentum in the ranks of organized labour to enable his Government to give the economy a major jolt forward.

It is easy enough to mock such an aim as harking back to the nineteenth century. But the truth is that the much more contemporary Tory approach, based on an appeal to common sense on both sides of industry, is still far from producing the desired effect. It could very well be, of course, that Mr Wilson's approach will make matters worse, and that the case for letting the Tories continue along their present sweetly reasonable lines is overwhelmingly strong. But let us at least realize that we are being offered a choice in this election, even if, as is unfortunately the case, it has not been properly spelt out. Mr Wilson would try to persuade labour to renounce restrictive industrial practices on the shop floor, as a *quid pro quo* for denying the managerial classes many of the social privileges and advantages which they at present enjoy.

That this would lead to intense bitterness is probably true, which is why only a radical leader of Mr Wilson's calibre would seriously seek to carry such a policy through. It would revive class passions which it has been the whole aim of Tory policy to damp down. But it is a policy which nevertheless merits serious attention.

There can be no doubt that any programmes for modernizing Britain are going to involve the workers in painful readjustments, involving in many cases physical uprooting. The essence of Mr Wilson's approach, as I see it, is that it is politically necessary that this pain should be seen to be shared. He has enough class sadism in his make-up—which Mr Gaitskell did not have—to enable him to do this job with determination and relish.

There is much to be said for the view that Mr Wilson is purposefully building up an exaggerated feeling of emergency—and has been doing so ever since he became party leader—so as to be able to justify carrying through the kind of drastic social changes that he would like to see anyhow, but knows would never be tolerated in normal times. This is what worries me about the Wilson appeal. I have a suspicion that for many reasons which, in a few years' time, may seem relatively trivial, we may be about to be tempted into electing the kind of dedicated, doctrinaire radical whom in the past, even in much more critical times, we have always avoided like the plague.*

Uppermost in my mind then was the conclusion that the only way for a Labour Government to bring about economic growth was through socialism, since only socialism could bring about that upsurge of working-class enthusiasm to compensate for the loss of business confidence. I still believe this to be true. But I am equally convinced, again with the benefit of hindsight, that such policies are outside the range of any Labour Government, however large its majority, for the most compelling reason of all: Labour Governments lack the authority to take the international risks inherent in such a policy, to set the country against the prevailing international trends; lack the authority, that is, to summon up from the deep the forces of nationalism and put them behind socialism.

* *Sunday Telegraph*, 11.10.64.

The history and composition of the Labour Party precludes such risks. I was casting Harold Wilson for a de Gaulle role. Seven years later I am increasingly convinced that no leader of the Labour Party can realistically be cast in such a role. Yet without a leader able to spark the flame of nationalism, socialism will not work in this country.

It is no accident, therefore, that Labour thinking before the election ignored the politics of economic growth. Any such frank assessment would have had to conclude that the Labour Party would prove sadly unable to cope with them. There were two broad possible approaches: skilful pursuit of stop–go, so as to maximize the 'go' and minimize the 'stop', which would require maximization of capitalist confidence both at home and abroad; or wholehearted adoption of a revolutionary approach, which would have involved swift devaluation, withdrawal from east of Suez—flouting both the dollar and the Pentagon—defiance of the international financial world, and willingness to snap the Government's fingers at official circles both at home and abroad. There can surely be very little doubt that in practice a Labour Government is bound to be too left-wing to command enough capitalist confidence to do the former and not right-wing enough to command enough national confidence to do the latter.

The truth is that the Labour Government in 1964 was faced with a tragic choice: either to continue the old policies, which it was doomed to make a mess of, or to strike out in uncharted and forbidding international waters, which no Labour Prime Minister could be expected to do, at least in the early days of office. Those who seriously supposed that Mr Wilson could have announced on taking office that it was Labour's intention to devalue the currency and wind up the empire and endanger the alliance seem to me to misunderstand the position of the Labour Party in this country; to overlook the crucial fact that, however many votes it may win, it is still not wholly trusted by any class in matters affecting the national interest. I doubt myself if any of the top Labour leaders at the time seriously considered such actions which must have appeared, as indeed they were, beyond their reach.

Professor John Vaisey describes that moment in these terms:

As the three men—Wilson, Brown and Callaghan, sat round the table on the first day in office, and decided not to devalue, I think they were deciding not only to try to preserve 'The City' but to abandon any possibility of serious economic growth. Upon what did this renunciation of growth rest? It was not a considered view, clearly, since the men involved were incapable at that flushed moment of power of that degree of forethought. Their unconsciouses spoke. And when the political unconscious speaks, it speaks on behalf of the lowest common denominator in all of us. Perhaps the British do not want growth.*

I do not think myself that this is quite what their unconsciouses told them. I think they realized unconsciously that a Labour Government is incapable of making these kinds of revolutionary changes; simply lacks the authority to do so. And their subconsciouses were quite right. I do not believe this option was open to a Labour Government in its first days of office; it would have meant saying, in effect, that Labour's first decision in office was to wind up the empire, renounce world status, and devalue the currency. Three years later, it is true, after economic disaster had imposed these courses on the Government, Mr Crossman was to say that they were British socialism's historic mission for the 1960s.

'Let me make a personal confession,' he said. (Note the revealing word *confession*, implying that he was about to say something that previously he would not have dared to mention.) 'During the last three years I have sometimes shared the concern expressed by party workers that this Government should fail to carry out the mission which history allocated to British socialism in this decade.' He went on to define this mission as: (1) to wind up the remains of the empire; (2) to renounce pretensions of world status; and (3) to develop a realistic foreign and defence policy based on a realistic parity of the pound.

Some mission! No wonder Mr Crossman mentioned it only in a confessional mood, and then only to justify the adoption of these policies under *force majeure*. Imagine what would have happened to the Labour Party in 1964 or in 1966 if it

* *Encounter*, February 1968.

23

had appealed to the country in these terms: 'We appeal to you, the people of Britain, to give us your votes so that we may wind up the empire, reduce Britain to the status of a minor power, and devalue the national currency.' It would have been political suicide. It might have helped the Labour candidate in Hampstead and in a handful of other constituencies where progressive intellectuals reside in large numbers. But throughout the rest of the country, particularly in working-class areas, it would have disastrously confirmed the deep-seated suspicion among all classes that in fact the Labour Party does not stand for Britain.

Mr Crossman gave no hint of why the Labour Government had found it so hard to fulfil this mission; why, indeed, it had struggled like a lion for three years to do exactly the opposite. Yet this is the crucial question. For if Mr Crossman was right about the contemporary mission of socialism, and if this is what the party faithful were working for, then how can the first three years of the Labour Government be explained, since their actual policies were overwhelmingly directed towards frustrating this mission? In the event, as we all now know, the Labour Government only came round to embracing socialism's 'contemporary mission' as a result of the failure of all its ardent efforts to escape doing so. This is really very odd and suggests some rather disturbing conclusions: either that the Labour Government was uninterested in embracing socialism's contemporary mission, or that it was unable to do so until it had engineered such a disastrous economic crisis as to leave the country with no alternative.

Mr Crossman did not go into these questions. It was sufficient for his purposes to leave his audience of party workers with the impression that all was eventually working out for the best even if this was not what the Labour Government had actually intended. Fate—he seemed to be implying—was on the socialist's side, even if the Labour Government was not. But this is not a very satisfactory conclusion from the point of view of the Labour Party, and must tend, presumably, to reduce the fervour of the party faithful, since if socialism is only likely to emerge from the defeat of Labour Government policies there is not much point in the party faithful sweating blood to get Labour Governments elected.

24

This brings us pretty near the heart of the Labour Party's problem. Let us assume that Mr Crossman was right—as I believe him to have been—and that British socialism's mission in the 1960s was as he described it. We immediately begin to realize how unsuitable an instrument the Labour Party is for fulfilling such a mission. The Labour Party is still essentially a working-class party, in the sense that it depends overwhelmingly on trade-union support. Its mission, therefore, has to correspond with working-class attitudes or, if you like, prejudices. Now, can it seriously be supposed that a party with its roots deep in trade-union soil could voluntarily fulfil what Mr Crossman confessed was the contemporary mission of British socialism? It may well be that devaluing the currency, welching on the United States, dissolving the remnants of empire, etcetera, were the absolute preconditions of any kind of socialist policy at home, and that without such socialist policies at home economic growth could not be achieved. This assessment is now the conventional economic wisdom, and I certainly do not feel qualified to discount it. What one can say, however, is that if these dramatic and challenging switches in traditional British foreign policy, and in Britain's position in the world, really were as necessary as they are now seen to have been, this triumphantly bears out my thesis that a Labour Government is doomed to ineffectiveness. For in terms of political reality they were simply out of the question, as Mr Wilson was the first to realize. Withdrawal from empire, flouting the United States, devaluing the currency to the fury of everybody else—all these could theoretically be presented as magnificent gestures of putting British interests first. It is not difficult to imagine a Conservative leader making them seem such, as de Gaulle did in France. But the leader of the British Labour Party is almost certain not to be the kind of man to carry off such a role convincingly, since if he were it is highly improbable that the Labour Party would ever have elected him in the first place. To get elected leader of the Labour Party it is almost mandatory to have said or done things which cast doubt on one's patriotic *bona fides*. This certainly applied to Harold Wilson with a vengeance. In other words, he was compelled to play safe.

What stopped Mr Wilson devaluing in 1964, and opting

then for withdrawal from east of Suez, was nothing more nor less than the realization that a Labour Prime Minister, before he does anything else, must first establish himself as a national leader; and that this must take precedence over any other consideration. So far as Labour is concerned, being elected is not by itself enough to confer unquestioned legitimacy. In this sense, the Labour Party is rather like the early Hanoverians in the eighteenth century, who, because of their German origins, had to demonstrate their over-riding concern for the British national interest and could not assume that the country would take it for granted. The same is true for a new Labour Prime Minister. Because of the nature and origins of the Labour Party, he has to prove himself a patriot first, before he can consider how to carry forward the socialist torch.

Right from the moment he entered Downing Street, therefore, Mr Wilson set out to assuage suspicions that a Labour Government meant an unpatriotic government. Against the strongly pressed advice of his Cabinet colleagues, he refused to devalue sterling, refused to abandon Britain's nuclear deterrent, and instead seized every opportunity open to a British Prime Minister to build himself up as a large enough figure to fill out the classical clothes of John Bull. In other words, he made it as clear as he possibly could that he had no more become Her Majesty's principal minister to preside over the disintegration of the British Empire than had Winston Churchill.

His instinct was dead right. This is the first task which a Labour Prime Minister must set his hand to. Here, then, is the irony of the situation. The first thing he has to do is to persuade the country that he is *not* going to fulfil what his most articulate Cabinet colleague describes as 'the mission of British socialism'. This, in my view, is the central fact in the Labour Party's predicament: what its socialist head recognizes to be its essential mission is in conflict with what its working-class heart holds most dear.

A Labour Government, in short, is blocked at every turn. It can neither risk releasing the enthusiasm of revolutionary change, for fear of frightening the old order on which it depends, nor risk calling out the forces of nationalism, because, first, this contradicts its internationalist traditions, and, secondly, its authority in these fields is highly suspect. The question which has to be considered is whether a Labour Government that is precluded from using these two most potent fuels can ever hope to get off the ground.

3

I should like to consider this question of nationalism, as it affects the Labour Party, a little more closely. For if I am right in suggesting that the Labour Party is peculiarly ill equipped to exploit this primitive but powerful force, then it surely follows that it suffers under a severe, if not crippling, handicap. Clearly any system of a collectivist kind requires for its successful operation a higher level of public spirit or patriotism than one based on private enterprise. Socialism, therefore, almost by definition, needs a more patriotic society than does capitalism, and if its aims are to be realized, it can only be through a man or a party able to arouse nationalist emotions. The paradox is that in Britain the instrument ordained by history to introduce socialism, the Labour Party, is peculiarly deficient in these particular skills, while the instrument ordained by history to oppose socialism, the Conservative Party, is peculiarly well endowed in these respects.

Socialism requires from all classes—but in particular from the working class—a degree of voluntary restraint and co-operation, a sacrificial renunciation of personal gain here and now, for the long-term communal good, and voluntary willingness to put country before self-interest, without its historic instrument's being able—in this country—to call upon the kind of emotional stimulus which traditionally evokes such responses from uneducated people. Ideally, and in the dreams of the socialist theorists, this public-spirited mood was to be engendered by the spectacle of expanding social justice. Theoretically, I suppose, this was a possibility. But in practice it is difficult to take this utopian aspiration very seriously, at any rate in a mass industrial society.

It is no accident, of course, that the conditions in which socialism has prospered most are those of wartime, when external dangers bring about the necessary popular mood of patriotic self-sacrifice, and when nationalist fervour is at its highest. But obviously the Labour Party cannot rely on further wars to promote the socialist cause. Its prospects have to be considered in the context not only of permanent peace, but of a peace the maintenance of which involves a clear acceptance by the country of a subordinate role in an alliance and a clear recognition of a reduction in independent national power. It is only reasonable to assume, therefore, that in the forseeable future British politics will be conducted against a background of national decline, highly unconducive to that spirit of national fervour in which collectivist policies are most likely to flourish.

This is a peculiar difficulty for the British Labour Party, and has a very direct relevance to its capacity to act as an effective instrument of government. Socialism, much more than conservatism, requires a corporate sense of national purpose. Under socialism the individual is expected to sacrifice personal advantage for the communal good. The individual is expected to trust the State as the instrument which will give expression to the communal good. If personal ambition and individual acquisitiveness are the fuel relied on to drive the capitalist engine, communal pride and social purpose are the fuel of socialism. It cannot be emphasized too strongly, therefore, that any democratic party which seeks to make socialism work needs to engender a powerful head of patriotic steam. This is inherent in any social or political system which places a high emphasis on the role of the State, since if the State is to enjoy the support it requires it must be able to arouse the passions and the loyalties of a wide section of the people.

But this is not easy for the Labour Party to do. It came into existence precisely because it did not believe, at the turn of the century, that Britain was a 'Land of Hope and Glory'. It was, and to some extent still is, a party of protest, concerned to arouse public awareness more about what is wrong and shameful in Britain than about what is hopeful or glorious. It can scarcely take pride in Britain's historic past, since its whole reason for existence is to ameliorate the abuses which disfigured 'the good old days'. It is difficult to debunk aristocracy, and attack its privileges, as the Left does, without debunking the whole pantheon of British national heroes, most of whom either sprang from its ranks or quickly joined them. In this respect, as in so many others, it is only possible to understand the peculiar disadvantages of the Labour Party by first appreciating the very special advantages of the Tory Party, of which the most striking is its monopoly of most of the best patriotic tunes.

History is on the side of the Tories, in the sense that most of the nation's myths and legends tend to induce a naturally right-wing disposition. Kings, noblemen, generals and admirals, wars, imperialism, all the ancient institutions of Church and State and the ceremonies and rituals attaching to them, in so far as they are today taken seriously at all, produce Tory-inclined reflexes. This is much truer in Britain than in the rest of Europe because the British Right, unlike its continental counterparts, has never decisively betrayed its monopoly of patriotism. The old order here has never been humiliatingly overthrown by revolution or compromised, as was the case in France, for example, by having to enlist foreign support against Napoleon, to win back its power and privilege. Indeed, in France it is primarily the parties of the Left rather than of the Right which can best evoke pride in the national past. Marching soldiers, military music, memorials to famous battles and famous generals, even street names —the majority of these recall the triumphs of the revolution or of Napoleon.

It is the Left which can sing the 'Marseillaise' with greatest enthusiasm and on whose platform the Tricolour seems most appropriate, with the Right always under suspicion—usually with good reason—of not being loyal to the Republic. French myths and legends, in short, being rooted in revolutionary and Republican—not to mention anti-clerical—soil, tend to fortify left-wing parties more than right—a tendency greatly strengthened by the appalling contrast between the role of the Right in supporting Pétain and the role of the Left in the Resistance. (De Gaulle is the exception that proves no rules and can be claimed equally by both Left and Right.)

The Right in Britain has a much better record. True, it has been associated with many failures and humiliations, but it has never been antinational. Moreover, by reason of its moderation and adaptability, it has never given the Left an opportunity for revolution. Thus there are in Britain no right-wing villains and no left-wing heroes; little right-wing shame and no left-wing glory.

This has had a number of consequences for the Labour Party which are of the utmost importance, and does much to explain why it is so ineffective in government. In the first place it has made it necessary for the Left to seek to denigrate British institutions, since it has never been strong enough to overthrow them. In Britain there has been no spectacular storming of the Bastille or glorious revolutionary war followed by the creation of new institutions and a new order. There has been instead a slow, gradual process of intellectual attrition, with the old order and the old institutions undermined from within by the corrosion of satire (Shaw and Wells) and the needling of detailed criticism (the Webbs). This is perfectly proper and in many ways a far more civilized process than revolution. But it has the effect of weakening the old order and the old institutions without evoking the kind of passionate desire for regeneration out of which a new order and new institutions can spring. In a way the British Left is in the same kind of position as so many of the former British colonies. Because they were handed independence without having to struggle very hard for it, and without having to win it by force of arms, they find themselves independent nations without having gone through the furnace which actually forges a nation into being a nation. The British Left has had a similar experience, in the sense that it has found its hands on the levers of power without going through the revolutionary struggle which forges a party with the will to govern.

This is much less obvious today, of course, than it was at the time of the first Labour Government in the 1920s. Then it was pathetic, as it was, in the circumstances, bound to be. Ramsay MacDonald's minority Government came to office by virtue of Tory goodwill. Baldwin felt that Labour ought to be allowed to win their spurs and advised the King to give them a chance. It is not very surprising that the Labour Government leant over backwards to prove themselves statesmen in the classical British manner, as indistinguishable from what had gone before as possible. This is the fate of a non-revolutionary party of the Left. Its very act of coming to power is a profoundly conservative development, since it illustrates to perfection the flexibility and viability of the existing political system which is willing to allow Labour to come to power. How wise, generous, statesmanlike, the old order is made to seem, encouraging Labour to have a go! Indeed, nothing so became the Tory Party in the inter-war years as its willingness to insist on Labour's being given its fair chance, although in fact the old parties, Liberal and Conservative, could have kept Labour out if they had chosen to do so.

Paradoxical as it may seem, therefore, the very process of winning office tended to guarantee that the first Labour Government was bathed in an atmosphere of mutual goodwill, with the old order positively basking in self-righteousness, fortified in the knowledge—which all sections of the community tended to share—that it had done the right thing. The truth is that the Labour Party first reached Downing Street by virtue of Tory noblesse oblige, which had the double effect of strengthening the complacency of the old order and weakening the will to change things on the part of the new.

In other words the Labour Party came to power in a manner which marked no violent break in the island story. This has been deemed a fine example of the genius of British politics. Yet from the Labour Party point of view it has had two effects. Having created no new national heroes of its own, no revolutionary legend with which to fire popular emotions, no 'Marseillaise', it has had to share with the Tories the old myths and legends, the old heroes, the old tunes of glory. This has put the Labour Party under a permanent disadvantage, since by and large the Labour Party cannot make the classical patriotic noises as convincingly as the Tories for the very good reason that a significant section of the Labour Party does not believe in them. One is conscious of this, for example, at the annual cenotaph ceremony. A morning-coated Labour Prime Minister lays his wreath. But to a sizeable minority of Labour M.P.s this whole ceremony is an ugly disgrace; war, to them, is a capitalist racket; generals and admirals figure half comic and half evil. Or at a coronation:

with the best will in the world a Labour Administration does not fit in too well, since these great State occasions cannot avoid being associated with, and evocative of, an England that the Labour Party has come into existence to change and even destroy.

Here lies the fatal ambivalence at the root of the Labour Party. It has to rely on the emotional symbols and legends and rituals of the old order, since when the national sense of patriotism needs to be stirred these are all that are available; while intellectually it has a deep-seated contempt for them. Or put it another way: precisely because the Labour Party has a left-wing element that does not love Britain—Britain, that is, as it is constituted here and now—any Labour Government has to lean over Rightwards to avoid being suspected of lack of patriotism.

It is a real problem to have to carry out policies aimed at changing Britain—policies which have been worked out by a process of intellectual analysis and involve debunking most of the assumptions and values of the old order—in a society whose emotional cohesion very largely depends on maintaining those values and assumptions. To be precise, it is more difficult for a man like Harold Wilson—who is manifestly less able to evoke emotional patriotism than most right-wing leaders—to lead the country than for a typical Tory P.M., which explains why he has had to prove himself more 'Tory' than the Tories. For a Labour Prime Minister to be a convincing national leader he has to behave like a Tory.

The Attlee administration was unusually well placed in this respect. Its leaders, Attlee, Bevin, Morrison, and several others, had won their spurs in the great wartime coalition; some of Churchill's stardust had rubbed off on them. No one could doubt their patriotism, and in Bevin there was a manifest member of the bulldog breed, a John Bull incarnate. At the same time, so deep and widespread was the disgust at the remembered social injustice of the 1930s that socialist measures could be presented in terms which caught the popular imagination. True patriotism seemed then very closely bound up with building a New Jerusalem. The British Welfare State was felt to be the cynosure of world opinion, and the process of building it seemed almost an extension of Britain's finest hour. Even the withdrawal from India, in those days when it was still possible to believe in the nobility of decolonization and in the constructive potential of commonwealth, had a certain grandeur about it—the authentic touch of statesmanship. Left-wing policies then, in short, could be filled into a convincingly patriotic framework, sounding notes that could evoke a genuinely national response.

But this was an exceptional period, with the Labour Party operating in a uniquely favourable context. Not only were its leaders associated with the glories of war and the Tory Party's still associated with the indignities of Munich and appeasement—Churchill himself was not regarded as a Tory—but they were operating in a society that had become accustomed to State direction and control, abandonment of individual rights and preferences, as part of the sacrifices necessary to win the war. The Attlee administration, in short, found a ready-made head of patriotic steam which they could channel into the engine of socialism. At that time, for a few years, the Left had the good patriotic tunes.

The Attlee administration, therefore, was able to withdraw from India, for example, with the minimum of difficulty at home. There were, of course, passionate arguments about the desirability or necessity of such a decision, but only a handful of critics saw fit to impugn the Government's patriotism; such a criticism, directed against Labour leaders who had shared the glory of Churchill's administration, just did not stand up. In any case, at that period, British people were sated with national glory. Imperial withdrawal then could still be presented as an act of splendid generosity—a decision taken from strength not weakness. Having won the war, Britain was proud enough nationally to make imperial concessions without recrimination. Indeed, she was proud enough nationally for imperial withdrawal to be presented as itself a new form of achievement which went by the name of transforming empire into commonwealth and which Labour was peculiarly suited to bring to fruition.

But it has to be understood that post-war Labour administrations—and this was true in the 1920s as well as the 1940s—are in peculiarly favourable circumstances, since if war itself, with its need for martial ardour, charismatic leadership, patriotic fervour, tends to give the Tory Party a natural edge —they are meant to know about strategy, foreign affairs and things like that—the challenge of peace and reconstruction tends naturally to favour Labour, since building New Jerusalems is very much a job for the Left to do. People feel it safe to forget about foreign affairs, defence and so on for a time, and more important to get on with promoting social justice. It is a period when people naturally talk about switching from waging war to waging peace, which is the ideal mood for a Labour Government to come to power. At such periods, the central requirement for an effective Labour Government—an ability to produce a popular head of steam powerful enough to drive a socialist engine—is more or less fulfilled. The right kind of popular slogans are at hand: homes fit for heroes to live in; if the State can spend £x billion on war, why can't it spend £y billion in peace? Moreover, a war economy has accustomed all classes to the idea of State control and direction. The wartime crusade is transmuted into a peacetime crusade, which is precisely the kind of popular climate that socialism requires, and which—at least in Britain—socialism, normally, cannot evoke.

But the mood in 1964–70 was sadly different from that of 1945. Seldom, if ever, has the communal impulse been so weak, or patriotism held in such low repute. There is, as I say, something ironic about this, since the Left played an immensely influential role in creating the present mood of national cynicism. Virtually every symbol of the collectivity —Parliament, the Monarchy, the armed forces of the Crown, the Church of England, and so on—has been mercilessly and ceaselessly derided, as have the individual heroes of the past, virtually all of whom, including Churchill himself, are now shown to have sensational feet of clay.

Let me make it clear that I am not in any way criticizing this cult of satire, or even the determined destruction of the nation's past. A liberal society has to be able to live with these passing fashions, damaging as they may well be. The question, however, is whether a society seeking to develop collectivist habits can live with them. Democratic socialism, as I say, much more than Toryism, requires a corporate sense of national purpose. Under socialism the individual is expected gladly to sacrifice personal advantage for the communal good. He is expected to trust the State as the instrument which will give expression to the popular good.

In 1945 this is what the State *could* do, which is why Mr Churchill's speech warning that socialism meant the Gestapo was so wide of the mark. In the postwar mood democratic socialism was certainly possible, since all classes were inspired by a remarkable upsurge of national pride. This was a continuation of Britain's finest hour. The patriotic soil was there in abundance for socialist sowing. Today's desert of cynicism, however, is a profoundly different matter. It does not mean the Gestapo, of course, any more than it did in 1945. But it does mean a less willing response to State appeals, less leverage for the State to get enthusiastic co-operation in painful or difficult ventures. The position can be stated very simply: in a society where the nation means less and less to the public, the public is prepared to do less and less for the nation.

This is surely a deadly disadvantage for a socialist party, much more so than for the Conservatives, who talk a lot about national pride but do not depend on it to anything like the same fundamental degree. The Conservatives believe in market disciplines and the profit motive as the source of economic energy. So far as the production of wealth is concerned the State is relegated to a relatively minor role. People are expected to work for their own good, not for the good of the community. But the Labour Party does not believe in private enterprise or the market. It believes in State control, in nationalization, in the ideal of all groups working together for the common good. Its whole ethos is deeply embedded in the idea of a highly self-conscious and corporatively cohesive society, in which the national interest comes before the whims or greed of private acquisition. This is the essence of collectivism, and an admirable essence in many ways it is.

But one crucial conclusion, which is seldom recognized, emerges from this. Whereas 'the authoritative state' and 'the patriotic people' are still part of Tory rhetoric, without having any longer much to do with Tory reality, they have everything to do with Labour reality, however little place they have in Labour rhetoric. Their absence from contemporary Britain, therefore, makes a mess of Tory speeches but not much difference to their ability to govern. For the Labour Party, on the other hand, their absence makes no difference to their speeches, but a profound difference to their ability to govern.

The paradox is that the Tory Party has the right emotional attitudes to make it an effective socialist instrument—reverence for the State, a sense of 'the nation', the ability to see authority as virtuous and worthy and to communicate this vision, a liking for the language of togetherness, and real patriotic fervour. These are the organ-stops it can pull out with genuine faith and zest, although the capitalist system, which it exists to promote, can get along very nicely without them. The Labour Party, on the other hand, which desperately needs to be able to exploit these tunes on behalf of socialism, and cannot make progress without doing so, is singularly unsuited to put them over, except in a miserably cracked way, its left wing exuding all the time a low indignant moan.

The tragedy of the Labour Party is that by an accident of history it was compelled into a posture and style which preclude it now from the kind of whole-hearted commitment to nationalism which its economic theories require if they are to work in a free society. Far more than the Tories it needs to be able to wrap itself up in the Union Jack and sing 'Rule, Britannia!'. But its history and composition do not allow it to do so convincingly, or without outraging the conscience of many of the party faithful.

It is clear today that the process of economic growth is going to be acutely painful, requiring a Government which can command exceptional loyalty, devotion and trust. Socialist and collectivist solutions have much to commend them. But if they are to work, they need an organ of government capable of breathing into the State machine a formidable spirit of confidence and authority, and into the workers a comparable and reciprocal spirit of fervour and expectancy. Can it any longer be seriously supposed that the Labour Party can forge such a Government? Realism suggests that its combination of right-wing fabianism, which rules out the impetus to be gained by militant radicalism, and left-wing internationalism and pacifism, which rule out the impetus to be gained by militant chauvinism, is almost doomed to produce variations of Wilsonianism which result only in disappointment and frustration all round.

Let me repeat: I am not concerned here to argue that collectivism or socialism are bad ideas in all conditions. The point is whether they are good ideas in the particular circumstances of this country at present; which means, in effect, is the British Labour Party in a position to make them work today? My answer is that in a society like that of contemporary Britain, where the old ruling class, which is still in control of the State machine, is so unsure of itself—its uncertainty being a direct result of Labour's own left-wing threats—and no new ruling class can be developed quickly enough to take its place, the Labour Party's right-wing fabians being opposed to such a root-and-branch transformation, the bureaucracy is likely to be totally unfit to shoulder the gigantic burdens of a collectivist grand design. This, I believe, it has proved itself to be. Secondly, in a society suffering from the shrinking pains of imperial diminution and from the fears and insecurities of technological change, the workers will be in no mood for voluntary co-operation for the good of the community, the community being a concept today in this country of unprecedented meaninglessness.

So we come back to the key question: how can a Labour Government create sufficient popular momentum to transform society by socialist measures? If it cannot have recourse to either the fervour of revolution or the passions of patriotism, from what other source can the necessary thrust and drive come? Six years under Mr Wilson showed up the inadequacy of the pre-1964 thinking on this question, which was best expressed in the now—with the benefit of hindsight —comical writings of Mr Anthony Crosland:

> I feel clearly that we need large egalitarian changes in our educational system, the distribution of property, the distribution of resources in periods of need, social manners and style of life, and the location of power within industry; and perhaps some, but certainly smaller, changes in respect of incomes from work. I think that these changes, taken together, will amount to a considerable social revolution.[*]

[*] Anthony Crosland, *The Future of Socialism* (Cape, 1964), p. 216.

John Vaisey summarizes the Crosland view:

> He argued in 1959 that what was needed was a better administration of a society that was rapidly solving its economic problems, and which found itself faced by a need to take certain measures to change the social tone. This implied of course measures that by traditional socialist criteria would be called modifications of the superstructure, and which were, in fact, of a fairly conventional Asquithian kind (the equivalent of disestablishing the Church of Wales).*

One cannot avoid the conclusion now, some twelve years later, that these Crosland thoughts were sadly unrealistic, since they took the basic problem of economic growth for granted, or assumed that it only required a little brainpower in high places—which they would supply *ad lib*—to bring it about. But it has not worked out like that. The problems are now seen to go much deeper. So much deeper that they raise doubts about the suitability of the Labour Party even to begin to cope with them.

In other words, we have today a disheartened bureaucracy and a suspicious workforce. To make a collectivist society out of such ingredients does not raise the old problem of freedom: how to make an omelette without breaking eggs. The Labour Party's problem is really not moral at all. It is severely practical. They are trying to make an omelette with no eggs. This is not immoral; it is just foolish. When the ingredients for an effective collectivist society are absent, as they are absent in Britain today, it is best not to try to create one.

* *Encounter,* May 1969.

4

In the last chapter, I referred to the problem posed for a Labour Government by the absence in this country of an authoritative ruling order. It may seem strange to refer to this as a problem, since the Labour Party is known to want to bring about precisely this state of affairs. But here, once again, we run into the extraordinary superficiality of Labour thinking. In fact, the problem of authority becomes more important, not less, in a society moving towards collectivism and socialism. Democratic socialism, far from being about equality, as Hugh Gaitskell once affirmed that it was, *should* be about authority, since no system is so dependent on its exercise. Failure to recognize this is a fundamental source of Labour weakness in government.

The first thing to note about a collectivist society is that it increases the range of decisions taken by officials; requires, that is, an enlarged bureaucracy. Decisions which in a predominantly capitalist economy are taken as a result of the dictates of the market are determined instead by central planners. This, indeed, is the supposed virtue of the collectivist system. It replaces the impersonal and often cruel pressures of the market, of the cold, invisible hand, by mortal men and women endowed with social consciences.

But let us be clear about the implications of this. It means that these men and women have to give orders, the authority behind which depends not on the impersonal forces of the market but on their individual judgements of what is right and wrong, sensible or stupid, in the public interest or against it. Clearly a local housing officer, allocating council houses, is in a different relationship to an applicant (one might almost say supplicant) than is a commercial estate agent seeking to sell a house to a client.

In the case of the latter, it is simply a question of cash. Has the client the money? If he has, he gets the house. In the case of the former, the housing officer is much more like God. He has to decide between one applicant and another; make highly subtle moral judgements. If his decisions and judgements are to be acceptable, he obviously has to be a rather special kind of person, somebody with just that bit of extra character, a leader of men. *Has* to be? I mean, of course, *ought* to be. But the point is that the Labour Party has given absolutely no thought to the problem—which is central to democratic social-ism—of making him so.

What I am arguing is that in a collectivist society, the authority of the official groups has to be of a much higher order than that of the capitalist 'boss' class. The boss gives orders within a system determined by iron laws of supply and demand, profit and loss, which he cannot control. It was these impersonal laws that sacked a man, or that led to unemploy-ment or to the poverty of one area as against the prosperity of another. The socialist or collectivist official gives orders that spring either from his own assessment or from those of his superiors, going up ultimately to the Minister himself. They are meant to represent the dictates of social justice as determined by men and women who are assumed to know best; not simply to be richer or better at manipulating the market or more inventive, but wiser, fairer; in a word, *superior.*

There is much to be said for this collectivist idea. That wealth should increasingly be produced and distributed according to rational patterns designed to maximize human welfare, rather than according to iron laws of the market, will always seem an aim worth struggling for, as long as men preserve their faith in human reason.

But the ideal, like all ideals, raises problems. How are we to develop these superior beings whose decisions and judge-ments in some of the most intimate and delicate areas of human life—the education of children, health, pensions, housing, and so on—will be voluntarily accepted; whose *orders*, to be blunt, will be willingly *obeyed*. This is the crucial problem in a society seeking to develop democratic socialism. How to get those who have to obey to want to obey, to want to co-operate? The surest way, of course, is that they should believe in the rightness of the orders, and of the fitness of those who give them; unless, that is, State compulsion is to play so large a part as to interfere with the requirements of a free society.

Let me repeat: a collectivist society rests on the assumption that it is possible to develop a minority which knows what is best for the majority. Nobody any longer can brush this fact under the carpet by pretending that in a participatory society, it is the majority which decides what is best for itself. Manifestly this cannot be so. Resources will never be unlimited. In practice, a collectivist society will require painful questions of priorities, taking away from one group to give to another and so on. While the general principles can be laid down by the people, acting through the political parties, their implementation will fall on the bureaucracy. Can it any longer be denied, therefore, that the authority exercised by this bureaucracy, by which I mean its ability to get its decisions willingly accepted and carried out, is an absolutely central problem for democratic socialism. Let me spell it out in a very simple proposition. Collectivist officials, much more than capitalist bosses, have to be able to elicit voluntary assent since, having done away with market disciplines, they can only compel adherence by recourse, in the final analysis, to the policeman's truncheon, which step in a free society they are naturally unwilling to take.

Yet if one looks at contemporary Britain this ability to command voluntary assent is unprecedently absent in all walks of life, as much in the schools and universities as in industry and the trade unions. Few deny that Britain today is suffering from a vacuum in leadership. People at the top know what needs to be done. What is lacking is their ability to persuade—inspire, if you like—those below them to do it. It is quite simply a failure of leadership, a collapse of authority. This diagnosis of Britain's ills finds widespread agreement. The inability of those in positions of command to give orders effectively, and the unwillingness of those underneath to receive them naturally, is so obvious that it has ceased to shock. Yet it is at the root of our contemporary ills; it is the canker at the heart of the body politic.

What is so pathetic about the Labour Party is that it refuses to recognize that this is a much more deadly threat to its own system of socialist organization than it is to the one it is seeking to replace. Although it seeks to promote economic changes which require an authoritative governing order, it at the same time presses ahead with social policies designed not only to weaken the governing class that already exists but also to prevent any new order taking its place. Its collectivist economic policies require a markedly hierarchic system of status and rank, while its egalitarian social policies are aimed at producing the opposite.

The explanation for this inconsistency is, of course, very simple. The Labour Party developed its emotional attitudes at a time when the problems of government did not need to bother it, and when its whole energy was concentrated on destroying the old ruling order rather than constructing the new. It was perfectly rational, therefore, to seek to weaken the old order, since this obviously had to be done first, and was going to be difficult enough to do anyway, without bothering unduly about such long-term—and at that time academic —problems as how to maintain authority in the new circumstances. But these same attitudes exist in the Labour Party today, when manifestly the urgent task for democratic socialism in this country is to create a new tradition or style of authority, a new kind of glamour at the top, a new élite, if you like, capable of getting its orders *willingly* obeyed.

This is another example of how impractical the Labour Party is as a base for effective government in contemporary conditions. It demands of its leaders two contradictory aims: that they should create and operate an increasingly collectivist economy, on the one hand, and promote an increasingly egalitarian society on the other; that is to say, build up an ever-expanding State machine while cutting down on the numbers of people fit to operate it. Here again the Labour theorists have lamentably failed in their task of intellectual analysis. They have failed to realize that far from collectivism's doing away with the need for authoritative leadership, for men and women with the gifts of winning voluntary obedience, it in fact vastly augments it, while bending every effort to guarantee that the need should not be met.

The trouble is, of course, that socialist theory assumes the existence of a co-operative society in which the masses have been educated to the point where they are eager to serve the public interest. The problem of the exercise of authority, therefore, is relegated to a very lowly place. Decisions would be reached in such a happy climate of communal solidarity that only the curmudgeonly and recalcitrant few would stand out against them. In the kind of mature democracy envisaged by the generation of socialist intellectuals, like Mr Crosland, who were in the Labour Government, a highly educated public, having participated in the decision-making process, would want to co-operate, it being taken for granted that by then social privilege would have been abolished.

It is now clear, as we have already seen, that this dream-world has not emerged and is not likely to do so in the foreseeable future. To a large extent it was wholly unrealistic to suppose that it would, since the kind of changes that would be required to build this utopia vastly exceeded anything that could be achieved through parliamentary reform. If the workers, for example, were to renounce their deeply ingrained habits of suspicion and non-co-operation, something far more radical was obviously required than the formal changeover from private ownership to nationalization, which from the workers' point of view changed very little. Quite clearly, to produce the kind of attitudes democratic socialism requires, Labour Governments would have had to overturn society, which they have had no mandate to do.

So much is now obvious even to the Labour leaders themselves. None any longer supposes that there has been or is going to be a moral transformation in the mass of the public. Maybe socialism would bring about such a transformation in ideal conditions. But the conditions are not going to be ideal. Indeed, from this point of view, they are getting worse. As affluence spreads it brings in its wake a new problem. In the nineteenth century the workers were too poor and primitive to understand the virtues of socialism, and too intimidated by the landlord and master. Today, they are too comfortable and selfish, and too corrupted by television and advertising. The socialist criticisms of the affluent society are so well known as not to need repeating here. What does need emphasizing.

however, is that the old assumptions about the nature of the society in which democratic socialism would be functioning make absolutely no sense today. Indeed, far from moving towards this kind of society, we are moving away from it.

But if the moral transformation of society cannot be relied upon—and nobody on the Left now believes that it can—what is the Labour Party's answer to the problem of authority in an untransformed and still unregenerate society? Pessimists might suppose, from the record of Mr Wilson's Government, that the trend is going to be towards compulsion. Certainly the prices and incomes legislation and the trade-union reforms lent substance to this suspicion. But in fact, no Labour Government, depending as it does on trade-union finance, can afford to go very far down this road, which, in any case, only traverses the strictly economic field. The problem of authority goes much wider than that. It affects all areas of the communal life, since, as I say, the essence of a collectivist society is that decisions affecting an ever-increasing range of activities are taken not by the citizen himself but by official bodies acting on his behalf. But from where are these official bodies going to draw their authority, in the sense defined above, if the community they now represent is not of the ideal kind which socialist theory supposed it was going to be? What we are moving towards is a socialist system of organization in a society without the spirit of socialist community required to give it legitimacy.

The Labour Party cannot any longer refuse to address itself to the problem of leadership in a collectivist society, since the justification for this refusal—namely, that the led would not need leading—has proved to be sadly unfounded. All the current trends suggest that modern industrial society, precisely because of its complexity, incomprehensibility, and moral ambiguity, will be much more difficult to lead, rather than much less; will require a much more impressive type of person at the top if the necessary degree of trust is to be engendered. It used to be argued that whereas the case for a ruling class might have made sense when there was an empire to govern, it makes no sense in the changed conditions of Britain today. Unfortunately, this facile optimism, so characteristic of the thinking of the Left, bears no relation to contemporary reality. Technology and science are all the time opening up new frontiers which reveal a world of terrifying mystery and challenge, inducing among the great mass of the people an almost unparallelled sense of insecurity and dependence on forces which they do not understand. Probably at no earlier period in history, therefore, has the need for authoritative leadership, capable of inspiring trust, been so great; or the danger of its absence been so overwhelming. In terms of popular understanding of the new forces which science and technology are unleashing, Britain today is comparable to a primitive African tribe in the nineteenth century suddenly finding itself faced with Western civilization. It is desperately in need of paternal tutelage, more so probably than at any other period. It is also, for this very reason, more vulnerable to exploitation and the depredation of irresponsible guidance. In other words, seldom have our circumstances put such a premium on the need to produce responsible rulers, who can inspire trust without exploiting it.

It is against this background that one must examine the Labour Party's commitment to egalitarianism, and to the creation of a classless society. It seems to me to show a staggering disregard for the deepest needs of democratic socialism in this country at the present time. For if it is agreed that democratic socialism involves an increase in the exercise of State authority across the board, and that this exercise should rely on the minimum use of compulsion; that the circumstances in which this increase is going to have to be made are not such as to inspire the public with a fierce spirit of communal patriotism—quite the opposite; that the decisions which will have to be implemented are likely to be both painful and unpopular—in many ways unprecedentedly so; and that the temptations to exploit public ignorance in a world where knowledge is increasingly esoteric are alarmingly great; then it follows that those who wield this power, the new technocrats and bureaucrats, will need to be, certainly ought to be, very superior people with exceptional gifts of responsible leadership—the very type of people which an egalitarian society is not only unlikely to produce but specifically designed to avoid producing. The irony is that although capitalism can work against a background of social egalitarianism—as America has demonstrated—democratic socialism, at least in a mass industrial society like Britain today, almost certainly cannot. The capitalist Tories really do not need those playing-fields at Eton. The Labour Party does.

What is so unfortunate about the Labour Party today is that it is still so obsessed by its traditional distaste for the old ruling class that it cannot get itself to give serious attention to the problem of creating a new one, since anything that helped to bring a new one into life would hinder the task of putting the old one to death. As a result, the whole thrust of Labour thinking is still geared to weakening and diminishing the old class system rather than building up a new hierarchy, relevant to present needs, to take its place. Instead of considering the potentially constructive role of privilege and property in contemporary society, and instead of seeking to adapt these two classical supports of authority to the needs of democratic socialism, it concentrates on rooting them out of capitalist society. They cannot be blamed for this. It is part of the Labour dilemma, part of the dilemma of the fabian approach. Being unwilling to make a clean sweep of the old order, the Labour Party has to adopt a squint-eyed approach to social problems, one eye on its commitment to get rid of the relics of the past and the other on its task of creating a social system to take their place. But this built-in ambivalence is a dreadful handicap to effective government, since it precludes clear recognition that social status is an integral part of social democracy, and that in seeking to destroy it, out of loyalty to its past commitments, the Labour Party is in fact frustrating its own chance of succeeding in its present aims.

For the truth is that once the market disciplines of a capitalist society are weakened, and State authority is increasingly relied on to take their place, those who operate the State machinery, if they are to command voluntary acquiescence, need to be endowed with all the mesmeric qualities which only a superior status can supply; need to be able to inspire a voluntary obedience which men do not normally accord to their equals; need, in short, to live in a privileged way that cuts them off from and raises them above the mass of their fellow citizens.

Of course it is easy to dismiss this as the worst kind of Tory reaction, and it is perfectly true that these are the views about authority which old-fashioned Tories do hold. As Samuel Beer puts it in his remarkable book *Modern British Politics*:

> Toryism is not a theory of oligarchy—a theory that the rich should rule because they are rich—although no doubt this is a corruption to which it is susceptible, and an interpretation that its opponents are prone to put upon it. The Tory argues that property should be adapted to the needs of the State, not vice versa. He does not argue, as Liberals sometimes did, that the protection of private property is the main end of the State and that, therefore, the well-to-do ought to rule. He does indeed say that the governing class ought to have wealth and social status. But these are not the justifications of its power. On the contrary, they are conditions auxiliary to its social function; they are 'privileges' necessary to enable it to rule effectively and well. 'Responsible government demands certain privileges in the way of leisure and culture,' writes A. K. White. 'Only those who are economically secure can acquire a culture which ... enables them to rule responsibly!' The governing class is not primarily an owning class or a class of elegance and culture. It is rather a class that governs—in business, education, and political party; in church, army and State. From this superiority its title to other superiorities is derived. If we may think of the class theory of the socialists as essentially a theory of 'economic' class, we may contrast the Tory view as a theory of 'political' class.*

The irony of all this is that this old and, to my mind, profound Tory insight into the source of social order is today far more applicable to the needs of modern socialism than to the needs of modern conservatism, and could be expected, logically, to appeal far more to Mr Wilson than to Mr Enoch Powell. Economic liberals, with their faith in the automatic mechanisms of the market, consider that order in economic life does not need more than an occasional touch of authority. There is no need, therefore, for a political class. To quote Beer again:

* S. H. Beer, *Modern British Politics* (Faber, 1965), p. 94.

48

On a deeper level, the moral philosophy of Liberalism held that a large part of the citizenry were capable of understanding and respecting the foundations of the social order. Such mutual acceptance of common purpose and interest, according to their way of thinking, opened the way for popular government and dispensed with the need for paternalistic guidance.*

But the Labour Party never shared the *economic* assumptions of liberalism, or at any rate not from the moment it adopted socialism, and would seem fairly rapidly to be losing faith in liberalism's moral philosophy. Mr Crossman, for example, confessed—he is always confessing, which makes him so attractive —that in many ways Britain today was less a participatory democracy than it had been in his youth.

When I was teaching W.E.A. classes in the 1930s I confidently anticipated that the number of citizens actively participating in public life, the number of self-governing groups and voluntary organizations, would increase year by year as education improved the political understanding of the electorate. Now thirty years later I have to admit that these hopes have not been justified. The active minority of citizens who participate has not grown as we expected....†

In other words, although the Labour Party is still as emotionally opposed to this ancient Tory insight as ever it was, the assumption which supported this opposition—namely, that a large part of the citizenry would be capable of understanding and respecting the foundations of the social order— can no longer be made with anything like the same confidence. But Mr Crossman's lecture went even further than that. He was not content merely to undermine one of the key socialist assumptions. He also paid perhaps unconscious tribute to the key Tory assumption about the need and value for a political class. 'In terms of universal suffrage,' he said, 'we may not have

* *Modern British Politics*, p. 94.
† *Three Studies in Communication* (Panther, 1969), p. 13.

had full democracy in the times of Gladstone and Disraeli. But in the terms of active participation by a voluntary minority our democracy was I fear more virile, more alert, more of a test for the real quality of a Government than it is today.'*

What Mr Crossman is in effect saying is that in contemporary Britain we have neither a majority nor a minority who wish to participate, which is really to admit that the drift towards the Left in recent years has resulted in doing away with the old ruling class without putting anything in its place except executive rule.

There can be little doubt, of course, that executive rule or, as John Mackintosh has called it, Prime Ministerial government has increased, in recent decades, while the power of Parliament has declined. 'In the absence of any written constitution,' Mr Crossman writes, 'this movement was inevitable as we gradually adopt universal suffrage. In the House of Commons we see the emergence of an ever stronger centralized executive.... Outside Westminster we see the decline of local democracy and the weakening of voluntary participation in most kinds of community life including politics.' Some British socialists might suppose that these trends would assist a Labour Government in the aim of introducing socialist measures, since they amount, in effect, to a general move towards plebiscitary democracy. In theory this should allow a Labour Government to use its grassroots support among mass opinion to impose its policies regardless of minority objections, as reflected in and outside Parliament, rather as Franklin Roosevelt, who was always appealing to the people over the heads of Congress, did in his New Deal days, or General de Gaulle did with his referenda.

The trouble with the Labour Party, however, is that it is not at all well suited to the practice of plebiscitary politics. Having developed during the late nineteenth century when success in Parliament was still regarded as the key to national influence, it has always sought to behave like a parliamentary party, eschewing vulgar recourse to demagogic appeals direct to the people. In this sense it is much more respectable than the Tories, whose roots go back to an earlier eighteenth-century approach of bribing the electorate with beer and cash.

* *Three Studies in Communication*, p. 13.

50

But in other ways, too, the Labour Party is far less plebiscitary in spirit than the Tories, for the good reason that most of the deeply popular tunes stick in its throat, as we have already seen.

It is bad at beating the nationalistic drum, unable to sound the chords of revolutionary memory about past glories or future aspirations. Equally important, it is highly suspect on certain issues of intense popular concern, like immigration and capital punishment, where its moral conscience precludes it from stirring the passions of the people, particularly of the working class. The Tories, perhaps because of their very primitiveness or coarseness, their lack of involvement with the non-conformist conscience in all its manifestations, from pacifism to teetotalism, their hearty patriotism and saloon-bar earthiness, their ability, that is, to appeal to a strain in the national character that transcends the Victorian age—in which the Labour Party has its roots—are better able than Labour to practise plebiscitary politics.

But if the composition and history of the Labour Party render it inept at whipping up the kind of popular enthusiasm which enables executive government to 'get things done', and it cannot rely on the existence of a civilized majority who want to participate in running the country, what alternative is there but to fall back on that essentially Tory solution of a civilized governing class?

Yet trying to follow this train of thought through the labyrinthine maze of Labour's mind one very quickly runs into a dead end—the commitment to egalitarianism. For how is it possible to re-create that 'voluntary minority' which, according to Mr Crossman, made 'our democracy more virile, more alert, more of a test for the real quality of a government' without encouraging it in ways that militate against the creation of a classless society?

This dilemma was beautifully illustrated in Mr Crossman's lecture from which I have been quoting. Its purpose was to plead for a more intelligent television coverage of politics, the aim being to get more programmes 'in depth' which might appeal to that 'voluntary minority' with a real interest in the subject. One sees the point. Most television programmes about public affairs are pitifully puerile. But the reason is that they are geared to a mass audience which likes triviality. From the point of view of a socialist bureaucrat seeking to operate an increasingly sophisticated post-industrial economy this is a major inconvenience. Issues are grossly oversimplified, reduced to questions of personality or, if they are really difficult to comprehend, simply ignored. But if they were discussed in an 'adult' way the great mass of the audience would switch off.

What is significant about this plea of Mr Crossman's—and similar pleas were made in the last few years by other Labour Ministers, notably Mr Wedgwood Benn—is that they are really asking for a television coverage of public affairs which would reduce mass interest and increase minority interest. They are really saying that public affairs are too serious and complicated a business to be left to the public, whose demands are for triviality and superficiality, and should be increasingly determined by the knowledgeable few, who have the necessary understanding of the problems.

This is all part of a growing recognition within the Labour Party of the incorrigibility of the masses, of the increasing difficulty of getting the requirements of socialist administration across to the working class, of the need, if socialist purposes are to be realized, of reducing the influence of the ignorant many and increasing the influence of the educated élite. The aim, therefore, is quite simply to disenfranchise the people, not of course by taking away their votes or anything reactionary like that, but by so elevating the level of public discussion, so reducing the content of what they call trivialization, that the expert view is always likely to prevail.

But boring the masses into passivity is hardly a serious answer to the problem of social authority in a collectivist society, and I only mention it as an example of how fanciful and unrealistic Labour thinking becomes when faced with it. They will chase any hare rather than risk shooting the socialist fox; think about anything rather than the central issue of whether socialism, in the particular circumstances of Britain today, can be successfully built without the aid of the very buttresses of property and privilege which previously it has been the Labour Party's purpose to knock down.

For it is now clear that socialist governments in Britain are not going to be able to 'get things done' by the dynamic exercise of executive power supercharged by regular draughts of referendum-type elections; cannot, that is, operate a plebiscitary democracy. As we have seen, the relationship between Labour Governments and the people is not of the inspirational kind which socialism requires. But this relationship was meant to be the soil in which, under socialism, State authority would be rooted and from which it would draw its strength. The assumption was that Labour would create so manifestly just a society that the servants of the State would enjoy a moral prestige which nobody would want to resist, except a few saboteurs whose actions would seem patently criminal to the great majority. Civil servants under socialism, or so the theory went, would be transformed from the bullying devils of old to the ministering angels of the new order. Socialism would beatify the bureaucracy: that was the hope.

But six years of Labour showed that this was an idle hope. No Labour Government, operating within the context of a mixed economy, and seeking to introduce technological change —much of it acutely painful—can expect, or fairly be expected, to bring about this kind of transformation, particularly at a period when the whole notion of the State is under severe attack. It is not necessary to blame Mr Wilson for failure here. No Labour Government, however skilful, could build up the moral authority of the State in present circumstances, without, that is, the aid of divine intervention. But if Labour cannot rely on an enhanced new public authority, rooted in respect for the State, and remains determined to continue undermining the old private authority of the capitalist class, rooted in respect for wealth, to whom is it going to look for drive and momentum?

The answer is that in the kind of society actually existing in this country, which is no longer capitalist in any socially meaningful sense and is not going to be socialist in any socially meaningful sense either, it is necessary to encourage the emergence of a new political class whose authority rests on neither capitalist nor socialist assumptions, both of which are no longer relevant to contemporary circumstances. It is necessary, in short, to recognize that the bureaucracy and technocracy, precisely because they are not going to be authoritative by reason of their function, being the personifications neither of social justice (socialism) nor of entrepreneurial skill (capitalism), cannot afford to be made up of impersonal, faceless men without individual qualities of leadership, but must instead be filled by individuals of conspicuous charisma, manifest superiority, impressive bearing; men and women to whom the public find it easy and natural to look up. The point that has to be grasped is that in a pure capitalist system the entrepreneurial skill legitimized a boss class, whose success at creating wealth endowed them with authority; and in a pure socialist society, social justice legitimizes the bureaucracy, which is endowed with authority by virtue of its role in administering such a blessed condition. But in the kind of mixed society which we have today, where the entrepreneurial function has been irretrievably undermined, and social justice has not been proportionately buttressed, authority has to look for other sources of legitimization, unless we are to fall into one or other of the twin traps of chaos and compulsion.

This is what I mean by the contemporary relevance of the Tory insight into the nature of authority, which has its roots in the pre-capitalist and pre-socialist periods. This recognizes that authority is not only a question of power, economic or political, but also one of social style. Clearly style divorced from economic or political power is insufficient; but so equally are political and economic power divorced from style. What is meant by social style? This is obviously a compound of many different ingredients, of which the most important is self-confidence, which in turn requires security. This obviously involves a measure of property and wealth, but not as ends in themselves; only as aids to the development of an authoritative social style. Capitalists do not need a social style; their money talks. Nor do communist officials; their power talks. But in the kind of society we are developing—or trying to develop—here, where neither the authority of office nor that of wealth can be relied on, this other factor, style, becomes crucially important. I hesitate to call it aristocratic style, because one has only to mention the word to hear the clicking of closing minds. But it is difficult to avoid doing so, because what I am really saying is that in a democratic socialist society an aristocratic style is in fact indispensable.

I hope it is not necessary to insist at this point that my mind is not filled with some fanciful idea of a return to rule by the ancient hereditary aristocracy. It is filled, however, with the urgent need to develop some of the qualities of the old aristocracy in the new bureaucracy and technocracy, so that in time they will acquire the habit of authority which at present they sadly lack.

Ironically enough, this aim is far more in tune, as I say, with the actual requirements of a liberal collectivist society than with those of a liberal capitalist one, since the existence of a high-principled, public-spirited, charismatic class of top people, imbued with a tradition of noblesse oblige, was a luxury for capitalism—an ornamental hangover which the bourgeois hung on to for largely snobbish reasons—whereas for democratic socialism it is much more like a necessity. That is why the modern Conservative Party, which wishes to promote capitalism, can afford to emphasize policies designed simply to increase economic incentives for the wealth producers; can afford to turn away from the emphasis on aristocracy. Being a capitalist party it believes that once the pacesetters start galloping, market disciplines will make sure that the rest of society keeps up with them. But socialists can have no such faith. Their leaders, precisely because they are not plutocrats, need to be aristocrats; not belted earls of old, but endowed with relevant new accoutrements of prestige designed to give them an aura of authority which the masses can recognize and respond to. This is not something which wealth alone can supply. (Only a capitalist party can believe that.) It is something that society has to nurture with the express purpose of producing an authoritative political class. It involves an educational system designed to this end; a system of privilege designed to this end; a social philosophy designed to this end.

This is the central problem for the Labour Party. For them it is not enough to encourage the few to set the pace. They have to be encouraged in such a way as to persuade the many to keep up with them. It is no good just tempting the innovators to give a lead unless the rest of society can be made to follow.

Incentives in a liberal collectivist society have to be

twin-purposed. First they have to be such as to prise the few out of the rut, and secondly—which is just as important—they have endow the few with enough magnetism to draw others after them. But the trouble is that the Labour Party has spent the last fifty years in making sure that the classical sources of such social magnetism are no longer effective. Thanks to their efforts, the traditional trappings of authority—titles, cultivation, superior education, breeding, background, property—instead of continuing to excite respect and awe, tend now to provoke ribaldry and ridicule.

What is more, this phenomenon is now so much an accepted part of the British way of life that we have ceased to find it amazing and disturbing. It strikes us as quite normal that people who go to the best schools, enjoy all the fruits of privilege and background, speak the best English, and so on, should nowadays find it more difficult to exercise authority than those who conspicuously lack these advantages. So much is this topsy-turvy posture accepted that we wholly fail to realize what a fantastic national handicap it is, forcing political leaders, for example, to buttress their authority not by demonstrating medals or orders, degrees or fine possessions—legitimate objects for respect—but by claiming acquaintance with the Beatles or the heroines of Coronation Street.

This is not a universal trend. It does not happen in the rest of Europe. General de Gaulle did not pretend a respect for pop culture; nor do even Social Democrat German Chancellors. It is an oddity peculiar to Britain, and illustrates what may be regarded as this country's peculiar weakness—the fatal inability, shared equally, although for different reasons, by all classes, to command authoritatively or to obey willingly, which stultifies action over the whole range of activity from the tea-shop to the board-room.

Yet the Labour Party cannot address itself to this problem. Such is its history and composition that it cannot even admit its existence. Socialism, in the famous phrase, is about equality. That is still the pathetic claim, which bears no relation to the contemporary challenge. Let me spell it out very starkly. So long as the Labour Party is precluded from recognizing the need to build up a new authoritative ruling order, which means putting into reverse its egalitarian priorities, it will be unable to make democratic socialism work in this country —except by moving towards compulsion, which it is equally loth to do. The truth which has to be realized is that democratic socialism in this country has reached the point where a continued policy of levelling, of undermining the security of the middle class, of frowning on wealth and privilege, of seeking to buy working-class co-operation by punishing the rich, of hostility to élitist institutions like Oxford and Cambridge and the public schools, far from being consistent with its aims, is diametrically opposed to them. One can almost sense this realization percolating down the ranks of the last Labour Government, as it had to cope with the breakdown of authority in virtually every field from the trade unions to the universities, with the breakdown of law and order in the cities, with the decline of standards in the Civil Service, with the collapse of civil pride—the realization that in undermining the old order Labour has not opened up the road to socialism but destroyed the very instruments and attitudes on which socialism, far more than capitalism, has to rely.

The irony is that socialism in Britain requires a hierarchical society and cannot function without it. Paternity, not fraternity, should be its watchword. What the Labour Party has done is to promote a paternalist society, while undermining the authority of the fathers; created a nation of sheep without shepherds.

5

This, of course, was not the intention. The intention was to produce a society that did not need shepherds because there would be no sheep. Surely even the most dedicated social democrat will now admit that this happy condition has not been met. The need for shepherds, instead of diminishing, has vastly increased. How could it be otherwise in a society which increasingly accepts a collective obligation for looking after the needs of the citizen to a greater extent than ever before? Clearly a Welfare State will require many more shepherds than one based on the principle of self-help.

The question which the Labour Party refuses to face is how to produce them. It seems to have been assumed that as society provides more and more equal opportunities for all, those who succeed will still feel just as responsible for those who fail as was the case in a society where success and failure had very little to do with individual merit; i.e., that the self-made man will develop the same sense of social responsibility as the beneficiary of hereditary privilege. This has always seemed to me a very peculiar assumption to make. For if socialism means equality, or even only equality of opportunity, then the more socialist a society becomes, the less necessary it is for those on top to feel any personal responsibility for those below —unless, that is, those on top happen to be individuals of exceptional sanctity. They may wish, out of the goodness of their hearts, to take pity on their less successful fellow-citizens. But an egalitarian social system cannot require this of them. Duty or obligation is the product of rights. But if nobody enjoys more rights than anybody else the successful man cannot be said to owe any duty to the unsuccessful.

This is a contradiction at the heart of socialism. It places on society a tremendous weight of social responsibility, but does nothing to create a class prepared to do all that is necessary to shoulder this burden. One can understand easily enough how hitherto this problem has been disguised. In the early days of the Labour Party there were such manifest conditions of injustice that the privileged class could be relied upon to throw up at least a minority of its number who, either out of feelings of guilt or out of an anachronistic hangover of an aristocratic tradition, were prepared to practise noblesse oblige. In other words, the Labour Party could rely on the hangover of an aristocratic sense of service to make socialism work. It could assume the continuation of the last remnants of the old order to operate the new order. It could avoid facing up to the inadequacy of its own social system because in its early days it could use up the capital of the social system it was seeking to replace, rather as the humanists can escape the consequences of their own debunking of Christianity by relying on the moral capital laid up in the Christian era.

But obviously this hangover from the past was bound to be a waning asset, since not only were the positive conditions which created a sense of social responsibility—the existence of privilege—undermined, but so were the negative conditions— shocking and obvious poverty—which previously could be relied upon to inflame the social conscience. The very success of the Labour Party in both reducing privilege and reducing injustice was bound to do away both with the soil out of which the seed of social responsibility could spring and with the climate in which it was likely to grow.

What has to be faced today is the problem of social responsibility in a society which lacks both the dying embers of an old aristocratic tradition and the fierce flames of early reformist zeal; which is sustained neither by the ancient Tory spirit of duty nor by the first flush of socialist pioneering. The situation was strikingly different in the 1945–51 period of Labour rule, when the guilt of the old order and the excitement of the new, both at their peak, combined to give a wholly misleading impression of the amount of social responsibility available for democratic socialism to tap. Today, however, after six years of Mr Wilson, the problem can be seen in a much more realistic fashion.

Contemporary Britain has rightly been described as 'a stalemate State'. The conservative elements in the nation have been forced by the Labour Party to accept a measure of redistribution of wealth on the condition that the socialist crusade stops short of draconian expropriation; and the reforming elements in the nation have reconciled themselves to a measure of inequality on condition that those who enjoy their privileges renounce any belief in an aristocratic system of government. Both sides, in short, have sacrificed the content of their faith, its essential virtue, in return for short-term concessions. In return for the Conservative Party's acceptance of the Welfare State, and of the principle of equality of opportunity, the Labour Party has agreed to do nothing vicious about the public schools, or about the continued upper- and middle-class domination of finance and industry and the Civil Service. In return for socialist toleration of the old order's *de facto* enjoyment of its traditional privileges, the conservatives have agreed to jettison their *de jure* claim to enjoy these privileges by right. Whereas before the war the situation was regarded by the Left as diabolical and by the Right as divinely ordained —a source of moral passion as much for the one as for the other—today it is passively accepted as a makeshift bargain which neither party loves or hates but everybody exploits as best he may.

This shoddy hodgepodge is often praised as a truly splendid example of the British gift for compromise. My own view is that it leaves Britain with the worst of both worlds; the empty shell of each system without its idealistic kernel.

What the Labour Party has done is to destroy Toryism without creating socialism; dishearten the middle class without invigorating the lower class; drain the blood out of the class system while leaving much of its outward form intact. Both Left and Right, looking at contemporary Britain, can only see reflected a caricature of their respective social images. Because neither side is strong enough to promote its ideals, both have agreed to compromise on a Britain reflecting the lowest common denominator of the philosophy of each.

The case against the first post-war Labour Government has been well put by Mr Paul Johnson, the former celebrated editor of the *New Statesman*, as far back as 1958:

Labour ... thought that vertical nationalization of key industries could place the centres of economic power in the control of the public, and that a limited redistribution of incomes would destroy the class structure. Neither of these things happened. Nationalization gave the State only a marginal increase in control over the direction of the economy, whilst high income-tax merely increased the power and importance of capital. Public ownership became discredited as a social objective because it was presented as merely an alternative system of management. Under high taxation, possession of inherited wealth, or any form of property, became not less but more valuable. Labour effectively prevented the poor or the hard-working from becoming rich, while allowing the rich to become richer. Nor has even the limited redistribution of income in the years 1945–58 produced any corresponding changes in the social structure. Where economic barriers between the classes were lowered or demolished, they have been speedily and effectively replaced by social ones ... more solid by their very nature, for they are largely immune to legislative attack. Social behaviour, as opposed to the distribution of wealth, is not a legitimate or even practicable field for political policy, but it is a vital factor in the distribution of political power. In this metaphysical citadel, which Marx and all his followers had ignored, the British class system was able to rest, recuperate and emerge stronger than before.

Our class structure has survived for two reasons. First, it is complex and finely graduated: the yawning chasms which breed violent jealousies, and therefore violent changes, have never been allowed to emerge. Second, it is inclusive, not exclusive. Rising economic groups have always been allowed to find their natural level in the social hierarchy, and the upper tiers have always taken care to come to terms with, and subsequently annex, emergent institutions. This dual process has been hard at work since the war. As full employment and high investment have increased the national income, so the dominant classes have welcomed new recruits and thus broadened their basis of acceptance. Equally, they have accepted and neutralized the new centres of power.

The leaders of the Labour Party, and the trade-union movement have been given their natural places in the establishment. The new graduates of the Welfare State were slowly and carefully digested. Many of them, of course, went into science and technology, still totally excluded from social and political power. But a number—too few to dilute the spirit of the existing structure, but enough when converted to bring it a perceptible accession of strength—went into those central citadels: the executive grades of industry, the Press, wireless and television, the Treasury, the Foreign Service and the law. As with working-class entrants to public schools, the proportion was never allowed to exceed ten per cent. For, although the higher classes have always opened their ranks to new recruits, they will never tolerate an influx of sufficient magnitude to produce a real change of character.*

After six years of Mr Wilson, the radical young are even more critical than Mr Johnson was thirteen years ago. From the way they put it, of course, one might assume that the conservative elements in the country had completely reversed the socialist tide and had no further reason to fear. Conservative publicists, however, paint a very different picture. While agreeing that the Tory counter-revolution has prevented the worst excesses of socialism, they emphasize the high cost which Toryism has had to pay. Its essential quality, they point out, is that it guarantees a ruling class sufficient security of tenure to enable it to perform its proper function of national leadership. It can afford to plan for the future, in every field, because its present is guaranteed. It can afford to take the long view because it can reasonably expect to be there to inherit the long-term blessings.

This is the basic argument for making property, birth and upbringing, rather than merit or ability, the determinants of status, power and income. It may mean that at any particular moment society is less well governed than it could be—in that the best brains and characters will not necessarily be on top—but at least there will be those essential elements of con-

* Paul Johnson, 'A Sense of Outrage' in Hugh Thomas (ed.), *Conviction* (MacGibbon & Kee, 1958).

tinuity and security which in the long run are even more important for the health of the body politic.

Continuity and security, however, are precisely what socialism has succeeded in undermining. Britain's old order has won a reprieve but not an acquittal. It is allowed to exist, but denied the climate in which it can function. As a result, although birth and upbringing still play a part in determining the composition of those who govern Britain—with all the disadvantages which this implies—they do so without any of the advantages to society which such a system should entail. The virtue of a hereditary system is not so much that the men in power should have succeeded their fathers but that they should feel confident of being able to bequeath to their sons. Under the present conservative–socialist compromise Britain has the disadvantage of the former without the advantages of the latter. There is, therefore, quite as much dissatisfaction on the Right as on the Left. The Tory counter-revolution has run into as frustrating a dead end as the socialist revolution.

The essence of a class system is that its various grades should accept the basic hierarchy as reasonable and right and permanent. It is no good allowing a Duke to be a Duke, a capitalist to be a capitalist, a landowner to be a landowner, or a working man to remain a working man if in fact the values which such a stratified society reflects are no longer held to be valid. If you allow a Duke to call himself a Duke but deny him the authority which gives any function to his title; if you allow a capitalist to hang on to his millions but deny him the freedom to use them as he thinks fit; if you allow the landowner to enjoy his land but take away the sense of responsibility that should go with it; and if you allow the worker to work but assure him that he ought to be enjoying power— then you get a society in which nobody can feel inclined to dig deep roots. Nobody is doing what he feels he ought to be doing. Guilt and resentment become the dominating emotions. Everybody feels out of place, insecure and on the move. Britain's social revolution, in other words, has killed the class system in theory without killing it in fact; has left the edifice standing but removed the cement which gave it solidity and endurance.

As a result, a generation has grown up which finds Britain

a peculiarly uninspiring society in which to live. Thousands of working-class or lower-middle-class young people feel that their talents, sedulously developed by Welfare State education, can find no satisfying outlet in the contemporary social system. Led to believe that they would inherit a socialist New Jerusalem, where demon snobbery had been exorcised and class barriers destroyed, they find themselves living in a society where snobbery and class barriers have never been so conspicuous. Although, thanks to the redistribution of incomes, they have more money in their pockets than their fathers ever had, and, thanks to the State educational system, more brains in their heads, they still cannot scale the citadels of social privilege.

So long as the socialist crusade carried conviction it was possible to replace contempt for the past by hope for the future. But today the young rebels are as critical of socialism as a means for improving the future as they are opposed to conservatism as a means of preserving the past. They find the Red Flag as irrelevant to their problems as the Union Jack.

There is an almost equally negative attitude in their public-school counterparts. It is negative for quite different reasons, of course, but negative all the same. With them the problem is not one of being cut off from the fruits of power and position, but of finding the fruits just not worth eating.

Take, for example, the public-school son of a senior industrial executive. His upbringing will not differ much from his father's or grandfather's—Eton, Oxford, perhaps the Guards, with an assured partnership in the family firm waiting in the background. Privilege will still smooth his way to the top. But the climate of values in which this process takes place will be profoundly different from that which shaped his father and grandfather. He will not regard these advantages as in any way imposing on him a debt of social responsibility. In the first place the existence of the Welfare State makes any such feeling of paternalism seem absurdly old-fashioned. Secondly, because he will be clever enough to realize that his advantages contradict the basic doctrinal assumptions of the society in which he lives, he will regard them as a piece of good fortune, like winning a football pool, which requires neither gratitude nor repayment. Privilege today has a black-market flavour.

Those who are lucky enough to enjoy it do not like to rationalize their good fortune, or to attempt to justify by accepting its obligations. It is regarded as a 'perk' which society dispenses for no particular reason. The less said or done about it the less likely society will be to have second thoughts. This privileged section of British youth enjoys life, but in a spirit of indulgent scepticism. In so far as they are interested in politics, it is as a means of protecting a cosy billet. But to sacrifice anything for a cosy billet is clearly a contradiction in terms, like dying for a standard of living.

There is, I should say, something in common between this kind of privileged negation and the attitude of the young rebels. Both these wings of the younger generation enjoy material well-being, the one nearly as great as that of their fathers and the other infinitely greater. But neither feels at all strongly about society itself, except a sense of disillusion and distaste.

It is, of course, wholly unfair to blame the Labour Party for the stalemate State. One could just as well blame the Conservatives. My point is not a party one at all. What I am trying to suggest is that, given the balance of the two parties, British socialism is bound to remain a hybrid affair; so, for that matter, is British Toryism. It is manifestly absurd to consider the future of British socialism without bearing in mind as a crucial determining factor the need to share power with a powerful Tory Party, just as the Tory Party has to consider conservatism against the background of a powerful Labour Party.

The trouble about the Labour Party is that its history and composition preclude it from coming to terms with the reality of the stalemate State; prevent it from making the best of it. The reality is that although Labour has succeeded in building a socialist structure in which the State is responsible for the people's major social needs and for a wide and crucial section of industrial affairs, it has not succeeded in bringing about a social revolution sufficiently far-reaching to produce a new kind of social being or do away with the old kind of social being. We have had a lot of new socialist measures since 1945, but there are probably fewer men and women prepared to make them work in the spirit of socialist ideals today than there were then. We have more of the machinery of socialism now but less of its flesh and blood. But the point is that British socialism, given the context of British politics, can never hope to create a new socialist social order. Assuming the continued strength of the Tory Party and barring unforeseeable upheaval, enough of the old social order will remain to be able to insist not that socialism should be reversed but that it can only be operated with middle-class consent and co-operation.

Yet in practice it is terribly difficult for the Labour Party to swallow this unpalatable conclusion. For once it is accepted, it becomes painfully clear that adjustments which in theory were meant to follow the social revolution, and be justified by it, are going to have to be made without the social revolution ever taking place. In other words, the Labour Party is going to have to start cosseting and comforting the existing bureaucrats and technocrats, the administrators of the Welfare State and the nationalized industries, the managers of the private sector, regardless of the fact that in many cases such cosseting and comforting will benefit not some new socialist governing order but the very capitalist middle class which the Labour Party thought it existed to destroy.

This is another major dilemma for the Labour Party. If socialism is to be made to work, there is obviously a need to promote the kind of conditions that will produce top-quality people to operate it. The Russians recognize this, as is well known, and are rapidly adopting the principle of selectivity in education and income differentials with the express purpose of encouraging a socialist élite. But in the case of Russia, of course, such concessions to inegalitarianism follow the social revolution and help to cement it. In Britain, however, the fact has to be faced that they would have the effect—indeed, are having the effect, particularly in the field of education—of strengthening the old order—the counter-revolution, if you like—since the old middle class is still likely to be first in the queue for all the socialist carrots going.

This is what forces the Labour Party into such contortions. In practice, as the record of the Wilson Government showed, great economic inequality is allowed to continue. Those six years saw no major redistribution of wealth. Nor is it conceivable that any Labour Government will be strong enough to take the necessary actions to bring about a redistribution on a scale likely to affect the social climate. This would require interference with basic freedoms—i.e., preventing the rich from taking themselves and their money out of the country—which is simply out of the question in the context of British politics, as successive Labour Chancellors were compelled to realize. Indeed, perhaps the most significant step taken by the Labour Government was anti-egalitarian—acceptance, at least in principle, of the need to pay senior executives in the nationalized industries salaries comparable to those earned in private industry.

In other words, the continued existence of a plutocracy of sorts is something which in practice Labour Governments have reluctantly come to accept. Money differentials are clearly here to stay, and even if Labour Governments squeeze more tightly on inherited wealth—as to some extent Mr Wilson's administration did—and on capital gains and other side-profits in industry, one can be pretty sure that great inequalities of wealth are bound to remain; not as great as they were but great enough to guarantee the existence at the top of society of a section of rich people whose power and influence will remain a pivotal factor in determining its quality. What I am trying to argue is that in practice British socialism has got to come to terms with the existence of a lot of rich people, many —perhaps most—of whom will either come from the *old* ruling class or have married into it. The real question for the Labour Party today should not be how to get rid of them, for that it cannot do. It should be, 'How does the Labour Party harness them to the socialist ideal?'

For if the existence of the rich is accepted—as it has to be in a mixed economy—it is clearly no good Labour thinkers carrying on their discussions of a socialist society as if the rich were somehow an unfortunate necessity which had to be tolerated temporarily, *faute de mieux*. Either the rich have got to be fitted into the socialist scheme of things, given a *constructive* role, recognized as being a crucial part of the socialist structure, or socialism cannot work. In other words, having found that in terms of British politics the rich cannot be beaten, the Labour Party has reached the point where it must either join them or make no further progress. For if the rich are simply allowed to be rich, as a reluctant concession to an economic state of affairs which the Labour Party would like to change but cannot, and are regarded as economically inevitable but socially undesirable, they will always be influential enough to corrupt socialist ideals—materialist serpents polluting the New Jerusalem—and never loyal enough to supply the social leadership which socialism so desperately requires.

For what I am trying to suggest is that if the rich are seen by the Labour Party as economic agents only—people who have to be allowed wealth so as to be able to produce it—and their social role is ignored, minimized or purposefully frustrated, then the way they live their lives will be plutocratic rather than aristocratic, geared to conspicuous consumption rather than community leadership—in a word Clores rather than Cecils. This seems to be the pitiful aspect of the contemporary Labour Party. Its term of office saw it rapidly coming to terms with the inevitability of greed and acquisitiveness as forces in human behaviour, and the need to adjust socialist economic theory accordingly—but not with the desirability of adjusting its social theories in such a way as to civilize these forces as well.

It has recognized the need to tolerate incentives for those at the top of industry—that is to say, to tolerate a plutocracy —but failed to realize that these concessions carry with them critical social implications. For if the successful administrators of the mixed economy are to be allowed to earn large salaries, they will obviously want to spend them, which raises the crucial question: on what? On superior consumer goods, cars, television sets, holidays on the Riviera, fur coats, and high living generally—on the principle of eat, drink and be merry today because nobody knows what the Labour Party will be up to tomorrow—or on the kind of cultural investment in the future which only a socially responsible class, with a tradition of service behind it and an expectation of service ahead of it, is ever likely to make?

The Labour Party so far has opted for the former. It is prepared to accept that conspicuous consumption is the price it has to pay to bribe the best industrial talents to serve the national economic interest. It has, in effect, abandoned the principle of economic egalitarianism. But the concessions have been made in a spirit that says, All right, we can no longer deny that you have got to be allowed to be richer than your neighbour, since the ugly facts of economic life make it inevitable that we should bribe you in this way. But do not imagine that you are superior in any other sense. We are determined in due course to prevent you giving your children a superior education, or passing on to them accumulations of capital that enable them to start life with unfair cultural advantages. The riches you enjoy are to be related exclusively to your services to the economy, to you in your capacity as economic man, in which respect we reluctantly have to admit that you are rather special. But there is nothing special about you socially; still less about your children. So just get this into your heads. You are jolly lucky to be allowed to be rich. Earlier generations of socialists would not have allowed you to be that, and truth to tell, we don't much like it either, and hope to put a stop to it eventually. But don't provoke us by seeking to behave as if you are more than just a lot of rich slobs by giving yourself class airs or any of that nonsense. You really ought to be rather ashamed of yourselves for refusing to do what you do for nothing. But since God or rather the Devil made you like that, there is nothing that we can do about it, at least for the time being. So keep your heads down at the trough, which is all you are fit for.

In other words, the Labour Party recognizes the need for an economic élite so long as it does not become a social class. But it is becoming overwhelmingly obvious that this is an impossibly unsatisfactory compromise. Rich people cannot be accorded *no* social role. If they are not given a constructive social role, they will play a destructive one. If they are not allowed to form themselves into a responsible governing class, with an exemplary sense of duty, they will form themselves into an irresponsible non-governing class, with an exemplary sense of non-duty. It is absurd to imagine that it is possible to pay the heads of businesses, both private and nationalized, hundreds of times more than the workers, in the name of economic efficiency, without recognizing that these potent economic figures will have an influence that extends well beyond the economic realm; or that these strikingly inegalitarian economic differentials will not have consequences that carry over into the social field, particularly since in many cases the differentials correspond so closely to the old class barriers.

The truth is surely very obvious. Economic reality has forced the Labour Party to accept the principle of massive salary differentials. However much may be taken away in tax, the fact remains that Sir XYZ and Lord ABC are assessed to be worth strikingly more than their workers. But the theory is that this superiority has only one purpose: to get Sir XYZ or Lord ABC to produce more wealth. It is a bribe to persuade him to use his organizational skills to their best advantage in the production of coal, or motor cars or ball-bearings. That is all that is asked of him. Once he leaves his board-room or his place of work, nothing further is expected. Socially, outside the factory, he is just like anybody else, except, of course, richer.

What I am saying is that the Labour Party has come to terms with the economic purpose of inegalitarianism—accepted the fact of rich *businessmen*—but so far found no social purpose for rich *men*; that is to say, it has not accepted the fact that rich men *per se* are potentially just as important socially as economically. This is really a vital point. If the Labour Party concedes that the nation's economic well-being requires that some should be paid very much more than others, it cannot avoid seeking to make sure that those who earn and spend these sums should be encouraged to do so in the most socially beneficial manner. But what is the most socially beneficial way? Should the rich simply buy more consumer goods; live out, so to speak, the fantasy life of all consumers, be exactly the same as the poor, except richer? Or should they be encouraged to maintain or develop a superior way of life, a superior culture, and constitute a class apart, to which the rest of society may aspire?

Left-wing socialists make it clear that they despise the conspicuous consumer-spending rich, but at the same time passionately oppose any attempt on the part of the rich to use their money in ways that give them cultural and social advantages, such as private education for their children, exclusive housing areas, accumulating capital for the next generation to inherit with a view to getting it off to a flying start, and so on.

But then they have not come to terms with economic differentials. The Labour Party, in general, has, and in practice they are at present choosing to tolerate a vulgar plutocracy, rather than consider the possibility that this constitutes a far greater threat to the future of socialism than the emergence, or re-emergence, of an upper class.

This seems to me to be why the Labour Party is moving into a position where paradoxically it may be less relevant to the future of socialism in this country than the Tory Party is. For if the need for economic incentives compels the Labour Party to accept inequality of wealth, it stands to reason that this concession must be made in such a way as to do the other socialist aims as little damage as possible; or, better still, as much good as possible. How to harness the rich to the purposes of socialism, instead of turning them into its enemy—this is now one of the key questions for socialists to answer. Economically, as I say, the question has been answered. Business people have shown themselves remarkably co-operative in the Labour Party's efforts at economic planning. But socialism is obviously much more than a theory of economic organization; it is an attempt to give practical effect to an ideal of collective responsibility for the social needs of all the people. That the rich can come to terms with the *economic* need of British socialism, and that British socialism can come to terms with the *economic* needs of the rich; so much Mr Wilson's Government made obvious. But what about the social needs of socialism? Can the rich come to terms with them, and can they be made compatible with the existence of the rich? This is the key question: can the rich serve not only the cause of economic planning but that of social planning as well? The Labour Party has recognized what it takes to win their economic co-operation. But what does it take to win their social co-operation, or at least avoid provoking their social opposition?

Just how fundamental a problem this is becomes clear when we consider some of the difficulties into which social planning is now running. While the State, thanks largely to Labour Party pressure and action, has taken over great areas of responsibility, in health, education, housing, and so on, this does not mean that there are not enormous gaps in these State services which need to be filled by the initiative and energy of private citizens. Indeed, it is becoming increasingly clear that unless a dedicated number of voluntary workers help to supervise the State services, and supplement them, and vast sums of private capital are made available too, standards can scarcely be maintained, let alone improved. It ought to be possible, of course, for the State to meet all these needs through public expenditure, which a grateful and public-spirited people would gladly pay. But we have already seen that such feelings of communal patriotism are not likely to be very prevalent in the years ahead and, in so far as Labour Governments accept the need for economic differentials, are more likely to diminish further than to grow. It is unrealistic not to recognize that, the more economic incentives are accepted as an important driving force in the economy, the less easy it becomes to raise taxes for social purposes, since people are not going to exert themselves for the carrot of incentives if it is taken away in taxation. The fact has to be faced, anyhow, that if there are to be a sizeable number of rich people, their consumption habits are bound to provoke material envy; are bound, that is, to make everybody down the social scale want to pay as little tax as possible so as to be able to spend more on himself. And in so far as the rich are encouraged to spend primarily on consumer goods, plutocratic consumption being less inegalitarian than aristocratic discrimination, this will further increase the resistance to high taxation among the non-rich, since the envied goods—fast cars, for example, rather than superior education—will be precisely those which public expenditure is not designed to supply.

But what is the socialist answer if it is accepted that public expenditure cannot go up fast enough to improve the social services, since in a mixed society—where economic differentials are unavoidable—the public will be too consumer-conscious, too concerned with the goods which only money in the private pocket can buy, to tolerate the necessary scale of taxation? I cannot see how the conclusion can be avoided that if the socialist ideal of universal welfare is not to be disastrously diluted the only answer is for there to be a major recrudescence of the spirit of voluntary social service, in terms of both people and cash.

In other words, if the Labour Party is to cushion the bad

effects of allowing greed to rear its ugly head, with all that this implies in terms of building up popular resistance to high taxation—in corrupting, that is, the social idealism of the poor—then it must do what is necessary to promote countervailing idealism among the rich. It has to be recognized that certain evil consequences flow from allowing the existence of rich people; consequences which only the rich can control. Awkward as it is for socialists to admit it, only the rich can civilize the rich. If the affluent society is to be a civilized society, the affluent have got themselves to be civilized, since if they are nothing but a moneyed élite they will infect the rest of society with vulgar values which make it impossible for the State to raise the revenue needed for the operation of a satisfactory Welfare State.

But how can the rich civilize the rich, if the socialist principle is adhered to that only earned income is respectable? How can the rich supply the spirit of voluntary service now desperately needed to augment the State services, or indeed to maintain them, if the only rich who exist with social approval, and with any sense of security, are those fully engaged in actively producing wealth? It is silly to suppose that granting incentives to the able has anything to do with promoting a recrudescence of a spirit of social service. That is only likely to emerge in a society that recognizes the need to promote an affluent, *leisured* class, many of whom have not had to fight their way to the top, who have enjoyed advantages which, precisely because they were not earned, inculcate a sense of obligation to do something about repaying the debt. If the rich are to civilize the rich, in short, it is vitally important that some of them should not be self-made, since a tradition of paternalist concern cannot grow up in one generation.

This brings us flat up against the problem of social leadership in a classless society which can be summarized thus: how to persuade those who have struggled to the top of the ladder to feel secure enough to bother about those who have not made the grade. Let us at least be clear about the measure of the problem, and not go on making optimistic assumptions about the role of the State in this respect. A mobile society, in which great emphasis is placed on the possibility of all ascending and descending, has two prime consequences. It means first that the successful are too busy staying where they have reached to bother much about anything else, and secondly that those who have not yet succeeded in climbing are likely to be so busy trying to succeed that they will be deeply resentful of any State demands on their purse which seem to burden their chances. Those on top will deeply resent the claims of the State; and so will those struggling to better themselves. The more open the society, therefore, the less easy it will be to finance a Welfare State. The idea of a competitive society with equality of opportunity relying on the State to make good its deficiencies is highly utopian. But so, in these circumstances, is the idea of a recrudescence of voluntary social leadership. The American experience here is extraordinarily revealing.

One of the disturbing aspects of the United States until very recently was that, although élites existed in profusion, they appeared to be prevented from fulfilling any general social function by the absence of any corporate or class cohesion. The politician, soldier, scientist, manager, technocrat, all wielded great power and influence within their own fields, but were socially neutral. That is to say, they accepted no social responsibility beyond their particular function. Not only did those at the top of the various hierarchies evade the social responsibilities which should properly accompany power, but their very failure in this respect was the necessary condition of their continuance in power. For the American élites to have practised benevolent paternalism would have involved their making an assumption destructive of the whole American dream: that the structure of society had been broadly settled and that those on top, because they were there to stay, owed a debt to those underneath, because they too, or at least a majority of them, were also there to stay. To take a paternal interest in the lower strata of society would have been to suggest that they could not look after themselves.

It is precisely to maintain its position at the top of the social pyramid that an aristocracy concerns itself with the proper maintenance of the base; it was precisely to maintain their position at the top of the American social pyramid that the American élites did not concern themselves with the proper maintenance of its base. Social irresponsibility, in fact, was the compulsory genuflection American élites made at the altar of equality. The resulting vacuum at the top was filled by the commercialized mass media which created fictional men of distinction who were not in reality allowed to exist.

What is so interesting today, however, is that those Americans who feel most concerned about some of the problems which spring from the non-socialist nature of American society, from its poor standards of social service, are precisely those who in fact, if not in theory, do constitute something approaching an upper class. It is no accident that the impulse towards a concept of social service in America today comes from such well established families as the Rockefellers and the Kennedys, rooted in inherited wealth, who are the nearest thing America has to an aristocracy. It is the offspring of established Eastern Seaboard wealth, the old rich, who are taking the lead in seeking to correct the imbalance of private affluence and public squalor. True, they are very far from being socialists in the full sense, and have no faith in socialism as an economic theory. But it is significant that the main thrust for social reform in America today springs from precisely those areas where egalitarianism has been least successful; that the seedbed of social service should be great concentrations of inherited wealth; that the spirit of social service should take the form of *noblesse oblige*. In other words, contemporary America suggests that such socialist or collectivist impulses as do exist there today arise more from the failure of the egalitarian ideal than from its success, and grow stronger as the class reality exerts itself over the classless fiction. Public opinion would not have tolerated a President Kennedy or a Governor Rockefeller a generation back. Their privileged millionaire background would have ruled them out of public life, rather as being a 14th Earl is today becoming a handicap in British politics. But that is precisely the point. Just at the moment when Britain is seeking to deny the advantages of privilege as a source of social leadership, the United States is beginning to accept the principle; just as we are seeking to do away with the class system as a threat to social justice, America is coming to terms with hers as a source of social justice.

But can the Labour Party's egalitarianism go through a comparable process of modification? Can the Labour Party come to see that socialism in Britain can only make progress by using wealth and privilege as an ally, rather than a bugbear; by creating among the rich and successful a sense of obligation and gratitude, rather than of fear and hostility; by giving those on top—whom it has failed to remove and knows now that it can never remove—a formidable vested interest in maintaining the socialist *status quo*? Can it come to see that, given the realities of British politics and the limitations which circumscribe the future of socialism in this country, it is more important for socialism today to enlist the energies and ideals of capital than those of the workers, to create a climate of security at the top rather than at the bottom, to concentrate, that is, not on getting rid of the class system because it is a threat to socialism in theory, but on getting the best out of it because in practice socialism in Britain can either live with it or be destroyed by it.

For if my analysis is right, certain conclusions flow from it. First, there is now no possibility of egalitarian measures being of such an extreme kind as to engender a new spirit of communal solidarity, fired by mass enthusiasm for a new social order. Even if the opportunity for creating such conditions ever existed, it was not seized by the Labour Party and has now passed for ever. Secondly, this being the case, the Labour Party is being forced to operate a system that involves accepting economic incentives, which in turn create a climate where conspicuous expenditure at the top prompts such a widespread popular concern with personal expenditure and consumption, with money in the pocket, that it becomes impossible politically to raise enough in taxes to fulfil socialist ideals through public expenditure. In practice, Labour Governments have to make too many economic concessions to the rich to prevent their way of life infecting society as a whole with the spending itch, which places very strict limits on the scope and scale of welfare-statism.

Thirdly, this means that it is very unlikely that a Labour Government will enjoy enough political backing ever to do very much to correct the imbalance between private affluence and public squalor, from which it follows, fourthly, that socialist ideals of a responsible and caring society will involve relying to a large extent on the potentially constructive elements of private affluence. This in turn means that those who enjoy private affluence must be encouraged to be responsible and community-minded, leaders of society, since the State is not going to be able to be nearly as responsible as much earlier generations of socialists assumed that it would be, which means, fifthly, that in so far—and it is very far indeed—as the new form of society will not be such as to inspire the socialist idealism and enthusiasm of the many it must be such as to inspire the idealism and enthusiasm of the few.

The pity is that the Labour Party is so constituted as to be unable to adapt its attitudes and policies to these new circumstances. It cannot, as I say, come to terms with the fact that its former policies have reached a dead end; that it has succeeded in creating a stalemate society which has corrupted the source of its old dynamic in the idealism of the working class without creating a fresh source of dynamism elsewhere; that socialism, in short, must either make new friends or perish. Its own character and composition and, even more important, the character and composition of its Tory rival preclude such a course. To attempt the transformation would involve such an internal blood-letting, and so play into the hands of the Tories, as not to be within the realm of practical politics. This is the Labour Party's dilemma. Practical politics preclude effective resource to its traditional policies as well as the necessary internal readjustments which would enable it to adopt new policies. It is caught in a trap that is at once ideological and structural, as I hope to show in the next chapter.

6

What I have been arguing in the last chapter can be summarized thus: since socialism in Britain has failed to produce a new social ethic based on fellowship and communal patriotism, and has been forced to fall back on self-interest and competitiveness as its driving forces, it is absurd to go on discussing the future of the Labour Party in terms of some ideal classless society which is manifestly not going to exist. The Labour Party's acceptance of the mixed economy means in practice that market forces, the search for profits, will determine the allocation of resources, human and material, over a very substantial sector. The social implications of this cannot be gainsaid. Whatever Labour Governments may succeed in doing to reduce the harshness of competitive striving and to mitigate the extremity of inequality, through both redistributive taxation and taxes on inheritance, the principal marks of a hierarchical society—differences in esteem and prestige—will remain.

Not only will they remain. In so far as Labour Governments succeed in their attempts to penalize inherited wealth and unearned income, they will actually be reinforced, since the effect of such policies will be to relate social status to social function, thereby legitimizing the social hierarchy. In short, the ideal of a classless society has been abandoned, in practice if not wholly in theory. This, it may be objected, is a very banal conclusion, amounting only to the truism that socialism has abandoned the hope of finding a substitute for ambition as the mainspring of society. So much the better, it is usually thought, for socialism. It means that it has at long last come to terms with human nature. These reactions are perfectly understandable, and in a sense reasonable. The abandonment of the classless ideal certainly makes it possible for the Labour Party to appeal to many members of the middle class who earlier dismissed it as committed to utopian rubbish. Nevertheless, it is my contention—which I hope to demonstrate in this chapter—that this abandonment of the classless ideal removes from the Labour Party its central pivot and compromises it to such an extent as to render it an unsuitable base on which to build an effective Government.

The first point to note is that although the Labour Party has renounced the ultimate social ideal of socialism—a classless society—it has not renounced its faith in the need for a planned economy and a centrally determined social system; that is to say, it still believes in a collectivist society. It follows from this that Labour Governments need to be able to rely on a very special kind of political party; something much more cohesive and unified than a Party designed to back a less ambitious kind of government. It is important to be quite clear about this: a managed economy requires a Government that can get its way in small matters as well as large, since a plan, by its very nature, stands or falls in its totality. In other words, a Government which sets itself the task of planning the economy not only so as to maximize its efficiency and growth but also to relate its workings to certain desiderata of social justice laid down at the centre, obviously needs to be much more strongly based in Parliament, and outside as well, than a Government which has no such comprehensive goals. Socialism as a theory of government—that is to say, central planning—cannot be separated, therefore, from socialism as a source of popular inspiration, because the former is absolutely dependent on the latter. Unless socialism as an ideal inspires a particularly cohesive and unified political organization, socialism as a system of government simply cannot work, or at least not in a democratic framework.

This is what distinguishes a Conservative Government or even a radical Government from one seeking to govern along collectivist lines. A Conservative Government *can* afford to rest on a party that is in effect only a coalition of interests since, not seeking to implement any grand design, it can adjust its policies as it goes along, retreating here, advancing there, balancing a concession to one interest against a sacrifice demanded from another, playing the whole operation by ear. A radical Government obviously requires to be more firmly based than a Conservative one, since it is committed to certain specific reforms. But even here there is a world of difference between a Government committed to specific reforms and one committed to an infinitely complicated and interconnected plan. A reforming Government needs to rally support in Parliament and the country for a specific purpose, Home Rule for Ireland, say, or House of Lords reform. But it does not need, as a Government committed to socialist planning needs, to maintain an unbroken buttress of support for a giant edifice of legislation which cannot be allowed to crumble in one place without endangering the whole structure.

This is what makes it so essential for the Labour Party to be a very special kind of political organization, more a movement or crusade than a mere party. A coalition of interests, each of which hopes to get something for itself out of its government and is prepared to back the other fellow simply so as to be backed in turn, cannot supply that steady, solid, loyal backing which socialist planning requires. Nor is this only a question of getting legislation through Parliament, crucial as this obviously is. If a Government is to succeed in implementing collectivist policies it must be able to feel supported, not only by a Parliamentary majority, but also by a great groundswell of popular backing; must be able to feel itself responding to the will of the people in a way that radical Governments only need to do very occasionally and Conservative ones do not need to do at all, except in time of war. This point cannot be underlined too forcefully. Any Government that takes upon itself the giant responsibility of not only planning the economy but also planning it according to certain moral principles— that is to say, takes upon itself responsibility for the moral as well as the material welfare of the people, and at the same time believes in and is determined to operate through democratic institutions—requires a kind of political backing fundamentally different from and superior to anything which an ordinary political party is able to supply.

Can the Labour Party supply that kind of backing today? This surely is where the abandonment of the ideal of a classless society enters the picture? For if the party gives up hope of creating this classless heaven on earth, and accepts much of the capitalist jungle as here to stay, what incentive is there for the workers to behave like angels, and resist the temptation to behave like tigers, here and now? Yet it cannot be too strongly emphasized that a Government attempting the immensely ambitious and exalted task of operating a collectivist society in freedom requires to be based on an inspirational movement, and cannot operate in a social jungle.

Originally, of course, this was only a theoretical problem. Such were the sins of capitalism in the nineteenth century and, until relatively recently, in this century as well, that a cogent case for the workers to put class solidarity before individual striving, and loyalty to the party before trade-union self-seeking, virtually made itself. The texture of industrial life, of the everyday experience of men and women in the factories, tended to inculcate a strong awareness of the urgent need for class solidarity in the face of the 'enemy'. The problem in these days was to make the workers politically conscious at all, so deep were the layers of apathy, ignorance and deference which first had to be broken through. But at least to a growing number of the politically conscious workers the need to band together in a tight political movement, disciplined, loyal and cohesive, was self-evident. The point is that in the early days of the Labour Party it was not necessary to place much emphasis on the vision of an ultimate classless heaven in order to weld the politically conscious working class together, since the bonds of unity were forged by actual experience of a capitalist hell. A few idealists may have been inspired to join the Labour Party by faith in a socialist god, but the great majority were frightened into it by fear of the capitalist devil.

In other words, in the early days of the class war what held the Labour army together was not faith in the ultimate peace terms but a feeling of backs-to-the-wall self-defence. Peace terms were left to the socialist theoreticians. So far as the rank-and-file were concerned it was a question of standing shoulder to shoulder because it was the natural thing to do.

Aneurin Bevan, in his *In Place of Fear*, explains that when he was a young miner in a South Wales colliery he was concerned with one practical question: 'Where does power lie in this particular state of Great Britain and how can it be attained by the workers?' This question, he says, did not shape itself in some such fashion as, 'How can I get on?'

> The texture of our lives shaped the question into a class and not into an individual form.... For us power meant the use of collective action designed to transform society and so lift all of us together.... We were the products of an industrial civilization and our psychology corresponded to that fact. Individual initiative was overlaid by the social imperative. The streams of individual initiative, therefore, flowed along collective channels already formed for us by our environment. Society presented itself to us as an area of conflicting social forces and not as a plexus of individual striving.*

But does the texture of working-class life today shape the question into a class and not into an individual form? Does it not seem perfectly sensible to a great many workers to ask not, 'How can *we* gain power?' but, 'How can *I* get on?' It is unquestionable that in contemporary circumstances the case for working-class solidarity is much less self-evident than it used to be. Skilled workers, for example, can obviously use their bargaining power to wrest great gains for themselves, at the expense of unskilled labour, if they so choose. If the industrial civilization of Aneurin Bevan's day produced a psychology conducive to class solidarity, the industrial civilization of today tends to produce a psychology very much more conducive to individual striving.

One must not exaggerate this point, since a great deal of class solidarity still exists. But it is a waning force, rooted more in ancestral memory than in contemporary necessity, engendered less by hard facts of material self-interest than by the hangover of a noble tradition. My point is simply that the vices of capitalism are no longer such as to prompt automatic or natural working-class solidarity, as a kind of reflex action. If working-class solidarity is to be maintained today, and all the centrifugal forces or temptations resisted, it will have to be because of the virtues of socialism. In other words, precisely because fear of capitalism can no longer be relied upon to

* Quoted in *Modern British Politics*, p. 84.

maintain the Labour movement, faith in socialism becomes all the more crucial. This is the awkward paradox for the Labour Party: the better it compels capitalism to behave, the better still it has to offer to behave itself, since it has to attract its support more through its own virtues than through the enemies' vices. The logic, therefore, of the present situation should be an escalation of socialist promises or claims; an increasing emphasis on the purity of socialist doctrine; a movement away from 'revisionism' back to 'fundamentalism'. Instead of being abandoned, the ideal of the classless society should be firmly reiterated. But, of course, it cannot be in practice, as we have seen, since any such commitment would involve retaining policies that would make it manifestly impossible for a Labour Government to operate a mixed economy.

A Labour Government, in short, is caught up in a dreadful dilemma. If it is to retain the cohesion of the Labour movement which is so vitally necessary for the support of collectivist aims, it needs to maintain an ideal of a classless society which in turn prevents it from operating effectively in the actual circumstances of the present time. On the other hand, if it does what is necessary to operate a mixed economy, this results in a diminution of working-class solidarity without which collectivist aims cannot be achieved.

The question that has to be asked is whether modified or revised socialism—that is to say, socialism adapted to the reality of a tamed and civilized form of capitalism—can possibly constitute a strong enough cement to hold together a Government seeking to implement collectivist policies. This was really the subject of the great revisionist debate within the Labour Party during the 1950s. Nominally it was about nationalization or Clause 4, with the fundamentalists pressing for public ownership to be extended until private ownership became no longer the rule but the exception. The revisionists, on the other hand, argued that public ownership was merely one of various means to socialist goals. They sought to show that it was perfectly possible for a Labour Government to plan the economy by occupying the commanding heights, etcetera, without nationalizing the means of production, distribution and exchange. Social justice, they argued, did not depend on nationalization and could be achieved just as surely without it.

Here is how Samuel H. Beer sums up the argument.

In the old orthodoxy for which the fundamentalists spoke public ownership was of central significance. It was an indispensable condition and a major expression of a radically transformed economy, society and culture. In the fundamentalist view, only by means of public ownership could the market be dethroned and public administration established as the central means of control over the economy. But for the revisionists the market rather than public administration would be the principal controlling mechanism. Admittedly, this market would be conditioned by heavily progressive taxation and massive welfare services and manipulated by broad controls, largely fiscal and monetary. Otherwise, however, competition among separate units would determine the allocation of resources, human and material.

This conflict over economic theory involved vital differences in social and ethical outlook and in the quality of life that revisionist and fundamentalist, respectively, thought socialism could and should achieve. Where the market rules, there self-interest is the dynamic of behaviour. The revisionists were ready to accept this implication. Indeed, one might say they started from it as a premise: 'Every economic system devised for ordinary human beings,' wrote Arthur Lewis, 'must have self-interest as its driving force.' In revisionist thinking and in the party documents that reflected it, there was during the 1950s a growing emphasis not only upon the private sector of the economy and the mechanisms of the market, but also upon the incentives of gain and competition.

The revisionists, to be sure, wished to reduce the scale of existing pecuniary differentials in the name of socialist equality. Yet they also expected that the old dynamic of the future society would enlist the support of other egoistic motives: the desire for prestige, power, status, 'esteem for success' and recognition of ability. It may be that no social system can function effectively unless it does enlist such motives. In this sense, the revisionist analysis may well have been correct. Whether correct or not, revisionism attacked socialist ideology at its heart—the doctrine of fellowship. For in this doctrine Socialism had not rejected merely comercialism and capitalism, but something more fundamental—moral egoism.*

Yet unless moral egoism is rejected, how can it be supposed that the working class will not break up into self-interested sections, pursuing their separate advantages as best they may? In Aneurin Bevan's youth, 'the streams of individual initiative flowed along collective channels already formed for us by our environment'. But the environment is not formed for the workers in that way today. The actual experience of living in contemporary society, with its glittering material temptations and opportunities for personal advancement, no longer forces the stream of individual initiative to flow into collectivist channels. Rather the opposite. If to this environmental change, which itself gravely weakens the working-class impulse towards collectivism, is added an ideological change—the abandonment of faith in a classless ideal—what is left of the cement which held the Labour Party together?

My point is that the less the capitalist environment imposes working-class solidarity the more necessary it is to have an ideological vision that can inspire it. Only a belief in a fundamentally different society at the end of the road, one in which individual striving has been replaced by social fellowship, can prevent the Labour movement from succumbing to all the temptations which will assail it at every turn. The truth has to be faced that the kind of society envisaged by the revisionists, although it has much to commend it in terms of social justice, is quite peculiarly unsuited to the maintenance of a cohesive political movement. It offers a lot *to* the workers, but in a manner least likely to evoke political loyalty *from* them. Equality of opportunity and greater social security— i.e., more chance to climb out of the working class for the ambitious and more State welfare hand-outs for the rest— that is the revisionist offer. But this surely is the very opposite of what is required to maintain a working-class spirit of

* *Modern British Politics*, pp. 236-7.

political militancy capable of breathing life into a Labour Government, since it is bound to produce a schizophrenic working class with the ambitious minority tempted to desert to the capitalist fleshpots and the unambitious majority tempted to relapse into passive acceptance of social largesse. A classless ideal is absolutely essential to any kind of dynamic working-class unity, since only if society is seen to be moving in that direction is there sufficient reason for the ambitious few to refrain from making their peace with the existing system and the unambitious many to feel politically active enough to keep up the fight against it.

This is much more than a question of the Labour Party's being in a position to win votes. One can assume, at any rate for the purposes of the argument, that the adoption of revisionist socialism will not necessarily affect its ability to do that, at least from time to time. Policies designed to do away with privilege and to improve the lot of the poor can be relied upon always to have a mass appeal. But that is not the whole problem. It is not enough simply to get in a position to govern, and to govern, as we have seen, along peculiarly ambitious lines. The question that has to be asked is whether socialist ideology so modified as to come to terms with the needs of the mixed economy—modified, that is, to the extent of doing away with the ultimate aim of a morally transformed society—can possibly forge a political instrument with enough cutting-edge to govern in this ambitious manner. For once it is accepted that socialism does not mean the end of social hierarchy, but only easier access to its higher rungs for those with talent and more comfortable conditions on the lower rungs for those who do not succeed in climbing—or do not want to climb— does it any longer remain a compelling enough doctrine to hold the Labour movement together, given that in this country the Tory Party can be relied upon to be plugging a very similar line of goods? Perhaps the problem can be best summed up in this way. Once the Labour Party is forced to admit that its best efforts cannot get rid of the ladder, and that there always have to be a few at the top and the masses underneath, it ceases to be able to enlist the special mass fervour and dedication which arose precisely from its earlier promise to do away with the ladder itself. For revised socialism

86

means, in effect, that although the masses will all enjoy better conditions, and a few of them will succeed in climbing to the top, most of them must resign themselves to a subordinate status, all the more shaming precisely because it will be clearly a consequence of their own inability rather than of the inequity of the system. Such a form of socialism will always have a certain appeal. But it is very doubtful whether it can be the soil from which a Labour Government can draw the necessary strength to impose a collectivist pattern of administration.

This is the crucial point. If the Labour Party is to be a governing party committed to a socialist method of planning, it has to have a special relationship with the working class, since this is not only the basis of its electoral strength but also the source of its moral authority. But in what does that special relationship consists? Not merely in the claim that it represented working-class interests in the sense of promoting policies from which the workers stood to benefit. Its special and unique claim was that it was advocating government *by* as well as *for* the workers.

The Labour Party, it should be recalled, came into existence as an independent national force first and foremost to facilitate the entry of working-class trade unionists into the House of Commons. This was its central raison d'être, the crucial germinal insight out of which its independence grew. The primary aim was not so much to promote particular policies beneficial to working men as to promote working men themselves.

After the First World War the Labour Party had to make a crucial decision: whether to carry on as part of a loose Lib–Lab alliance—dominated by the middle-class liberal 'inner circle'—or to break away from the Liberal embrace and go it alone. There was a strong case for remaining linked to the Liberal Party, since at least its radical wing was in favour of many of the same policies as the Labour Party itself. If the aim had simply been to bring about reforms which would have benefited the workers, a Lib–Lab coalition might well have done better than a Labour Party fighting on its own.

The Labour leaders of the day, however, were quite clear that this was not the primary aim. They realized that, however satisfactorily the Lib–Lab alliance might represent the interests of the working class, it would never result in enough working-class candidates actually getting into the House of Commons. Middle-class radicals with all the right ideas might do as much *for* the workers as would an independent Labour Party, but only the Labour Party, fighting on its own, could produce Government *by* as well as for the working class.

This overriding desire for the working class to take active control of its own destiny also played a crucial part in the Labour leaders' decision to write socialist economic theory into the party's constitution. They did not do so only because of the theoretical persuasiveness of the socialist doctrine. They did so with the express purpose of adopting policies which would henceforth make it impossible to blur the differences between the Labour and Liberal parties.

It is fascinating to read the debates of the period. What comes out with overwhelming clarity is the realization by the Labour leaders of the day that radicalism alone—which was what the radical wing of the Liberal Party espoused—would never galvanize the working class into active participation in politics, or maintain the unity of the movement once it got going. Socialism was seen as the best way of giving the workers a unifying ideology of their own—different from the radical idealism of the middle-class progressives—on the strength of which they could themselves claim a right to govern and occupy the seats of power. Socialism, in short, was not an end in itself. It was a means to the end of giving the working-class movement a unifying political purpose independent of the essentially middle-class ethos of liberal radicalism.

If the last Labour Government did nothing else it unquestionably dissolved that unifying political purpose. It cannot reasonably be blamed for doing this, since it is manifestly impossible to run a mixed economy within the capitalist system without running this risk. This, of course, was what Mr Ray Gunter was railing against in his letter of resignation from Mr Wilson's Government. His complaint was that the Labour Government was becoming increasingly dominated by middle-class intellectuals to the exclusion of working-class trade unionists. This charge, incredibly enough, was widely regarded by the pundits as puerile or frivolous. If he had chosen to make a stand on, say, prescription charges or nuclear weapons, or on one or other of the innumerable issues which are regarded in modern Labour circles as being proper grounds for resignation, his action would have been accorded much more serious attention. Yet Mr Gunter was drawing attention to the terribly important fact that in 1968, fifty years after the Labour Party decided to break away from the middle-class radical embrace, it was back where it began, with a smaller proportion of working-class representatives in Parliament now than it had then.

One suspects that for some of the most prominent Labour leaders of today, Roy Jenkins and Anthony Crosland for example, this reversal does not terribly matter. They are more concerned with measures than with men, and if Labour Governments can best pursue what they regard as reasonably progressive and civilized policies under the influence of middle-class intellectuals, then let there be more middle-class intellectuals, however much this may contradict the original aim of the Labour Party. And the truth is that the kind of policies they do want to pursue, and indeed did pursue—incomes policy, restructuring of industry, national planning, prison reform, abolition of capital punishment, legalized homosexuality, race-relations laws, trade-union reform, and so on—are all essentially causes that make more sense to the radical middle class than to the working class.

It is no accident, therefore, that the Parliamentary Labour Party is increasingly dominated by middle-class intellectuals —or those who have shaped themselves in that mould—to the exclusion of working-class trade unionists. This is the kind of party that such policies require. But it is absurd not to recognize that the adoption of such policies, with the implications that this has for the kind of people needed to implement them in government and support them in Parliament, cannot fail to have a baleful effect on the great purpose of the Labour movement, which was to galvanize the working class into seizing control of their own destiny. The burden of Mr Gunter's complaint was that the middle class was taking over the Labour Party. If Mr Jenkins ever got to Downing Street, he implied, this would be like the days of Asquith all over again.

From the country's point of view, this may be an excellent

idea. But from the point of view of the Labour movement it would be the end of a dream. The particular promise of the Labour Party was that it would transform society in the image of the working class; create a new kind of society, as different from middle-class England as middle-class England was from upper-class England. In the event, under the impact of the Labour Government, the movement is becoming just another ladder on which the brighter members of the working class can rise into, and take on the colouring of, the middle class itself.

It can be argued that this was inevitable; that the Labour Party was bound to develop in this way. But this is what made Mr Gunther's resignation so poignant and so significant. It was a cry of despair, and as such much more disturbing than any reasoned argument.

Conventional wisdom has it, of course, that this is all just part of the process of dragging the Labour Party kicking and screaming into the second half of the twentieth century. But is it certain that the 'kicking and screaming' is so irrational and the 'dragging' so rational? It is possible that there is a fundamental flaw in the logic of the revisionist school, in that they are envisaging the possibility of maintaining a socialist system of government, i.e. central control over the economy, which requires a massively authoritative executive, while abandoning the only real justification for such a system, which is the claim not so much to represent as actually to be the party of the people. The reality may be that a Government seeking to implement collectivist policies, if it is to work, really needs to be backed by a party able to galvanize the working class into wanting to seize control over its own destiny. A middle-class Labour Government, largely made up of progressive intellectuals, cannot rely on enough active support to enable it to implement its plans; in other words, the more élitist Labour Governments become, in response to the needs of sophisticated socialist administration, the less popular support will they enjoy, so that just at the moment when the complexities of socialist planning in an advanced economy require party backing of a specially loyal and comprehensive kind, this is precisely the kind of backing that will not be forthcoming. Contemporary socialism may require a Jenkins-type Labour Party, if it is to throw up the necessary talents for planning a highly advanced economy, but if the cost of such adaptation is a party without deep working-class links, the result is a beautiful socialist administrative engine without enough fuel in the tank to make it turn over.

The point is a fundamental one. Modification of socialist doctrine so as to bring it into line with the realities of capitalism in the second half of the twentieth century shows a nice understanding of the new possibilities of operating a planned economy without the cumbersome and old-fashioned methods of outright nationalization. No longer is it necessary for the State to own the means of production and so on for it to be able to exert great influence. The last Labour Government certainly demonstrated that, and I know no Labour Minister who would argue that his problems arose from lack of control over the private sector. The problems, I suggest, did not arise principally from lack of control or lack of power, or from resistance by recalcitrant industrialists to central planning. There was fantastically little such resistance, as Enoch Powell was always dolefully pointing out. Private industry, for example, showed endless patience in supplying data to the Prices and Incomes Board and co-operated almost enthusiastically in the drawing-up of the George Brown national plan. No, the principal difficulty experienced by the Labour Government in the years of office was a much more basic one from the point of view of democratic socialism. It was not that the Government lacked the power to do what it wanted; nor even that it lacked the will. It lacked something much more fundamental: the firm support of a united political movement.

What had been overlooked in the process of adapting socialist administration to the needs of modern capitalism was that although a form of State capitalism makes sense administratively, it does not make sense politically. By this I mean that although the basic socialist aims of social justice can be promoted theoretically by an élitist Labour Government's influencing the economy from the commanding heights— rather than the workers' physically taking it over—this scheme in practice falls down through lack of any general agreement about what social justice in such circumstances actually amounts to. The administrative means to promote social justice are available to a Labour Government, but the political momentum is not.

This is the point which needs very close examination: the effect which the modifications of socialist doctrine have had on the homogeneity of the Labour movement, without which —however much a Labour Government may seek to promote social justice as a general aim—it constantly finds itself baulked by disagreement among its supporters about what social justice actually consists of in particular cases. For social justice only becomes a practical political aim for a Government supported by a homogeneous political movement able to agree on what it involves in each situation; able to agree, for example, on what social justice means in the matter of allocating aid to one area of unemployment as against another, in the matter of deciding between spending more on free false teeth and spectacles and less on comprehensive schools, and in all the other areas where the choices are such as to raise infinitely complex questions of social priority.

Old-fashioned socialism had a ready-made answer to this problem. The postulate was that in time, through ownership by the State of all the means of production, distribution and exchange, a classless society would be fashioned in which there were no longer competing and rival interests—a homogeneous society possessed by a common interest. And during the years while that goal was being struggled towards—before, that is, a homogeneous society had been achieved—Labour Governments would make do with the next best thing: a homogeneous working class which would be so inspired by the glory of the struggle as to put aside sectional interests for, so to speak, the duration of the class war. In other words, the premise was that a Labour Government would never have any problem in knowing where the path of social justice lay, since it would be guided initially by the infallible inspiration of the Labour movement, and ultimately by the inspiration of a new social ethic which would have dissolved the corrupting bonds of acquisitiveness and self-interest.

In a sense, therefore, the central difficulty of democratic socialism—how to guarantee enough popular backing for controversial interpretations of what social justice means in particular cases—was simply evaded, since it was assumed that while the class war was still raging the difficulty would not arise—the discipline of battle and the esprit de corps of a crusading movement would see to that—and once it was won, the texture of society would be so transformed as to render the difficulty irrelevant.

But the facts of contemporary society obviously do not allow the Labour Party to make any such assumptions. What we have today is a kind of stalemate in the class war. The goal of victory has been abandoned. A classless society is recognized as utopian. But if victory is utopian, so is the idea of working-class homogeneity during the period of battle. While it made sense to take for granted an almost military standard of Labour Party discipline and a crusading sense of comradely esprit de corps as a temporary phenomenon during a period of critical class warfare, it clearly makes no such sense to assume that it can carry over into a period of permanent stalemate. In other words abandonment of the long-term goal of a classless or homogeneous society leads ineluctably to loss of the short-term instrument for achieving that goal, a homogeneous and disciplined Labour movement, since the instrument can only really be conceived of in relation to that goal, just as an army can only be conceived of in relation to the job of fighting a war.

In other words, in coming to terms with the realities of capitalism in the second half of the twentieth century, and in making its peace with them, democratic socialism has been forced to accept a social context where it can no longer rely on a homogeneous political movement to give effect to its purposes. But without such a political movement, the task of planning the economy in the light of social justice becomes politically impracticable, since virtually every decision is open to challenge and dispute. But since Governments *have* to reach decisions, the practical consequence is an ever-widening rift between a Labour Government and the Labour Party; an ever-accelerating drift towards Government by bureaucracy. The lack of agreed guidelines laid down from below means imposed decisions determined from above. I am not suggesting for a moment that this is what Labour Governments want. What I am suggesting, however, is that this is what is bound to happen, since in a stalemate society, which is neither homogeneous and classless nor so at war with itself as to create conditions of working-class homogeneity, the pursuit of social justice can only be an élitist activity, with the few setting the pace, determining the paths down which the hunt should go, and choosing which quarry to chase or not to chase.

This, of course, is precisely what happened in the Wilson years, much to the distress of the Labour movement. On a whole host of major issues, incomes policy and trade-union reforms being the most controversial, the Government had to insist that it and only it knew what was right for the country. This, of course, was a perfectly acceptable claim. Mr Wilson was well within the British political tradition in claiming that the Government was there to govern, so long as it was able to summon up a Parliamentary majority. But the fact has to be recognized that this doctrine grew up in a period when Governments were not seeking to plan prices and wages or to interfere with trade-union freedoms; during a period, that is to say, when governments were much less ambitious than Mr Wilson sought to be. Manifestly the claim of a Government that its job is to govern, if need be against the will of a large section of its supporters in Parliament, against the will of its party executive, and against the will of one of its party's major elements—in the case of the Wilson Government, the trade-union movement—not to mention a hostile national Press, is very different when made by a Government with far-reaching interventionist aims to the same claim made by one with a much more modest idea of the frontiers of governmental power. A Tory Prime Minister does not—or at least did not—set out to run a planned economy; to plan prices and wages, to determine investment, to interfere with collective bargaining and so on. In his mouth, the claim to carry on the Queen's Government means little more than a claim to be allowed to preserve the security of the realm, law and order, and the value of the currency, all basic responsibilities which no Government can afford to renounce. And precisely because they are such minimal aims, it can be assumed that there will always be a consensus which accepts the Government of the day's responsibility to seek to achieve them.

But what the six years of Wilson Government began to demonstrate was that this assumption cannot be made about the aims of a socialist Government, since they are so complicated as to make it extremely improbable that any consensus can in fact exist. The needs of central planning require a Labour Government to claim the right to get on with the job of governing; yet they also tend to provoke such widespread opposition as to preclude the existence of that minimum consensus which previously legitimized that claim. In other words, the very fact that a Labour Government's ambitions make it require more freedom to govern as it thinks best tends to guarantee that it will not get it.

This is a problem which the advocates of democratic socialism have largely ignored. They assumed that the purposes of planning would always be so generally popular that a Government embracing them would be able to rely on a great upsurge of popular support to overcome sectional objections. But this assumption was rooted in a period when the sins of capitalism were so crimson that planning could be conceived of in simple, demagogically compelling terms: pursuit of social justice, eradication of poverty, and so on. However, that period is long since past. Planning today involves doing things which hurt the many as well as the few. The old idea, therefore, that the pursuit of social justice is so overwhelming an aim as to create a kind of wartime national will behind it is seen to be wholly illusory. Yet without this national consensus, it is terribly difficult to see how a Labour Government can avoid falling back on the increasingly élitist claim that it knows best what is good for the country—a claim which is guaranteed to make its task more difficult since the Labour Party is quite peculiarly ill designed to be able to accept it.

The experience of the Wilson years suggests very clearly that ambitious social planning in pursuit of something so abstract as social justice requires either a mass political movement bound together by a common ideology—something so cohesive as to constitute a virtual general will—which contemporary circumstances do nothing to encourage, or an authoritative élite whose interpretations of what constitutes social justice are by and large acceptable to the mass of the public; that is to say, either a society so morally homogeneous as to make it easy for the Government to decide on all the innumerable questions at issue—whether, for example, the North-East should benefit at the expense of the South-West, or the miners at the expense of the engineers, or even, at another level, whether health should take precedence over education —or a society in which the élite enjoys such prestige and authority as to be able to make its decisions in these matters generally acceptable. The support for these infinitely delicate decisions has got to come from an exceptional solidarity of purpose either at the bottom or at the top; either from a popular ideology that amounts to a moral consensus, or from a charismatic élite that can put its judgements over as part of a gigantic confidence operation.

The difficulty in this country, however, is that democratic socialism has modified its ideology to a point where it cannot hope to arouse any solidarity of purpose at the bottom, but not far enough to have any hope of arousing any solidarity of purpose at the top; destroyed its mass appeal without constructing an élitist magnetism to take its place. So what we have been witnessing is a Labour Government forced to behave in an élitist manner—what could possibly be more élitist than Harold Wilson's repeated claims that the Government knew best?—which is also forced to rely for its support on a party deeply rooted in a profound distrust for élitism in all its forms; a Government, that is, whose administrative head is at bitter war with its ideological heart.

This is the crux of the problem. Operating a planned but mixed economy in a mass industrial society and pursuing at the same time the ideals of social justice tends inevitably to involve the Government of the day, and its attendant bureaucracy, in vastly complicated technical decisions which have to be taken at the top. It is really rather naïve to suppose that such a complicated operation can avoid creating a gap between leaders and led. What is required, therefore, to make such an arrangement politically practicable in a democracy is a party organized around a principle of paternal authority; that is to say, a political party whose own internal values and traditions correspond to, or at any rate do not dramatically conflict with, the élitist pattern of government inherent in the situation.

The supreme irony of contemporary British politics is that the Tory Party is precisely such an organization, while the

Labour Party is precisely the opposite of such an organization. The Tory Party sees its function as being the seed-bed of strong government; the instrument, if you like, for giving effect to an hierarchical view of society which accepts the need for a governing class. Its whole purpose is to make it possible for a governing class to get on with the job of governing, within the context of universal franchise; to relate the practical requirements of good government to the contemporary circumstances of majority rule, to translate the idea of aristocratic rule into terms which make sense in a democracy, which means organizing mass support for what is basically an élitist or paternalist system of government. If it is meaningful at all to talk about a Tory ideology, it is simply this: a recognition of the inevitability of authority and hierarchy, and a determination to guarantee the availability of enough men and women who can meet this requirement, and enough popular support for them to be able to get on with the job of governing. It sees its function, in short, as twofold: to promote policies designed to nurture habits of command and habits of deference; to produce a relationship which allows the leaders to lead and the led to be led in such a way as to result in mutual satisfaction.

The Labour Party is organized around a profoundly different principle; almost the opposite principle. Not only does it not believe in the inevitability of authority and hierarchy as permanent needs of human society, but it came into existence with the express intention of demonstrating the possibility of organizing a new kind of society which could do without them. What is more, it adopted a theory of social organization, socialism, which was guaranteed to contain the secret of how such a society could be brought to fruition. This is not to argue, of course, that the Labour Party has not come to terms with the need for authority and hierarchy in its own structure. But it has always been a highly conditional acceptance, the condition being that the parliamentary leadership should be allowed to lead only so long as it led in the right direction—that is, towards a classless society which would no longer need to suffer the evils of authority and hierarchy. In other words, hierarchy and authority have been accepted by the Labour Party as short-term necessities; evil in themselves and only to be tolerated as a means of fighting the class war to a victorious conclusion; and only to be tolerated, furthermore, because of the existence of clear guidelines, in the form of socialist doctrine, which were assumed to guarantee that the party leadership could not stray from the straight and narrow path, even if it wished to do so. The whole concept of leadership, therefore, was fundamentally different from that of the Tory Party. While it was accepted, for purposes of practical administration, that the leaders had to have a tactical freedom of manoeuvre—otherwise it would have been impossible for them to govern—this was always seen as a temporary concession; never as a permanent principle. One could liken the attitude of the Labour Party towards authority, hierarchy and discipline to that of a volunteer army which is prepared to accept the need for generals and all the rest for the duration of the war, it being clearly understood that they were bad in themselves and only to be tolerated as means to an end, to be got rid of at the first possible opportunity; to that of men and women voluntarily agreeing to form themselves into an army, and to accept the rules and discipline and to obey commanders, not because this was a natural thing to do, but because this was temporarily necessary for the purpose of bringing about a society where the army could be disbanded, and the rules, discipline and generals consigned to oblivion. Although in the past this attitude has enabled the Labour Party to overcome its basically democratic inclinations, and to tolerate a high degree of actual authority in practice, this has most emphatically not been because of any understanding, still less approval, of the principles of authority and hierarchy, or of the need to organize society around them, but because of a reluctant recognition that they could only be overthrown in the long run by accepting their dictates during the process of destruction.

Not surprisingly, these somewhat grudging attitudes have never encouraged a very happy relationship between the Party leaders and the rank-and-file. But hitherto the differences have been of the kind—if one may continue the military analogy—which bedevil a democratic nation at war: arguments over tactics, timing, speed of advance, the need for tactical withdrawals, individual struggles for command between the various wings of the army, and so on. But all these internal quarrels between the party leadership and the National Executive Council, or Conference, have been conducted within the context of a basic consensus as to broad strategy. The rank-and-file, so to speak, have often disagreed with what the generals have seen fit to do, or not to do, and, being a rough-and-ready lot, have even wondered from time to time whether it was really necessary to have generals at all. On one terrible occasion, in 1931, they even went so far as to mutiny against the generals' decision to accept an armistice with the enemy. But surely there is a fundamental difference between these past disputes and what is taking place today. For what is taking place today must be likened to the disintegration of an army after the hope of victory has been abandoned; the refusal of the rank-and-file to accept the continued need for discipline and subordination, since some no longer believe that there is a war to fight and others do not believe that the generals are any longer fighting it on the agreed strategy.

What this means is that just when the practical logic of democratic socialism requires the Labour Party to become more willing to accept authoritative leadership, the basis for justifying such leadership is found to be weaker than it has ever been before; just when a Labour Government needs to be able to rely on a Party prepared to support a paternalist approach to leadership, the likelihood of the Labour Party being able to meet that need has never been so remote. In short, just when a Labour Government needs to enjoy the maximum latitude, the party is inclined to allow it the minimum.

This is the contradiction at the heart of democratic socialism today. In practice, as the class war develops into a stalemate, the problems facing a democratic socialist government are such as to raise questions of choice which cannot be answered by the simple test of what is good for the working class. They therefore require for their resolution a party attitude to governmental authority which allows for policies to be carried through even if the working class are sometimes victims rather than beneficiaries. Yet the fact has to be recognized that the Labour Party's attitude to its leaders is deeply rooted in the assumption that governmental authority is only justified for class-war purposes; for use, that is, against the class enemy.

In other words, there are two contradictory forces at work. On the one hand, there is the cold logic of democratic socialism adapted to the needs of the stalemate society, which requires, precisely because peace has come, that party discipline should be tightened rather than weakened, since if a Labour Government is to be as firm with its class friends as with its class enemies, its leaders obviously have to be given more authority rather than less. On the other hand, again precisely because peace has broken out, a working-class party is obviously much less inclined to grant that authority, since the whole attitude to leadership rested on a view of society which no longer applies.

The problems inherent in this contradiction were beautifully illustrated by the battle over trade-union reform. If it is assumed—as it has to be in a stalemate society—that industrial relations are no longer a battle between God (the workers) and the Devil (the employers), but rather an argument between two equally legitimate interests, then it follows that a democratic socialist Government has to assume the role of arbitrator between the two interests rather than that of protagonist on the side of one. It makes obvious sense, therefore, for a Labour Government to seek to curb improper use of trade-union independence; just as much sense as to curb improper use of capitalist power. Manifestly, a Labour Government's attitude to the exercise of trade-union power must be fundamentally different in conditions of class peace to its attitude in conditions of class war. In the former, anything a trade unionist wants to do is fair, since war is war. But in the latter, all is not fair, since the interests of management become just as deserving—and their protection just as important in terms of planning—as the interests of the workers. So much is obvious. But it is equally obvious that this conclusion raises vast questions for the Labour Party. For if industrial relations are accepted as a prosaic struggle between two equally legitimate interests, rather than a struggle between right and wrong, and a social democratic Government becomes therefore an arbitrator rather than a protagonist, then it obviously cannot expect to enjoy the same kind of working-class support as it did when its whole claim to obedience rested on its commitment to fight the good fight.

First and foremost, of course, there is the effect on the relationship of the trade-union movement to the Labour Party. No one, I imagine, would deny the inevitability that this relationship will be very profoundly modified by the increasing evidence of the Wilson years—of which the Industrial Relations Bill was only the climax—that a Labour Government cannot be relied upon always to take the side of the workers. It is perfectly true, of course, that such a development was always implicit in the theory of democratic socialism, since even the most diluted form of milk-and-water socialism must entail some State intervention in the Labour market as well as in other spheres. But there is obviously a major difference between something's being theoretically implicit and its being explicitly spelt out in the cold terms of legal statute. In any case, the trade-union movement was always more interested in Labour Party practice than socialist theory, and so far as practice went, there had been a long-standing convention, dating back to the formation of the party, of mutual non-interference between the political wing and the trade-union wing; each agreeing to recognize the other as supreme in its own sphere.

As Mr David Marquand, M.P., put it in *New Society*:

From time to time the agreement has broken down. One obvious example was the split in 1914, when most trade unions rallied to King and Country, and most of the socialists remained loyal to the International. Another was the 1926 general strike, when the T.U.C. found itself—albeit to its own astonishment—challenging the constitution and embarrassing its political allies in the process. A more recent example was Frank Cousins's use of the Transport and General Workers' block vote in the debate on nuclear disarmament.

On the whole, however, the agreement has been honoured. The trade unions have rarely used their power at Labour Party conferences to coerce the political leadership. When the party has been in office, they have refrained from exploiting their position as its paymaster to dictate to

Labour ministers. By the same token, the political wing of the movement trod warily in industrial questions.*

What the Industrial Relations Bill did was to make it unmistakably clear that democratic socialism has reached the stage where this tacit agreement can no longer be honoured on either side. This certainly does not mean that the alliance between the two wings is about to break up; still less that it necessarily should. As Mr Marquand also points out:

> Left-wing parties in industrial countries always have close ties with the unions, even if they are sometimes informal rather than formal, for the obvious reason that the interests of their members coincide. Industrial Relations Bill or no Industrial Relations Bill, most Labour voters will still be trade unionists or the wives of trade unionists; so long as the Labour Party stands for the have-nots against the haves, this will continue to be the case.
>
> Equally, the unions will always need a left-wing Party at least as much as the left-wing Party needs them. Even under this rather unadventurous Labour Government, they have done better than they would have done under a Conservative Government faced with the same economic circumstances; and if the Conservatives win the next election, even those trade unionists who now call a plague on both parties will look back with sentimental nostalgia to the good old days of Roy Jenkins and Barbara Castle. Unless the unions lose all interest in the wider aims of their members, and concentrate solely on sectional wage claims of the narrowest kind, this, too, will continue.†

It may continue up to a point. Indeed, it obviously will. Loyalty to the Labour Party runs very deep in trade-union folklore. But it has to be recognized that the old pattern of mutual non-interference has gone for ever. Mr Marquand may well be right in arguing that on balance the trade-union movement will go on supporting the Labour Party at election time, and continue its financial support. But it will be forced to interfere with the political wing more and more, just as the political wing will be forced to interfere with it.

* *New Society*, 29 May 1969.   † *New Society*.

What this means is that a Labour Government will find itself engaged in a permanent argument with the trade unions; an argument, moreover, conducted in public. The marriage, so to speak, may carry on, but it will be an increasingly acrimonious marriage, marked by recurring rows and recriminations. This is bound to affect the ability of a Labour Government to provide the kind of clear-cut leadership which ambitious social planning requires.

The hope is, of course, that the trade-union leadership will make it unnecessary for Labour Governments to act the policeman by itself taking on this role. But it is very doubtful whether this is quite the panacea that it seems. For the trade-union leadership to take on the role of policeman means transferring the tension which is bound to exist in an industrial society to the trade-union movement itself; enlarging the gap *there* between leaders and led. One proposal, for example, for strengthening the trade-union leadership is that union leaders should be paid salaries comparable to the scales enjoyed by senior management. This might well add to their authority. But it would also add to the gap dividing those who give the orders from those who receive them. It might mean that trade-union leaders would see problems from the same viewpoint as ministers—and as management, too, for that matter— thereby facilitating the administrative requirements of democratic socialism; but only at the price of further alienating and isolating the workers on the shop floor and further underlining the fact that democratic socialism, far from bringing about a classless society, means in practice introducing hierarchical distinctions even into the trade-union movement itself.

Try as one may, there is no escaping the conclusion that democratic socialist government will either find itself arguing with the trade-union movement as a whole or, if its present attempt to force the trade-union leadership to take on the onus of arguing with the workers on its behalf fails, entering into a partnership with the trade-union establishment to keep the workers in line as a joint endeavour. It is difficult to see either development creating a context conducive to effective socialist planning. An alliance between the Labour Party and the trade-union leadership would create a political super-structure for economic planning—an apparatus at the top for drawing up the plan—but only at the cost of alienating the workers on the shop floor and increasing the likelihood of unofficial industrial strife, and thereby endangering the plan because of resistance to it at the bottom. On the other hand, if the Labour Party finds itself in permanent argument with a united trade union, having failed to prod the trade-union leaders into policing their own affairs, then socialist planning will fail because of the absence of an effective political superstructure at the top.

This brings one back inexorably to the root dilemma of the Labour Party. The administrative logic of democratic socialism compels a Labour Government to move in an élitist direction towards an alliance with enlightened management and enlightened trade-union leaders. That is what is required to make democratic socialism work. But the whole ethos of the Labour Party is profoundly unsympathetic to such a trend. The more inevitable it is seen to be, therefore, the less united is the Labour Party likely to become. So a Labour Government is forced into an impossible posture. It has, for compelling administrative reasons, to seek to promote policies, like an incomes policy and trade-union reform, which are profoundly élitist in their implications, while at the same time, for compelling political reasons, continuing to affirm its faith in a non-élitist ideology. Its actions have to be based on the assumption that the class war is over, but its language has to remain militant. One part of contemporary reality is that democratic socialism requires a cohesive élite, confident in its own values, and able to win the confidence of the masses—an élite which can make its claim to be governing for the people acceptable and plausible. But another part of reality is that the Labour Party draws its strength from an egalitarian or classless inspiration that cannot survive the conscious acceptance of such a need. The truth is that democratic socialist government needs the strength that can only come either from dedicated working-class support—a condition of which is commitment to a transforming social ideal—or from a middle-class élite that is capable of inspiring exceptional trust and loyalty. The conclusion can only be that the Labour Party must move either very much further to the Left or very much further to the Right. But in practice it can do neither. It is blocked on the Right by the existence of the Tory Party, which has already pre-empted the paternalist approach, and is manifestly the most suitable instrument for operating a meritocratic society; and on the Left by the limitations imposed by its commitment to democratic procedures, which force it to accept the necessity of operating a mixed economy. In practice, therefore, it cannot appeal wholeheartedly either to the middle class or to the working class; can build neither the administrative power superstructure needed to make democratic socialism work at the top nor the popular working-class base on which it needs to rest at the bottom. Its efforts to succeed in doing the former guarantee its failure in doing the latter, and its efforts to do the latter conflict with its efforts to do the former.

Let me sum up the burden of this chapter. My contention is that a democratic socialist Government in the circumstances of a mixed economy cannot hope to arouse the solid loyalty or fervent enthusiasm of working-class political movement, since not only are the economic and social conditions of such a society likely to dilute any sense of solidarity among the working class but the necessity of winning the confidence of the other interests—notably, of course, private enterprise—compels a democratic socialist Government to treat the working class—and the trade unions—as only one of many interests which need to be considered. This does not mean that most working-class voters and most trade unionists will not continue to be loyal to democratic socialism in general and to the Labour Party in particular, but it does mean that their loyalty will be highly conditional, far from wholehearted, and dismally different from the almost religious commitment which the implementation of socialism was thought to require; sufficient perhaps to guarantee that Labour Governments get elected but very far from sufficient to guarantee them the kind of sustained momentum needed to make a success of democratic socialist central planning.

It has to be recognized, therefore, that the kind of mass grassroots support which a Labour Government hoped to be able to rely on—something so purposeful and powerful as to constitute a wholly new force in politics—is simply not going to materialize; is likely indeed to decrease rather than increase, as the gap between the new reality of democratic socialism in practice and the old rhetoric becomes ever more glaringly apparent. So democratic socialism will increasingly have to look elsewhere for its momentum. But where? The answer seems to me to be: to the new élites or leadership groups, bureaucratic, trade-union, managerial, commercial, academic, on whose co-operation and enthusiasm democratic socialist government in effect depends. Unable any longer to rely on harnessing the fervour of the have-nots, democratic socialism must increasingly fall back on the enthusiasm of the haves.

This does not mean, of course, renunciation of the ideals of social justice. It means accepting the logic of a mixed economy in which the old socialist idea of social justice determined from below by a kind of classless general will has to be abandoned in favour of a new socialist concept of paternalist social justice determined from above. The point is that as the implementation of democratic socialism weakens the solidarity and idealism of the have-nots, thereby weakening and dissolving its traditional source of guidance, it is forced to seek to strengthen and solidify the enthusiasm and idealism of the haves, as a new source of guidance. As the old working-class consensus is eroded, a new middle-class consensus must take its place, since without either the one or the other a democratic socialist Government cannot hope to know what to do, let alone be in a position to do it.

The trouble, unfortunately, is that the Labour Party is quite peculiarly unsuited to make this switch. Its structure and ideology were not designed for this purpose. They were designed for the purpose of fighting the class war, for the purpose of overthrowing the capitalist establishment, and cannot come to terms with the present task—which is to operate in the context of a new democratic socialist establishment— without undergoing such a revolutionary transformation as to tear the Party apart. The necessity is clear: to reorganize the structure of the party so as to allow the Parliamentary leadership the same kind of authority and latitude as that enjoyed by the Tory Party, and to reinterpret the ideology so as to allow the adoption of policies likely to promote a new democratic socialist political class. But this would involve a fundamental change of nature for the Labour Party: from

106

a party seeking to change society, to shake up the existing hierarchy and to harness the discontent of the have-nots, to one determined to stabilize society, get the best out of the existing hierarchy and harness the contentment of the haves; would involve the Labour Party's coming to see itself as the instrument for operating democratic socialism here and now, making the best, that is, of the present stalemate conditions, with all that this would imply in terms of new rhetoric and policies, rather than as an instrument for transforming the *status quo*. My contention is that only such a fundamentally altered instrument can succeed in operating democratic socialism in the circumstances of a mixed economy, since unless it believes in the compromise, and promotes a governing class with a vested interest in the compromise, and seeks to inculcate a popular acceptance of that compromise and that governing class, conditions cannot exist for effective government.

This is the crucial point. Given acceptance of the mixed economy democratic socialism cannot hope to galvanize the working class into an effective dynamic for purposeful government. It must either lower its sights and accept a reduction in the range of government—that is, try to do less in terms of central planning—or seek to galvanize the middle class into becoming, in effect, the democratic socialist political class; must renounce either the social ends of socialism—egalitarianism—or the economic means—central planning. Unless the Labour Party can resolve this dilemma, its Governments are condemned to go on setting themselves unachievable goals, since they will be committed both to reliance on a political dynamic—the working class—which will be on the wane, and to egalitarian policies which preclude their bringing into existence a new political dynamic to take its place.

Two very significant political developments can be noticed in post-industrial, affluent, mass societies: first, the growth and importance of their intellectual communities, and secondly, the inability of Governments to act and speak in a manner that commands the allegiance of this constituency, which is expanding so rapidly both in numbers and in power.

This raises very serious questions, first as to the nature of the intellectual—what are his distinctive attributes to the exercise of power?—and secondly, as to how Governments in a democratic society can satisfy the requirements of this new power-group—for such, as we shall see, the intellectuals have become—without being false to their larger responsibilities to the nation as a whole.

What has to be realized is that intellectuals make demands on Governments which are rather different from those of other power-groups; that they require for their satisfaction a moral as well as a material response, a pattern in the exercise of power that conforms to an ideology and does not just serve a vested interest. If intellectuals are to constitute a new ruling order, then Governments can no longer afford to operate pragmatically or in the light of expediency, since it is of the nature of intellectuals to insist on adherence to principle.

It is scarcely an exaggeration to say that if a landed ruling class demands from Governments protection of property, and a capitalist ruling order demands protection of the market, an intellectual ruling class will demand protection of its conscience. Irving Kristol writes in *Foreign Affairs*:

> What creates a community of intellectuals, as against a mere aggregate of individuals, is the fact that they subscribe —with varying degrees of warmth, or with more or less

explicit reservations—to a prevailing ideology. This ideology permits them to interpret the past, make sense of the present, outline a shape for the future. It constitutes the essence of their rationality, as this is directed toward the life of man in society.*

The greater the importance of intellectuals in the community, therefore, the greater will be the pressure for ideological government. Yet the ideology favoured by intellectuals is by no means certainly shared by the rest of the community; nor will it be easy to make the exercise of power in a pluralist society conform to their requirements, particularly in the field of foreign relations which are peculiarly intractable to principle. The point is that a ruling order dominated by intellectuals poses problems for democratic government of a new and baffling kind, since they are likely to ask for something much more difficult to supply than protection and promotion of their material well-being. They are likely to ask for the protection and promotion of their moral sensibilities.

One of the more interesting political developments in the years 1964–70 was the hostility which grew up between the intellectuals and the Labour Government. In theory most intellectuals would probably describe themselves as democratic socialists. But a democratic socialist Government, in practice, found itself compelled over and over again to act and speak in a manner that deeply offended them. There is nothing surprising about this. Intellectuals always find themselves out of sympathy with Governments, since the inevitably pragmatic approach of the latter can never conform to the principles enunciated by the former. Intellectuals, therefore, are always complaining about the gap between what ministers preach and what they practise. Not only do democratic socialist Governments do more preaching than Conservative ones— and therefore present so much broader a target for criticism, are so much more susceptible to the bitterness of disillusion— but they also depend far more on the approval of intellectuals, who have traditionally been one of their most important constituencies.

* I. Kristol, 'American Intellectuals and Foreign Policy', *Foreign Affairs*, Vol. 45 (July 1967).

This, of course, has been largely for historical reasons. So long as democratic socialism was an instrument aimed at undermining a predominantly capitalist society it was bound to be popular with the intellectual community, since criticism of the prevailing patterns is their function, as well as their pleasure. But in the years 1964–70 a democratic socialist Government began to act and speak as if it saw itself as part of a governing order. This was certain to raise the hackles of the intellectual community, which is instinctively hostile to such an attitude. In so far as the Labour Party transforms itself into a natural governing party—which under Harold Wilson it went a long way towards doing—to that extent it will increasingly find itself opposed by intellectuals, which means, in effect, being opposed by most of those in a position to influence public opinion about public affairs.

This difficulty seems to me particularly relevant to the future of democratic socialism, which has the effect not only of elevating brainpower at the expense of other wealth and rank, but also of producing Governments which are peculiarly unsuitable to cope with the consequent problems. But before we consider the reasons for this, let me be a little more explicit about what is meant by the intellectual community, and about why, in contemporary society, it is coming to play so crucial a role.

An intellectual is not someone simply of intelligence and education, nor even an expert in some particular branch of knowledge. A historian, for example, writing about the 1867 Reform Bill, is being an historian, not an intellectual. But a historian signing a Vietnam manifesto *is* acting as an intellectual. An intellectual, in short, is a thinker, scholar, scientist, journalist, economist who sees himself, and expects to be seen by others, as having some authority, by reason of his superior education, to influence society in general far beyond the limits of his particular expertise.

An analogy, perhaps, may help to illustrate the point. A large landowner, so long as he limits his activities to taking care of his estate's fencing and drainage, is simply a man who owns many acres. But if he starts thinking that ownership of so much land confers upon him some special status and authority as a result of which he must be allowed to determine the country's morals and generally run its affairs—and society is prepared to accept his claim—then he becomes something more than a great landowner; he becomes, in fact, an oligarch or a member of a ruling class.

The same goes for scientists, writers, artists, academics and even actors and actresses. So long as they were content simply to exert influence in their own fields, then they were simply so many scientists, writers, artists and so on. But today they are increasingly claiming—and being accorded—the right to influence society in every way, from the Vietnam war to abortion, not as talented individuals but as an authoritative group; as, in effect, a new ruling class. Their names, backed by a string of degrees, as the head of a manifesto carry the same weight today as the names of the great landowners, backed by a string of titles, did fifty years ago.

Yet as Henry Fairlie once reminded us:

> Removed from his own discipline, no one is more vain than the intellectual. Precisely because his mind is able to handle ideas with ease and excitement, it is all too easily turned when he is invited to discourse outside his own field. Inside his own field, the intellectual would never lay claim to omniscience, and seldom to authority. Outside it his claim to both is breathtaking. A man who, having devoted his life to the study of some exact historical event, would hesitate to suggest the multiple reasons why it occurred, has no hesitation in analysing the situation in Vietnam and predicting, say, the Vietcong reaction to a hypothetical situation.*

The intellectual may be defined, in short, to quote Kristol again:

> ... as a man who speaks with general authority about a subject on which he has no particular competence. This definition sounds ironic, but is not. The authority is real enough, just as the lack of specific competence is crucial. An economist writing about economics is not acting as an intellectual, nor is a literary critic when he explicates a

* Quoted in 'American Intellectuals and Foreign Policy'.

text. In such cases, we are witnessing professionals at work. On the other hand, there is good reason why we ordinarily take the 'man of letters' as the archetypical intellectual. It is he who most closely resembles his sociological forbear and ideal type: the sermonizing cleric.

Precisely which people, at which time, in any particular social situation, are certified as intellectuals is less important than the fact that such certification is achieved—informally but indisputably. And this process involves the recognition of the intellectual as legitimately possessing the prerogative of being moral guide and critic to the world. (It is not too much of an exaggeration to say that even the clergy in the modern world can claim this prerogative only to the extent that it apes the intellectual class. It is the 'writing cleric', like the 'writing psycho-analyst', who achieves recognition.) But there is this critical difference between the intellectual of today and the average cleric of yesteryear: the intellectual, lacking in other worldly interests, is committed to the pursuit of temporal status, temporal influence and temporal power with a single-minded passion that used to be found only in the highest reaches of the Catholic Church.*

And it has never been so easy for him to achieve that status, influence and power. In the first place, in an ever more complicated society, possession of specialist intellectual skills assumes a significance and importance which society as a whole is forced to recognize and admire. Never has expert knowledge been so valuable, not only to Governments, but also to industry, indeed to organizations of every sort. None of the major programmes of the planned society is possible without the participation of intellectuals. The corridors of power are chock-a-block with economists, statisticians, social scientists, sociologists, psychologists, psephologists, public-relations experts, educationalists, to mention only the most obvious of the new specialisms. Indeed, no government department today would have the nerve not to 'intellectualize' itself. Such an omission would inevitably draw down upon its head the wrath of a Royal Commission, itself made up of intellectuals. Daniel Bell writes in *The Public Interest*:

* 'American Intellectuals and Foreign Policy'.

The ganglion of the post-industrial society is knowledge. But to put it this way is banal. Knowledge is at the base of every society. But in the post-industrial society, what is crucial is not just a shift from property or political position to knowledge as the new base of power, but a change in the *character* of knowledge itself. What has now become decisive for society is the new centrality of theoretical knowledge, the primacy of theory over empiricism and the codification of knowledge into abstract systems of symbols that can be translated into many different and varied circumstances. Every society now lives by innovation and growth: and it is theoretical knowledge that has become the matrix of innovation.... In all this, the university, which is the place where theoretical knowledge is sought, tested, and codified in a disinterested way, becomes the primary institution of the new society. Perhaps it is not too much to say that if the business firm was the key institution of the past hundred years, because of its role in organizing production for the mass creation of products, the university will become the central institution of the next hundred years because of its role as the new source of innovation and knowledge. To say that the primary institutions of the new age will be intellectual is not to say that the majority of persons will be scientists, engineers, technicians or intellectuals. The majority of individuals in contemporary society are not businessmen, yet one can say that this has been a 'business civilization'. The basic values of society have been focused on business institutions, the largest rewards have been found in business, and the strongest power has been held by the business community, although today that power is to some extent shared within the factory by the trade union, and regulated within society by the political order. In the most general ways, however, the major decisions affecting the day-to-day life of the citizen—the kind of work available, the location of plants, investment decisions on new products, the distribution of tax burdens, occupational mobility —have been made by business, and latterly by government which gives major priority to the welfare of business.

To say that the major institutions of the new society will be intellectual is to say that production and business decisions will be subordinate to, or will derive from, other forces in society; that the crucial decisions regarding the growth of the economy and its balance will come from government, but they will be based on the government's sponsorship or research and development, of cost effectiveness and cost benefit analysis; that the making of decisions, because of the intricately linked nature of their consequences, will have an increasingly technical character. The husbanding of talent and the spread of educational and intellectual institutions will become a prime concern for the society; not only the best talents, but eventually, the entire complex of social prestige and social status, will be rooted in the intellectual and scientific communities.*

There remains, of course, the question of the so-called literary intellectual, the writers, journalists, television pundits, for whom the mass media now offer such a phenomenal expansion of opportunity to influence both the educated classes and the masses. It is the influence of intellectuals of this kind that Charles Frankel had in mind when he wrote: '... the stability and strength of social and political institutions depend not only on their practical performance but on their symbolic *legitimacy*. And to a considerable extent, the secular intellectuals of modern nations have supplanted the clergy as the principal suppliers and endorsers of the symbols of legitimacy.'† So the intellectual community is not only playing a far more central role in the operational side of modern society, in, so to speak, its nuts and bolts. It is also increasingly the crucial factor in determining its moral climate, its heart and soul.

The question that has to be asked, therefore, is what kind of a society is likely to emerge when 'the entire complex of social prestige and social status' is 'rooted in the intellectual and scientific communities', and when they determine its moral climate. The answer is already fairly clear. It will be a society extremely difficult to govern by democratic methods, since whether the intellectual and scientific communities favour a left-wing or a right-wing ideology, they will find

* Daniel Bell, 'Notes on the Post-Industrial Society' in *The Public Interest*, No. 6.
† Quoted in 'American Intellectuals and Foreign Policy'.

themselves deeply out of sympathy with the style of democratic government, which is inevitably non-ideological; and all the more non-ideological in practice the more the Government concerned is involved on the international scene, since international affairs, even more than domestic affairs, cannot be determined according to a moral pattern. An intellectual community which was predominantly right-wing would find a Tory Government as ideologically unsatisfactory as a left-wing intellectual community finds a Labour Government.

The fate of the intellectual in all societies is to be critical of government, since even ideological dictatorships, like that of the Soviet Union, find it impossible to avoid shoddy compromises which outrage the doctrinaires. But in a democracy, these shoddy compromises are of the essence of government, its constant practice. In no other system, therefore, is the intellectual desire for principled government so difficult to satisfy. This difficulty applies to all ideologies and all Governments, but with particular relevance to left-wing ideologies and left-wing Governments, as I hope to show.

And in this country, of course, ever since the end of the First World War, the intellectual community has tended to be predominantly on the Left, concerned with social justice at home, with opposing imperialism abroad, against the nation state, for multiracialism, for sexual permissiveness, against organized religion, suspicious of power, contemptuous of authority, in favour of disarmament, opposed to war and so on. These have been the prevailing attitudes, so to speak, of the raw intellectual, of which, of course there have, until recently, been relatively few. The existence of a class society saw to that. A working-class boy, or an upper-class boy, or a middle-class boy, however intellectual he might be, however influenced by the university, would be unlikely to throw off his class coloration entirely; would be unlikely, that is, to become a raw intellectual. Some did. But the great majority did not. The effect of being brought up in a class background was to dilute the intellectual experience, or render the individual less responsive to it. In so far as the old ruling class, or the old business class, or even the old working class was intellectual, to that extent it was affected by the prevailing Left-wing progressive ideology. But, as I say, they were all only

115

fractionally intellectual; their university education—in so far as they had one—was only part of the formative influence of their lives, the rest being made up of traditions which were overwhelmingly non-intellectual or even anti-intellectual. In other words, ideological considerations were only part of the concern of the old educated classes, which were also deeply shaped by other non-intellectual traditions, aristocratic, commercial, entrepreneurial, military, bureaucratic, which in many respects were in conflict with the prevailing progressive ideology. And they were in conflict with the prevailing progressive ideology from positions of strength; not only material strength, rooted in property, but moral strength, rooted in function. The aristocratic tradition, the military tradition, the entrepreneurial tradition were still accepted as relevant and valuable. Today, however, the intellectual tradition is infinitely more potent and seductive, because class traditions and the functions out of which they arose have become infinitely less so. In the old days, class habits and values blocked the ears of the great majority who passed through the experience of higher education. But today these class habits and values are infinitely less solid. Instead of the student's going up to university rooted in a class background and coloration, and therefore to a large extent immune to intellectual indoctrination, he goes up far more open to it than ever before, far more likely to emerge at the end of the process as a 'raw intellectual'.

In the old days, such was the social magnetism of the establishment that the raw intellectual looked for a niche within it, and for the most part became more an establishment man than an intellectual man, more a supporter of the *status quo* than a critic of it. But today, as the social magnetism of the establishment is progressively weakened, and the power and status of the intellectual aggrandized, the process works the other way, with the intellectual imposing his values on the establishment instead of having its imposed on him.

Several processes have to be noted. In the first place there is the development of technology which requires a system of organization based on brainpower—a system, that is, which tends to enhance the importance of the intellectual, at the expense of all the other social categories. In the second place,

116

there is the dissolution of the class system, which not only accorded intellectuals a subordinate place but also guaranteed that those who benefited from higher education were only partially affected by its process of ideological indoctrination. In the old days an educated man would regard himself as first a gentleman, or a clergyman, or a businessman, or a civil servant, as the case might be, and only secondly as an intellectual. But in the more classless society of today, he is first and foremost an intellectual, because the process through which he became one, that of higher education, is much more influential in his life than his social background, a much more distinctive experience, and one of which he is much more aware and proud.

In other words, as modern society becomes much more dependent on the intellectual community, it becomes more dependent on a community that is peculiarly unsympathetic to the problems of democratic government; one whose most formative experience has been indoctrination by an ideology that fits it ideally to be the critic and conscience of society but by no means ideally to be the basis of a political class charged with the responsibility of operating society as it actually is. The old ruling classes were brought up in traditions that all had to do with the defence of society, with maintaining its institutions, and burnishing its image. Those that came from military families were concerned with one aspect of serving society, those from bureaucratic families with another aspect, and so on. But today we have a situation where the most crucial segment of society, the intellectual community, sees its role as that of reforming rather than defending society, of subverting rather conserving it, of undermining its institutions instead of building them up, since this is where its most formative influence encourages it to conceive its duty to lie.

Way back in 1797, Benjamin Constant observed that 'in the new society where the prestige of rank is destroyed, we—thinkers, writers and philosophers—should be honoured as the first among all the citizens'. The only reason Constant did not say 'we intellectuals' is that the term had not yet come into common usage. But he did not consider the implications for democratic government of this development. What I am saying is that it is of the nature of intellectuals to dislike all government, since all Governments are inevitably non-ideological, in the sense of being unable to hew to a particular abstract principle. But democratic Governments are particularly unsatisfactory in this respect, particularly prone to shoddy compromises, to pragmatism, to all the blurring of principle inherent in the business of reconciling the various interests and aspirations of a free and pluralist society. All Governments, therefore, tend to be offensive to the intellectual community; but democratic Governments most of all. And all intellectual communities tend to be unsympathetic to Governments, but a liberal progressive one, because its ideology is critical of authority and suspicious of power, is likely to be doubly critical, since the gap between its principles and the practice of government will be even wider than that between a right-wing ideology and the practice of government.

What we have to realize is that given the prevailing liberal progressive ideology, which could only make sense if everybody at home and abroad behaved like progressive liberals, and given the growing status and prestige of an intellectual community committed to the defence and promotion of this ideology, there is bound to be a mounting tension between democratic government which has to operate in the real world —where the majority are not made up of liberal progressives —and the intellectual community on whom Governments are increasingly dependent. Or put it another way, democratic Governments will be more and more unable to offer the key echelons in society the moral satisfactions for which they yearn. This is the fascinating new dilemma in the contemporary situation. Democracy has evolved a new ruling class based on brainpower which insists on being appeased by the one privilege which democracy is peculiarly unfitted to supply: moral satisfaction.

The history of the last hundred years or so suggests that democracy can come to terms with and tolerate a governing class based on land and a governing class based on a combination of land and capital, and that these two governing classes can come to terms with and tolerate democracy. But what the last few years are beginning to show is that a governing class based on brainpower is going to find democracy, and be found by democracy, far less tolerable. There are two reasons for this. Not only does the intellectual community yearn for a kind of society governed by values which the uneducated do not share—permissive, multiracial, internationalist, ordered to ideological patterns that allow no place for custom and habit —but it is instinctively suspicious and contemptuous of the morally blurred manner in which democratic Governments are compelled to frustrate these yearnings. Democracy, one might say, is the most political of systems, since it depends essentially—as we have seen—on the arts of compromise and negotiation. It is, therefore, of all political systems the least suitable for ideological government; the least suitable, therefore, for a society ever more dominated by intellectuals, whose predilection is precisely in favour of ideological government. Reliance on expediency, on pragmatism, willingness to reach shoddy compromises, inability to pursue principles to their logical conclusion—these are the essential characteristics of democratic government. All of these characteristics, however, are repugnant to intellectuals as a class, since they all have the effect of rendering intellectuals so much the less indispensable: to the extent that expediency, pragmatism, and compromise are necessary principles of action, to that extent the sovereignty of intellectuals is automatically circumscribed.

If one were to try to summarize the attitude of Britain's traditional political class, and the difference between it and the contemporary intellectual class, it would be difficult to improve on these words of Sir Thomas More in his *Utopia*:

> If evil persons cannot be quite rooted out, and if you cannot correct habitual attitudes as you wish, you must not therefore abandon the Commonwealth.... You must strive to guide policy indirectly, so that you make the best of things, and what you cannot turn to good, you can at least make less bad. For it is impossible to do all things well unless all men are good, and this I do not expect to see for a long time.

Here, one might say, is the quintessential wisdom of a non-ideological political tradition. But what a world of difference from the writings of the contemporary intellectual community which, unlike Sir Thomas More, is quite convinced that all men are indeed good and that any such modest and compromising involvement with political power can represent only a corruption of the spirit. But the point to notice about Sir Thomas More was that he was not primarily an intellectual. He was an educated gentleman, whose roots lay in a social background that helped to induce an instinctive understanding of the art of politics. The difficulties inherent in the exercise of power, in governance, were something that he understood, not from books, but from life. It was bred into him. By this I do not mean, of course, that a respect for democracy was bred into him, which it certainly was not, but that he had a recognition of the limitation of politics, of the frustration of power, of the absurdity of ideologies. The point I am trying to make is that the more dominant the educational process alone is in forming a governing class—as it increasingly is today—and the less its members come from backgrounds where the true nature of the political process is instinctively understood, the more impatient such a class will be with the frustrations of politics. And since democratic politics are the most frustrating of all, this means, in effect, that such a class will be peculiarly undemocratic in spirit.

The British political tradition, as is well known, is not easy to codify; is not easy, therefore, to learn; take, as Michael Oakeshott says, 'in the most favourable circumstances, two or three generations to learn'.* The essence of it is that it is rooted in the practice of politics, the theory, in so far as it is a theory, arising from the practice. A very large part of it amounts to little more than the accumulated experience of a ruling class that has discovered what can and cannot be done, and passed on the lessons from generation to generation. Probably in no other country, therefore, is the human element so important, the tradition residing essentially in the hearts of men and being transmitted by example. But what will be the impact on this tradition of the rise to influence of the intellectual community, which is strikingly out of sympathy with the art of politics? What will be the impact on this tradition of the replacement of the old social class, out of which it sprang and by whom it was preserved, by an intellectual community whose ideological approach to politics is

* 'Rationalism in Politics' and Other Essays (Methuen, 1962).

almost the opposite of the British political tradition? That it will be profound cannot seriously be doubted. The point that has to be noticed is that until very recently British politics were shaped and determined by a political tradition that depended vitally on hunch and instinct, and could afford so to depend because the social system guaranteed the existence of a stratum which possessed hunch and instinct. But that social stratum is now disappearing and being replaced by an intellectual stratum which is the product of a wholly different experience, and not only lacks the hunch and instinct, but is possessed of an ideology that positively despises hunch and instinct.

This seems to me a much more important development than is generally realized. British politics have moved from feudalism through capitalism to the present mixed economy with astonishingly little change in the composition of the political class. Measures have changed out of all recognition, but enough of the same kind of men have continued to sit in the Houses of Parliament to preserve the political tradition. Capitalism transformed Britain, but left the political tradition intact. Indeed the political tradition absorbed capitalism; businessmen were absorbed by the political class and rendered indistinguishable from it.

But the intellectual community looks like proving a far tougher nut to absorb, since not only is the political class in a far less favourable position to do the absorbing, but the nut itself is far less willing to be absorbed. Businessmen as a class were willing to be absorbed; were willing to leave politics to the governing class, provided of course that its material affairs were suitably attended to. Intellectuals, however, are not. They are passionately interested and involved in politics, but interested and involved in an ideological manner that is profoundly different from the traditional manner.

Now, it may be objected that this is a transitional phase, and that as the intellectual community becomes accustomed to its new position of status and prestige, it will itself develop an understanding of the inevitable limitations of power; that it will cease to find the words of Sir Thomas More not only incomprehensible but reprehensible. To some extent this can be said to be happening, and nowhere is this process more obvious than in the changed attitudes of the Labour Party which gets steadily less ideological as it moves from being a party of opposition to being a party of power. One can see the process at work too in the increasing numbers of academics who are being drawn into the processes of government. It is therefore probably only a matter of time before the intellectual community as a whole develops the instincts and hunch of a political class. Many writers and thinkers—and not only on the political Left—have viewed this prospect with the greatest unease, for it seemed to them to threaten the continued existence of the intellectual community as a critical moral force in British life.

They need not have worried. For although it is true that a minority of intellectuals have moved in this direction— crossed the barrier, so to speak, which divided the supporters of the *status quo* from the opponents—their numbers have been made up a thousandfold by the new recruits to the intellectual community brought about by the phenomenal expansion of higher education. The reasons for this expansion are so well known as not to need elaboration here. They are partly technical—the fact that a technological civilization needs more brainpower—and partly moral, in the sense that it is felt to be right that higher education should be made available for all who can be induced to use it. Joseph Schumpeter gave a warning about these developments some thirty years ago in his great work *Capitalism, Socialism and Democracy*.

One of the most important features of the later stages of capitalist civilization is the vigorous expansion of higher education. This development was and is no less inevitable than the development of the largest-scale industrial unit, but unlike the latter, it has been and is being fostered by public opinion and public authority so as to go much further than it would have done under its own steam. Whatever we may think about this from other standpoints and whatever the precise causation, there are several consequences that bear upon the size and attitude of the intellectual group.

First, in as much as higher education thus increases the supply of services in professional, quasi-professional and in the end all 'white collar' lines beyond the point determined by cost-return consideration, it may create a particularly important case of sectional unemployment.

Second, along with or in place of such unemployment, it creates unsatisfactory conditions of employment—employment in sub-standard work or at wages below those of the better paid manual workers.

Third, it may create unemployability of a particularly disconcerting type. The man who has gone through a college or university easily becomes psychically unemployable in manual occupations without necessarily becoming employable in, say, professional work. His failure to do so may be due either to lack of natural ability—perfectly compatible with passing academic tests—or to inadequate teaching; and both cases will, absolutely and relatively, occur more frequently as ever larger numbers are drafted into higher education and as the required amount of teaching increases irrespective of how many teachers and scholars nature chooses to turn out. The results of neglecting this and of acting on the theory that schools, colleges and universities are just matters of money, are too obvious to insist upon. Cases in which among a dozen applicants for a job, all formally qualified, there is not one who can fill it satisfactorily, are known to everyone who has anything to do with appointments—to everyone who, that is, is qualified to judge.

All those who are unemployed or unsatisfactorily employed or unemployable drift into vocations in which standards are least definite or in which aptitudes and acquirements of a different order count. They swell the host of intellectuals in the strict sense of the term whose numbers hence increase disproportionately. They enter it in a thoroughly discontented frame of mind. Discontent breeds resentment. And it often rationalizes itself into that social criticism which is in any case the intellectual spectator's typical attitude towards men, class and institutions especially in a rationalist and utilitarian civilization.*

* Joseph Schumpeter, *Capitalism, Socialism and Democracy* (Allen and Unwin, 1947), p. 152.

This prophecy has been fulfilled down to the last detail. So although it is perfectly true that a minority of the intellectual community has been absorbed into the power structure of modern technological society, the majority has not and cannot be, and is in many ways much more like a 'mass' than an élite, with its own mass movement situated in the universities. The top of the intellectual community is to some extent being drawn off into the political process, and thereby 'corrupted by power', but these desertions from the cause of ideological commitment are more than made up for by new recruits from the bottom, who bring a fresh whine of material frustration to add to the existing moral moan.

What has all this to do with the future of democratic socialism? It has, I think, a very great deal, since the question that has to be considered is how democratic socialism can hope to operate in the context of an alienated intellectual community; alienated in part because of an ideological distaste for, or misunderstanding of, the democratic political process and in part because of genuine fears and resentments arising from economic insecurity. The contemporary intellectual community is dissatisfied on two counts, first moral—ideological distaste for contemporary society on account of its imperfections—and second, material, the fear of unemployment being far more real for them than it is for the manual worker. Yet this intellectual community, so fraught with frustration and resentment, is the raw material on which democratic socialism has to rely for the implementation of its grandiose plans, since it is determined to destroy, and already has largely succeeded in destroying, the political class which capitalism was wise enough to use. What has to be realized is that the intellectual community was intended to be the executant class of democratic socialism, the instrument by which the new Jerusalem would be engineered. But just how suitable is it going to prove to be? May it not be that an alienated intellectual community will constitute a far more damaging and corrosive element in a democratic socialist society than ever it was in a capitalist one! May it not be that in releasing this genie democratic socialism has not only dealt capitalism a death-blow—which was the intention—but also prevented itself from ever coming properly to life?

After the six years of the Wilson administration this cannot be said to be an academic question. One of the more remarkable developments in the years 1964–70, as we have seen, was the hostility which grew up between the intellectual community and the Labour Government. Opinion in the universities about Labour was far more bitterly critical than it was even in the City, the organs of the intellectual Left no less censorious than those of the intellectual Right. The complaint was very specific, and repeated over and over again: that Mr Wilson lacked principle, that he was a pragmatist who would do anything to stay in power, that he 'played' politics, that he lowered the tone of public life. It is probably true to say that no Prime Minister before in our history has been subjected to such *moral* obloquy. When one tries to discover what it was that Mr Wilson had done to deserve such indignant reactions, it is difficult to find enough crimes to explain them. Of course it is very easy to find fault with the Wilson administration and to criticize it on the grounds of economic incompetence. But this is not enough to account for the peculiarly moral note of so much of the criticism. It seems to me that Mr Wilson was being judged by different standards from those traditionally applied to political practice, that he was being judged by ideological standards, by the standards of the intellectual community rather than those of the political class. I almost suspect that it was not Mr Wilson's economic failures that made him so morally objectionable but his political successes—the fact that he was such a superb politician. When the public-opinion polls kept on giving him a lead during the election campaign, it was widely felt that he did not *deserve* such success, that he had won it unfairly by 'double-talk and double-cross'. One cannot recall the same moralistic reaction, to anything like the same extent, to the success of Mr Harold Macmillan in 1959—a success, of course, that was carried over into polling day, as Mr Wilson's was not. Mr Macmillan, like Mr Wilson, was a master politician, and much criticized by the intellectual community for lack of principle, but never with the same degree of vehemence and passion.

The point I am trying to make is that much of the criticism of Mr Wilson was not because he was an exceptionally bad politician but because he was an exceptionally good one; that it was rooted less in condemnation of his failures than in abhorrence of his successes, that it was based less on an objective assessment of his policies than a subjective evaluation of his character. I suspect that Mr Wilson has all the qualities and skills necessary to make a highly successful political leader in a democratic society, but that these skills and qualities, which were once enormously admired by a political class capable of appreciating them, are precisely those which the intellectual community finds least to its taste. The truth is that the more one knows about the democratic political process, the easier it is to admire Mr Wilson; while the more one thinks of politics in ideological terms the more difficult it is. Reporters, close to the political scene, were fascinated with Mr Wilson, and pundits, looking for ideas and patterns, were revolted. But the degree of moralizing about Mr Wilson, which was more intense than that directed against any Prime Minister in modern history, tells us more about the state of British society than about Mr Wilson. It is surely a sign of the extent to which the intellectual approach to politics has strengthened its hold; of the extent to which pragmatism and expediency—the hallmarks of democratic politics—are now anathema to a segment of society whose influence is growing, not least, of course, because its members play such a dominant role in the mass media. By any traditional political standards Mr Wilson's achievement was very remarkable. He has transformed the Labour Party from one associated in the public mind primarily with opposition to one than can contend for power on at least equal terms with its Tory rival. It is now much more a political party than an ideological movement. Judged by traditional political standards, as I say, this is a great achievement. But how relevant are traditional political standards in a society where, because of the growing importance and numbers of the intellectual community, ideological commitment is now the fashionable demand? Mr Wilson's non-ideological approach to politics certainly reassured the old middle class, because he seemed much less of a threat to their pockets than they had feared. After all, he seemed at times almost like a Tory, particularly in foreign affairs. But what this overlooks is the fact that the middle class is no longer the same as it was; that its new generation is more characteristically intellectual than bourgeois, more concerned with its conscience than with its pocket. By making the Labour Party less ideological Mr Wilson certainly rendered it more acceptable to the traditional middle class. But he has made it less ideological just at the moment when this is exactly the opposite of what the new middle class most fervently desires. The situation is full of irony. Mr Wilson has transformed the Labour Party's image to conform with a bourgeois approach to politics, oblivious of the fact that in an increasingly classless society, where higher education has become the meritocracy's most formative experience, the bourgeois approach repels rather than attracting.

It may be, of course, that such a transformation of the Labour Party's image was inherent in the responsibilities which holding office entails; that governing Britain in a democratic manner—that is to say, accepting the necessity for operating a mixed economy at home and serving the national interest abroad, and paying attention to the non-ideological prejudice of the uneducated mass—inevitably meant governing in a manner that would offend the intellectual community. This would certainly seem to me to be the case. I do not see how Mr Wilson, given the actual problems which he faced, could conceivably have pursued policies that satisfied the liberal progressive conscience. The British economy is peculiarly dependent on world trade balances, and the area of manoeuvrability is cruelly limited. In fact, in the managerial revolution which has silently emerged, technical decision-making by the economic expert now shapes the politician's pronouncements. That this would preclude ideological government should always have been obvious, and socialist theorists have only themselves to blame for overlooking the obvious. Socialism was primarily a redistributive philosophy. Marx's manifesto assumed that the problem of production had been solved by capitalism and that the function of socialism was to redistribute the fruits in more equitable fashion, a task calling more for an understanding of morals than for an understanding of politics. Yet, as the last six years of Labour Government have made all too clear, the nineteenth-century problems of capital growth, of incentives and productivity, are very much alive today, for none of which is there an ideological or moral solution. Nationalization was an ideological solution, in the sense that it was meant to transform the moral climate of industrial relations. But in practice workers no more feel they own the nationalized industries than sailors feel they own the Royal Navy. The truth is that there is no ideologically satisfying way of managing the British economy, as Labour Ministers would now be the first to admit.

Still less is there an ideologically satisfying way of operating foreign policy. This, of course, has always been true. As Irving Kristol has written:

> ... it is the peculiarity of foreign policy that it is the area of public life in which ideology founders most dramatically. Thus, while it is possible—if not necessarily fruitful—to organize the political writings of the past 300 years along a spectrum ranging from the ideological Left to the ideological Right, no such arrangement is conceivable for writings on foreign policy. There is no great radical text on the conduct of foreign policy—and no great conservative text either. What texts there are (e.g. Machiavelli, Grotius, in our own day the writings of George Kennan and Hans Morgenthau) are used indifferently by all parties, as circumstance allows.

And we find, if we pursue the matter further, that the entire tradition of Western political thought has very little to say about foreign policy. From Thucydides to our own time, political philosophy has seen foreign affairs as so radically affected by contingency, fortune and fate as to leave little room for speculative enlightenment. John Locke was fertile in suggestions for the establishment and maintenance of good government, but when it came to foreign affairs he pretty much threw up his hands: 'What is to be done in reference to foreigners, depending much upon their actions and the variation of designs and interests, must be left in great part to the prudence of those who have this power committed to them, to be managed by the best of their skill for the advantage of the Commonwealth.'

The reasons why this should be so are not mysterious. ... whereas a national community is governed by principles by which one takes one's intellectual and moral bearings, the nations of the world do not constitute such a community and propose few principles by which their conduct may be evaluated. What this adds up to is that ideology can obtain exasperatingly little purchase over the realities of foreign policy—and that intellectuals feel keenly their dispossession from this area.... It is only where politics is ideologized that intellectuals have a pivotal social and political role. To be good at coping with expediential situations you don't have to be an intellectual—and it may even be a handicap.... No modern nation has ever constructed a foreign policy that was acceptable to its intellectuals. True, at moments of national peril or national exaltation, intellectuals will feel the same patriotic emotions as everyone else, and will subscribe as enthusiastically to the common cause. But these moments pass, the process of disengagement begins, and it usually does not take long for disengagement to eventuate in alienation. Public opinion polls generally reveal that the overwhelming majority of ordinary citizens, at any particular time, will be approving of their government's foreign policy; among intellectuals, this majority tends to be skimpy at best, and will frequently not exist at all. It is reasonable to suppose that there is an instinctive bias at work here, favorable to government among the common people, unfavorable among the intellectuals.*

The problem is particularly acute in the United States today, since the intellectual community has risen to domestic power just at the very moment when the country's imperial position in the world involves her in all sorts of foreign responsibilities which brutally affront the historic ideology. Hitherto American intellectuals have been very spoilt in this respect. For most of American history their ideological distaste for the use of power has corresponded—thanks to the Royal Navy—with a perfectly viable diplomatic and political assessment of the national interest. In other words, there has

* 'American Intellectuals and Foreign Policy.'

been no cause for tension between the keepers of the American conscience and the guardians of American shield. Isolationism and anti-imperialism made sense in both moral *and* practical terms. More and more, however, America's ideological approach to foreign affairs is at war with American reality, with the intellectuals continuing in ever more strident terms to affirm their faith in a set of moral principles which the politicians, with mounting impatience, are compelled to ignore. The American intellectual community has probably never before felt itself so cut off from, and in conflict with, the thrust of governmental policy. To them the Vietnam war, and much else besides, seems to outrage every principle for which the U.S. is meant to stand. They are disgusted by, and wholly unable to understand, the true explanation that a great power with world responsibilities cannot avoid this kind of ugly action. As a result, just at the moment when technological developments, notably the vast expansion of university education, have created more intellectuals than ever before—more American citizens, that is to say, who operate in ideological terms—America finds itself compelled to act with less and less respect for ideology. The resulting tension is tearing the body politic apart.

It would be comforting to suppose that as Britain becomes less of a world power, the provocation offered to the intellectual conscience by the inevitably non-ideological nature of foreign affairs will decline in intensity since, being less involved, there will be few causes for offence to be given. This seems to me an optimistic view. It would be much more realistic to assume that we are moving into a period when the clash between liberal–progressive ideology and international reality will become fiercer than ever before. All the signs suggest that divergence of interest between the underdeveloped third world and the West is likely to involve a mounting conflict between expediency and principle, with the liberal–progressive conscience in a permanent state of indignation about the failure of Government to hew to the supposedly moralistic line.

The problem of South Africa illustrates this difficulty with particular acuteness. The liberal–progressive view, so beloved of the intellectual community, is that the most crucial battle in the world today is in the field of race, and that Britain, for reasons of morality and expediency, must throw in its lot with the coloured peoples, for all their imperfections. But one can only doubt whether any Government in fact will pay more than lip-service to this view. During its last period of office Labour was able to blur the issue in a way that gave some satisfaction to both the realists and the idealists, backing the liberal–progressive view in words but only very partially in actions. It did not sell arms to South Africa, but it carried on cynically enough with trade and defence co-operation.

But as the pressure on South Africa from its black neighbours grows in intensity, this double-faced attitude will become far less easy to maintain. The moment of truth will dawn. And when it does, can one really suppose that any British Government, Labour or Conservative, will support the coloured crusade, which will probably have the support of Russian and Chinese arms to overthrow the South African regime by force? It is much more probable that if Labour is back in power at the time we shall hear Mr Michael Stewart's successor arguing the obvious point that South Africa is a fellow-member of the Western world, an erring member, certainly, but none the less, for all its faults, part of our culture and civilization in a way that no black African State is likely to be for many generations. He will not like so arguing, any more than the last Labour Government liked holding on to nuclear weapons or supporting the Americans in Vietnam. But that is how the facts of power will compel him to argue, when it comes to the crunch, since like it or not, white South Africa *can* be relied upon to stand with the West against the Communist super-Powers, while the black African States are at best either non-aligned or neutral and at worst potentially, if not actually, hostile.

In other words, it is not the importance of the Cape route (which is the Tory kind of double-talk) that forces Britain to support a hateful white supremacist State. It is the fact of white supremacy which makes the relationship so peculiarly irresistible. Of course it would be much less embarrassing if white supremacy was exercised in a less morally obnoxious manner. But if it was not exercised at all, the relationship would lose much of its point. The harsh truth, which will become clearer and clearer as time passes, is that Britain, far from being neutral in the race struggle, let alone on the coloured side, is positively on South Africa's side, since in the crucial battle in the world today—which is not between North and South but between East and West—Britain has no alternative but to throw in its lot with the white peoples, in spite of their imperfections.

Such a view, of course, flouts all the prevailing assumptions about both morality and expediency, since it is based on the conclusion that the underdeveloped world, being made up of have-not nations, has no true interest in supporting the West against Soviet hegemony, is in fact basically on the side of world revolution, and therefore, knowingly or unwittingly, likely to play the Soviet game, at least for the foreseeable future. It follows from this, however, that any British Government, mindful of Britain's interests, will be compelled into a mounting conflict with liberal–progressive ideology. The intellectual community sees the African struggle against South Africa as a moral crusade against colour discrimination, an attempt to redress a particular injustice which, if realized, would be the end of the matter. But in fact it is something much broader and deeper—a revolution not simply aimed at the overthrow of apartheid—that is only the immediate objective—but at the overthrow of the whole structure of Western superiority and security. The struggle would not end with the overthrow of the South African regime, since apartheid is only the excuse, albeit an outstandingly good one. The true target, the real source of provocation, is Western power itself.

As the implications of this truth become inescapable we shall see a reversal of Britain's postwar diplomatic and even internal policies, whatever Government is in power. In the 1950s and 1960s Britain, in common with all the Western countries, assumed that the Third World could be rallied to the Western cause. This was the basis of our attempt to create a multiracial Commonwealth, of our agreement to work within the United Nations—where the Third World enjoys a majority—even of the hope at home of integrating large numbers of coloured citizens into a multiracial community. The underlying assumption of all these policies was that it was worth while leaning over backwards to woo the underdeveloped world, to the point even of being blackmailed by it. The Tory decision to sell arms to South Africa was only the first sign of a spectacular break with this fundamental estimate, an indication of a new note—which Governments of the Left will have no alternative but to echo—of growing scepticism about the value of the underdeveloped world, a clear sign of a willingness to call its bluff. And not only *its* bluff, but also the bluff of all those in this country who advocate elevating racial accord into the primary aim of British statesmanship. The racial issue will be seen by policy-makers as an instrument which is being used by the enemies of this country for purposes which have nothing to do with morality and that this thraldom around our hearts has to be broken, since it is in danger of becoming a noose around our necks.

What is becoming clear is that apartheid is not at the heart of the racial issue. At the heart of it is the fact of Western superiority, resentment of which would remain even if revolution came to South Africa. This is what the liberal–progressive ideology so dangerously overlooks, and why it will find itself more and more at war with official policy, whichever party is in power. The struggle for racial equality will be seen as a power struggle and because of this intimately bound up with all those revolutionary forces, both within these shores and outside them, aimed at weakening the West. The West in short can never hope to win the hearts of the Third World except by ceasing to be the West, since in reality it is its virtues, quite as much as its vices, that cause the hostility. It is in this sense that the liberal–progressive obsession with Britain's being on the right side of the race war is so unrealistic. It inculcates a Western inclination to self-abasement that plays into Soviet hands.

The truth will get harder and harder to burke: racial equality will never be achieved by raising the Third World up; it can only be achieved by casting the Western world down. The Soviet Union knows this full well, which is why it supports the coloured cause. The West will also come to realize the truth, which is why British policy is likely to give more and more outrage to the liberal–progressive community. While it is doubtless true that the next Labour Government will do so less tactlessly than the present Tory Government, it will have to do so enough to damn it irretrievably in their eyes.

Nor is it only abroad that the question of race is going to raise its ugly head. The race problem here at home is far more complicated than is generally recognized, even perhaps by Mr Enoch Powell. Almost everybody fails to understand it, anti-blacks quite as much as those who wish them well. One can only be appalled at the gap that exists between the real nature of the problem and the illusions about it held so passionately by the intellectual community. But it is the real nature of the problem which Governments will be compelled to deal with in the coming decades, with all that this will imply in terms of shattered Left-wing illusions.

The problem of the multiracial society today, at any rate so far as this country is concerned, does not begin to be understood in its entirety if it is seen as one of simply assuring coloured people a square deal; that is to say, preventing discrimination against them. That is an intolerably patronizing white *de haut en bas* approach. It assumes that the coloured minority will always remain a timorous passive group of railway porters, low-paid clerks and crossing-sweeps in need of white protection. At the risk of putting it too crudely, it has to be recognized that future black *power* is quite as much part of the problem as is present black *weakness*. Here and now, of course, the coloured communities are very vulnerable. But it is intolerably insulting to them to suppose that they are bound always to remain underprivileged. It is equally insulting to them to suppose that as the years pass they will be content simply to merge into their existing surroundings, becoming black and brown equivalents of their white fellow citizens. The much more respectful and realistic assumption to make is that as they find their feet, and feel the ground under them secure, they will seek to create communities which correspond to their own cultural needs and aspirations, however much these needs and aspirations, conflict with those of the natives.

Just as the British in India and Africa sought to create oases in those continents where they could live according to their own mores and values, so will the Africans, West Indians and Asians seek to do the same in Britain. I see no reason to suppose that the coloured immigrants in these islands now will be more prepared to become British than the British emigrants to their own continents then were prepared to become Indian or African. The fact has to be faced that large-scale coloured immigration has taken place at a time when the African and Indian races are rediscovering pride in their own ancestries; when the impulse to demonstrate the quality of their own cultures is growing stronger all the time. Indeed the dynamism of cultural pride, even of colour consciousness, is much more marked today among the black and brown races, who feel that their glories lie ahead, than among the whites— or at least the European whites—who feel that their glories lie in the past.

The American Negro experience is quite different, dominated by its origins in slavery. Nearly two hundred years of humiliation and servitude deprived them of pride in their own ancestry, of cultural identity—created, in short, a de-racinated mass which has and had no alternative to integration. The problem there, at least until very recently, was white pride and black inadequacy. But this is not the problem here. The problem here, at any rate in the long run, will be black and brown racial (in the best sense) pride. In other words, although the phrase *Black Power* has been invented in the United States it is not nearly so relevant there as it is, or will be, here. There it is real only in the sense of pointless violence, since the great majority of blacks know in their hearts that they are not African, are doomed by fate to be American or nothing. Black Power extremists may pretend otherwise, but it is a futile, tragic pretence, flying in the face of fate. But it is not flying in the face of fate in Britain. Precisely because the coloured immigrants are still genuinely Indian and Pakistani and Sikh (admittedly this applies much less to Caribbean immigrants), with real roots in their countries and regions of origin, they do not need to become British any more than the British who sought their fortunes in Africa and India needed to become Africans or Indians.

My point is that Britain is not faced by the relatively simple problem of coloured ghettoes in the major cities. There may, of course, be ghettoes, but sensible and generous provision and

135

planning may, one hopes, be able to prevent that. It is faced by a different kind of colour problem: that the centre of many of our major cities should become civilized communal oases of men and women who are proud of not being British—foreign oases with their own culture, their own language, political leaders and separate destinies. It is faced, in short, by a form of coloured power which will not (one hopes) be mad or violent or evil, but which will be all the more significant precisely because of being perfectly respectable and legitimate. But *foreign*. Of course this may not come about. The immigrants may prove themselves a feckless, disorganized liability, a coloured proletariat, which would create grave practical problems comparable with those which the United States is experiencing at the present time. But such an estimate of immigrant potentiality is shockingly dismissive, insulting both to them and to our own determination to create conditions in which they can prosper.

No, let us assume that they do prosper, that we do give them a chance, as I am sure we will. Let us assume, in other words, that they prove true to themselves and we prove true to ourselves. Only then will the true proportions of the problem become manifest. For what will emerge as the result of their and our best efforts is a much more intractable problem than that faced in America—coloured foreign communities, in key areas of the country, who are economically and administratively integrated into the country, essential parts of its physical life, but emotionally, culturally and mentally still belonging to other lands.

Not to take this problem seriously is only explicable in terms of a truly ineffable assumption of British racial superiority. It is to assume that foreign minorities, if they are black and brown, are not foreign in the accepted sense of being a potential threat, are not really foreign at all since they came from countries and cultures that do not properly count. It is to assume that such communities will prove incapable of organizing themselves into effective units of power which could prove potentially hostile. It is to assume, in short, that it is utterly inconceivable that the African and Asian settlers here could prove as disruptive to our national cohesion and identity as British settlers proved to theirs.

Yes, settlers. This is what they are, and it is contemptuous to see them as anything else. They do not want to be dissolved into the great pool of British life. In time it must be assumed that political leaders will emerge who will articulate this sense of separateness and that this in turn will lead to tensions which are much more serious than street rioting and ghetto violence, since they will be the result not of economic grievance, or of social deprivation—although these can be expected to play some part—but of straight communal rivalry: that most fateful canker in the body politic.

I am paying the immigrants the courtesy of seeing them as they ought to be seen, not as they are now, weak, vulnerable and in need of protection, but as they will become—strong, purposeful and potentially disruptive. With the benefit of hindsight it is now clear that British emigrants should never have been financially encouraged to settle in Africa, that they should long ago have been encouraged financially to come home. To urge that this lesson be applied to the problem of coloured immigrants in this country is the opposite of racialism. It is a tribute to their future strength, and markedly less patronizing than the attitudes of those who dwell only on their present weakness.

I fear that this view, which seems so heretical and obnoxious today, will soon seem the merest common sense. For if I am right in suggesting that Britain will never be able to support the Third World in its struggle against Western superiority— a struggle for which white supremacy in South Africa is more the excuse than the cause—then it has to be recognized that the coloured immigrant population will find itself opposed to —if not literally up in arms against—official British policy. The truth is that in the event of a black uprising in South Africa, supported by Russian-armed guerrillas from the north, the immigrant population would be on one side and the British Government on the other. Can there really be any doubt that on any issue where Third World interests clash with those of the West, the immigrant population will side with the Third World? This is not a criticism. It is perfectly natural that they should. But it would be wholly unrealistic not to conclude that problems of race are going to be at the centre of British politics for many years to come, and that they will not easily be resolvable in a fashion acceptable to liberal–progressive ideology. One must, in all honesty, go further. If anything is certain, it is that Labour Governments, no less than Tory ones, will be compelled to give offence to the liberal–progressive conscience even more in the future than in the past. To suppose, therefore, that the intellectual community's loss of faith in Mr Wilson's Labour Government was due to special circumstances, or to particular errors on his part—or that of Mr Stewart—is to miss the crucial point. The loss of faith is likely to be a continuing factor in the political situation, getting worse rather than better.

But if this is so, how is it going to be possible for democratic socialist Governments to engender that fierce surge of public enthusiasm, and that cohesive and united popular movement, which their ambitious policies so crucially depend on? We have already noted that the responsibility of operating a mixed economy involves adopting policies which displeases the working class. If the responsibility of operating a realistic foreign policy also involves provoking the intellectual class, we have to conclude that the amount of support democratic socialist Governments are likely to receive, while possibly sufficient for very limited and modest aims, will be wholly inadequate for the kind of grandiose transformation of society inherent in the idea of a planned society. What has to be recognized—and one cannot make this reminder too often—is that a climate of moral legitimacy is absolutely crucial to the successful implementation of democratic socialist policies. But moral legitimacy is precisely what it is in the power of the intellectual community to give or to withhold.

That it was increasingly withheld during the years 1964–70 can hardly be gainsaid. Mr Wilson liked to imagine that the cause was unfair Press and television coverage, much of which he attributed to Tory ownership of so many newspapers, commercial control of independent television and general bloody-mindedness in the B.B.C. This explanation greatly underestimates the seriousness of the problem from the point of view of the future of democratic socialism. It suggests that all would be well if there could be a change of ownership in the newspapers, if the capitalist proprietors were replaced by working journalists, or if Tory sympathizers could be routed out of the B.B.C. The truth, however, is that the last Government's most fervent critics were not the Tory newspaper proprietors, or the capitalist television tycoons or the B.B.C. senior administrators; they were the socialist working journalists and producers who write the stories and put out the programmes. The mass media were not critical of the Labour Government because of lack of sympathy in high places, but because of lack of sympathy in relatively low ones, because those who work in the media are members of an alienated intellectual community. Whereas a generation ago it was rare for a newspaper reporter to have a degree, today it is more the norm than the exception, with the result that the world is presented through jaundiced intellectual eyes—eyes which are far less understanding of the inherent difficulties of democratic government, far more cavalierly irrevent and iconoclastic, far more moralizingly censorious, far more ideologically committed. The media are more and more dominated by raw intellectuals: that is to say, men and women who have been made by their university education —which in many cases is woefully bad—more than by anything else. They are not products of working-class, bourgeois or aristocratic culture. They are products of the university.

That such people should be responsible for the way in which national and international affairs are presented to the public, and for the way in which institutions are described, means in effect—at any rate for the foreseeable future—that the climate in which Governments operate will be acutely unsympathetic, that cynicism and scepticism about government will be kept at a high pitch. And the irony is that all the socialist ideas for reforming the Press, for making it less biased in favour of Toryism, would only make this condition more extreme. Criticism of the Labour Government would almost certainly have been more virulent if the Press was not Tory-owned, if it was owned by the journalists themselves under the kind of syndicalist arrangements favoured by the Left, since most professional journalists today, being raw intellectuals, are far less tolerant of government, of all government, than are newspaper proprietors. Take, for example, the Labour Government support for the Americans in Vietnam, or their decision to make cuts in the social services, or limit entry of Kenyan Asians or a whole host of other so-called 'unprincipled' measures which were imposed on Mr Wilson by the responsibilities of office—measures of a kind which, if one is realistic, will be as much, if not more, part of any future Labour Government as they were of Mr Wilson's. A non-Tory Press, operated and controlled by journalists, would have been far less sympathetic to all these policies than the Tory Press actually was. Mr Wilson, or any future democratic socialist leader, should not hoodwink himself on this point. Unless they are prepared to consider Government-operated and controlled newspapers and T.V.—which they are too democratically respectable to want to do—they are probably better off with Tory proprietors than under any alternative arrangement, since at least Tory proprietors, however anti-socialist they may be, are basically pro-authority, basically pro-government, basically on the side of the established institutions—through which democratic socialist Governments have to work as much as Tory Governments do—whereas most journalists, however pro-socialist they may be, are constitutionally disposed to oppose and criticize.

The B.B.C., after all, is not Tory-owned. But precisely because of this it reflects the new spirit of irreverence and iconoclasm, and the liberal–progressive ideology, more completely than the Press or commercial television. In many ways the B.B.C.-producer type embodies all that socialism would wish a man to be. It is inconceivable that any B.B.C. producer would ever disapprove of any popular revolution anywhere in the world—whatever the express or implicit principles of this revolution. It is inconceivable that a B.B.C. producer would ever approve of the British Government's suppressing, or helping to frustrate, any popular revolution by poor people— whatever the nature or consequences of this revolution. The B.B.C. producer finds the idea of a gradual evolution of traditional societies thoroughly uninteresting; has an instinctive detestation of all traditional societies as being inherently unjust and an equally instinctive approval, as being inherently righteous, of any revolutionary ideology which claims to incorporate the people's will. It would be totally alien to a B.B.C. producer's mentality to recognize that support of revolutionary intentions is inconsistent with a prudent and responsible British foreign policy, because Britain, as a rich country in a poor world, is likely to suffer rather than gain from revolution. (To hear this point made nowadays one has to go to the Soviet Union, where intellectuals are not allowed to dabble in foreign affairs.) Tell a B.B.C. producer that he is a disturber of the intellectual peace, and he is gratified. Tell him he is a reassuring spokesman for calm and tranquillity, and he will think you have made a nasty accusation. The B.B.C. producer, if you like, is the *New Statesman* incarnate, the raw intellectual personified, about as unhelpful to government in the real world as it is possible to be.

It is perfectly true, of course, that once upon a time, in the old Reithian days, the B.B.C. was a prop of authority, an organ of the conservative establishment. But that was within the context of class structure wherein intellectuals were kept in their place—a situation which socialism was determined to upset and has very largely succeeded in upsetting. In the kind of classless society which socialism has done so much to create, intellectuals are no longer processed by the social system into public-school types—either the genuine article or copies of it—as used to be the case for all but an incorrigible minority—but are increasingly the 'raw' variety, with their natural bias against authority exerting itself untempered by loyalty to a ruling class.

In other words, it has to be assumed that the communications media will grow less and less sympathetic to the problems of authority—that is to say, to the problems of government—the more socialist society becomes, since the more egalitarian the society the more dominant is the role of the raw intellectual. Paradoxical as it may sound, future Labour Governments may come to look upon Tory-owned newspapers as an oasis of 'responsibility', compared to the B.B.C.—the one part of the communications media least under the influence of bloody-minded intellectuals.

The point that has to be grasped is that it is totally unrealistic to assume that some future Labour Government will find the media more responsive and understanding. The opposite is much more probable, since the media are likely to get more censorious and critical the less they are controlled by people with a vested interest in supporting authority, the more, that is, they correspond to the socialist ideal of being run by those who work in them. No doubt in some utopian democratic socialist State, where the Government always lived up to its socialist principles, this would not be the case. But in the real world this will prove to be the case. Democratic socialist Governments will operate against a background of a public opinion that is increasingly stirred up against them; that is increasingly influenced by the anti-authority bias of the intellectual community.

To some extent, of course, a free Press is always the enemy of the Government. This is part of its job. And if it is to be in a position to stop a Government doing evil it also has to be in a position to stop it doing good. But the position today is more complicated than that. In so far—and it is now very far indeed—as the media is overwhelmingly operated by intellectuals it is likely to be much more obstructive of government than ever before. The situation is really rather ironic. One of the results of socialism is to create a society in which democratic government becomes more difficult—a society which at once immensely elevates the function of government and magnifies the critical element which has no understanding of the problems of government; that more and more relies on government but at the same time guarantees that government should be denied the support it needs.

For if what I am saying is right one inescapable conclusion flows from it: that the climate of society today is such as to preclude ambitious government. Nobody would deny that the power of the intellectual class has been vastly augmented; nor that its beliefs are profoundly hostile to the responsible exercise of power. The power of the intellectual class has grown as the power of the political class has declined. Never in British history have there been so many people in positions of influence who have not the slightest understanding of what power is about and so few who have been brought up in a background where the exercise of power is a customary and habitual activity. This, then, is the paradox of democratic socialism. It depends vitally on the credibility of government, on the moral legitimacy of government; yet promotes the very social element most likely to undermine this credibility, this moral legitimacy, and demotes all those social elements likely to build them up.

The point I am trying to make—and have been trying to make throughout this book—is that the social aims of socialism, which can be seen in the expansion of the intellectual community at the expense of the political class, are at war with its political aims, which depend on a strong political class. Socialism has a conception of the role of government which can only be realized in a social system that exalts authority; that inculcates habits of command in those who wield power and habits of deference in those who do not; that generates a ready supply of leaders with a fine political sense; that protects and cherishes its institutions, surrounding them with such awe and majesty as to elicit maximum popular respect. Only in such a context can ambitious central planning hope to survive the inevitably fissiparious tendencies of a free society. Yet, as we have seen, society today, largely thanks to the social trends of socialism, fulfils these conditions to an ever-declining extent. Politically speaking, socialism requires an ideally smooth and well-oiled governmental machine. Yet socially speaking, it makes sure that as much sand and as many spanners as possible are thrown into it. This is why socialist Governments, by promoting a system of political and economic organization that extends the frontiers of governmental intervention, succeed only in enlarging the frontiers of their own frustration.

Tory Governments, of course, are also frustrated by the hostility of the intellectual community, manifested in critical mass media, although, less being expected of it, the disillusion is less bitter. Also, because Tory Governments seek to do less than Labour ones, they expose much less backside to be kicked. Because they preach less there is less of a gap between their precepts and their practice. But in any case the moral standing of a Government seeking to operate a capitalist system is much less important than the moral standing of a Government seeking to operate a socialist system, because the forces that keep the capitalist wheels running are economic rather than political, draw their strength from the market rather than from the institutions of the State. But the success of a socialist system depends crucially on the authority of

Government and on the respect in which the institutions of the State are held. In a socialist system a slump in the standing of the Government is the equivalent of what a slump in the market is in a capitalist system. Just as the decline in the value of financial stocks and shares depresses the dynamism of a capitalist economy, so does a decline in the value of a Government's public-opinion stock depress the dynamism of a socialist economy. Intellectuals, however, are the arbiters of a Government's standing, the stockbrokers, so to speak, in the market of public opinion, and if they lose confidence in a socialist Government, the effect is to paralyse the system in all its parts.

Yet the central fact about the contemporary situation—and this is as true in America as here—is that the intellectual community *has* lost faith in government; not so much in any particular Government as in the whole idea of government. The significance of this development cannot be exaggerated, since faith in government lies at the root, constitutes the very foundation, of the case for socialism. The central plank of left-wing ideology is the belief that by turning tasks over to government, conflict and decision would be made to go away. As Peter Drucker puts it—referring to socialist intellectual attitudes in the 1930s—in his remarkable *The Age of Discontinuity*:

> Once the 'wicked private interests' had been eliminated, the right course of action would emerge from the 'facts', and decision would be rational and automatic. There would be neither selfishness nor political passion. Belief in Government was thus largely a romantic escape from politics and responsibility.... The argument was simply: 'private business and profits are bad—ergo government ownership must be good'.... But the conflicts, the decisions, the problems would be eliminated by turning things over to Government. Government, on the contrary, has itself become one of the wicked 'vested interests' for the young. And few even of the older generation expect any more that the political millennium will result from Government control.... In fact most of us today realize that to turn an area over to government creates conflict, creates vested and selfish interests,

and complicates decisions. *We realize that to turn something over to government makes it political instead of abolishing politics* [my italics].*

What we have to realize is that socialism was conceived of as a system that would put an end to the unpleasant side of politics, the unpleasant side being attributed to capitalism's reliance on the base motive of private gain. Under socialism it would be possible to organize society according to the humanitarian patterns of social justice. Politics, in short, which is essentially the art of reconciling conflict, would no longer be necessary, since conflict would have been eliminated. The need for a *political* class, by the same token, would disappear. In a socialist society, the intellectual community, who are the natural *moral* guides, would govern in the light of principle. Socialism, in short, was envisaged as a non-political system, one suitable for ideological administration, heaven-made for the intellectual community to take over.

The agony of the Left today is rooted in the realization that socialism, in fact, means a society that is more political rather than less, peculiarly *un*suitable rather than peculiarly suitable for government by the intellectual community—a society that, far from being able to dispense with a political class, needs one more urgently than ever before. Socialists thought they were creating a society which would be easier to govern along moral lines, because the sources of political conflict would have been eliminated; and find that they have created one which is infinitely more difficult to govern, since the sources of political conflict have been immensely enlarged. They thought they were creating a society where the intellectual approach to government would be ideal; and are realizing now that they have created a society where the intellectual approach to government is calamitous. They thought they were creating a society where, because power would be dissolved, its exercise would present no problems and require no skilled practitioners, no ruling class. They have succeeded in creating a society where, because power is concentrated, a ruling class is absolutely vital.

Two conclusions flow from this: either the Left lowers its

---

* Peter F. Drucker, *The Age of Discontinuity* (Heinemann, 1969), p. 215.

sights as to the role of government—that is, abandons the ambitious aims of socialist organization, reconciling itself to trying to plan less—or it accepts the need to build up a political class skilled in the arts of politics, a task which cannot be done without abandoning the ideal of egalitarianism. The choice is between more socialism and less egalitarianism or more egalitarianism and less socialism. For if the role of government is to be expanded, then society must be geared to the production of rulers, and if rulers are not to be produced, then the role of government must be minimized.

Joseph Schumpeter saw this very clearly thirty years ago when he pointed out that Britain at *that* period was ideally suited to the practice of democratic socialism precisely because it boasted a political class, rooted in a privileged social stratum:

> There may be many ways in which politicians of sufficiently good quality can be secured. Thus far, however, experience seems to suggest that the only effective guarantee is in the existence of a social stratum, itself a product of a severely selective process, that takes to politics as a matter of course. If such a stratum be neither too exclusive nor too easily accessible for the outsider and if it be strong enough to assimilate most of the elements it currently absorbs, it will not only present for the political career products of stocks that have successfully passed in other fields—served, as it were, an apprenticeship in private affairs—but it will also increase their fitness by endowing them with traditions that embody experience, with a professional code and with a common fund of views. It is hardly mere coincidence that England, which is the only country to fulfil our conditions completely, is also the only country to have a political society in this sense.*

Note this last sentence: England is 'the only country to fulfil our conditions completely ... the only country to have a political society in this sense', in the sense, that is, of having this essential social stratum. But the point today is that this essential social stratum is under attack, under attack from the very democratic socialists who need it so badly. This essen-

* *Capitalism, Socialism and Democracy*, p. 291.

tial social stratum has increasingly been replaced by an intellectual stratum, whose characteristics, as I have sought to show, are the very opposite of those required to produce a political class.

It follows that the Labour Party must ask itself some very profound questions. Is it prepared so to order society as to preserve this social stratum instead of destroying it? Is it prepared to promote a social system which will transform the new intellectual élite into a social class? Is it prepared to provide the soil of privilege into which the new men will dig such roots that they will cease to be like reeds swaying this way and that in the winds of protest, and become instead, as other ruling classes before them, the buttress of the State? In a word, is it prepared to renounce egalitarianism?

The fact has to be faced that hierarchy based on brainpower alone, or brainpower predominantly, which is what egalitarianism means, produces a governing order that is totally unsuited to work contentedly within the confines of a democratic system, since the intellectuals who rise to the top constitute an element of permanent disruption, spreading alarm and despondency instead of calm and reassurance. So long as they remain primarily intellectuals, shaped predominantly by the experience of higher education, indoctrinated in loyalty to an ideology rather than to a class, they will yearn for an ideal society which cannot be realized in freedom. In other words, they will constitute a social stratum ideally suited to produce a non-political class, if not an anti-political class.

That brainpower *is* the relevant form of power in the contemporary technological society cannot be denied, any more than it could be denied that property was the relevant source of power in the capitalist society. But the *political* success of the capitalist system in this country—in such marked contrast with its failure in France and Germany—was precisely due to its willingness to maintain a social system that produced leaders of men, in addition to makers of money. There is no reason—except doctrinaire Left-wing prejudice—why enough of the old social system should not be left intact to fulfil the same political function for the technological society as it did for the capitalist.

In many ways capitalism, which gave power to the business-man, presented as acute a political problem for democracy as does the advent of technocracy, which gives power to the intellectual. The businessman, like the intellectual, tends to be a non-political animal, since the counting-house does as little as the university to inculcate the arts required for political leadership. The bourgeois, again like the intellectual, is essentially rationalist and unheroic and, being so, can only use rationalist and unheroic means to bend a nation to his will. There is no trace of any mystic glamour about the merchant or the industrialist which is what counts in ruling men, and counts all the more in a democracy where magnetism has to take the place of power. 'The stock ex-change,' as Schumpeter put it so well, 'is a poor substitute for the Holy Grail.'* But then so are the senior common room and, even more, the junior common room. But the point is that the bourgeoisie accepted the political leadership of the old ruling class, and the social system on which it rested, merged their fortunes with it, used it, with results that played a significant part in helping Britain to escape the ravages of revolution.

What I am suggesting is that the success of democratic socialism depends on the new élite based on brainpower being subjected to the same process of assimilation and transmogrification. But this cannot happen if the social stratum needed to do the job is regarded, as it is by the Labour Party, as the enemy to be taxed out of existence and relegated to the dustheap of history; if its educational base, the public-school system, is undermined; if its security is threatened and way of life rendered morally and materially impossible. In one sense, as I have noted earlier, the Labour Party had already had second thoughts about the value of this social stratum, moderating its destructive egalitarian fervour to the extent of recognizing the *economic* value of the old bourgeois stock, which is being allowed—indeed encouraged —to carry on managing the socialized sector of the economy. To this end the last Labour Government made immense ideological concessions by allowing a scale of monetary re-wards which would have deeply shocked its founding fathers.

* *Capitalism, Socialism and Democracy*, p. 137.

They even went so far as to recognize, in the appointment of the 3rd Lord Melchett as chairman of the nationalized Steel Corporation, the value of the hereditary principle—for economic purposes. No ideological scruples about the sufficiency of altruism and duty are going to be allowed to stand in the way of exploiting bourgeois aptitudes and traditions for the purpose of supplying socialist economic leadership. Why then should not aristocratic aptitudes and traditions be exploited for the purpose of supplying political leadership? If socialist principles can be compromised so as to harness the bourgeois stock to the socialist cause, does not the real world demand comparable concessions in the political field with a view to harnessing the talents of the most successful political class in modern history? If it is desirable to put third-generation business tycoons to work in the socialist vineyard, and all right to accept the social values of the capitalist class for purposes of economic management, is it not desirable to put hereditary members of the political class to work in the socialist vineyard and all right to accept *their* social values for purposes of political management?

Until this question is affirmatively answered I do not see how the Labour Party can hope to govern effectively. Just as the classical socialist prescription for an efficient economic society overlooked certain basic truths about human nature—truths which the Labour Party is now belatedly coming to recognize—so does it overlook certain basic truths about human nature in politics. A successful political society is a very subtle, delicate plant, the social roots of which require special nurturing. A successful democratic political society is a particularly subtle and delicate plant, the social roots of which require nurturing of a most particular kind, and a successful democratic socialist political society is the most delicate, subtle plant of all. I do not see how it can grow in an egalitarian society which has the effect of guaranteeing the worst kind of gardeners—an intellectual community whose dispositions guarantee that they are more concerned to nurture the weeds of dissent than the flower of loyalty; how it can grow in a climate so dismally uncongenial to the art of politics. My contention is that leadership does not grow out of a social topsoil that is being permanently dug up and turned over; that is denied the fertilizing enrichment of tradition and continuity, that is denied the shelter from the winds of change which only property and privilege can properly supply. Britain still has the remnants of a social stratum capable of absorbing the new intellectual élite, and welding it into an effective instrument of government. None of the other great democracies is so fortunate. But if it is to be preserved, and put to the purposes of socialism, the Labour Party has to recognize certain truths: that there is a social value to wealth, over and above its use as an economic incentive, in that its possession from generation to generation inculcates a class with a vested interest in serving the State; that there is a social value to inherited rank in that it inculcates the habit of authority, thereby minimizing the need for reliance on naked power; and that without the support of rank and wealth no élite, least of all one based on brainpower alone, will enjoy enough political skill or social authority to dare to rise to the challenge of socialism. Up to now, democratic socialism has only worked successfully anywhere for very brief periods and in exceptionally favourable circumstances. It worked for a few years under Attlee, when war engendered unity and discipline smoothed the way; it works in Scandinavia—an area uniquely blessed by a highly educated working class, which, moreover, is spared the necessity of operating in the field of international politics. But normally its inherent contradictions produce either breakdown followed by dictatorship, as happened in France in both 1848 and 1958 (Louis-Napoleon and de Gaulle) and in Italy and Germany after the First World War, or a retreat into the Conservative embrace, as was the fate of British Labour Governments in the 1920s. These were not just accidents; still less can they be attributed to personal failure by individual democratic socialist leaders. However purposeful a democratic socialist administration may be, and however able its leaders are, the inherently contradictory aims of democracy and socialism, of freedom and planning, produce an eventual stagnation of will. Respect for liberty quite simply blunts the cutting edge of socialist administration.

The Labour Party is naturally reluctant to recognize this; for years it preferred, for example, to blame Ramsay Mac-

Donald personally for the failure of the first Labour Government. In any case, the apologists then argued, it never enjoyed a working majority. Given an absolute majority and a courageous leader, it was said, the story of the next Labour Government would be very different. This was always a profoundly optimistic view, as Elie Halévy,* the distinguished French historian, warned at the time, a warning which today has a devastatingly prophetic ring. Writing in 1934 about the first Labour Government's failure to cure unemployment, he observed:

> Of course I know they had their excuse: they could do nothing because they had not a clear majority, but were they at bottom not glad not to have it, because they were afraid of the responsibilities of power? I tell you frankly that I shudder at the thought of the Labour Party ever having a real majority, not for the sake of capitalism, but for the sake of socialism.*

The events of the last few years have shown how right he was to shudder. What the optimists overlooked is the central problem facing any democratic Labour Government, however large its majority may be—the profound conservatism of the British working class. To the Left, socialism means the replacement of the authority of the ruling class by the power of the State. But most workers are much more suspicious of the power of the State than they are hostile to the authority of the ruling class. They are primarily interested in shorter working hours and higher pay. Nor are they inspired by the prospect of exchanging the existing ruling class, which largely shares their prejudices, for an intellectual élite which passionately opposes them. The Labour Party is an essentially timid political force so far as the implementation of socialism is concerned, precisely because, relying on the working class, it relies on the very segment of society that, for deep historical reasons, is least sympathetic to the exercise of State power. The more Labour M.P.s there are in Parliament, therefore, the less likely are we to see bold and courageous advance towards socialism. Listen again to Elie Halévy: *

* Elie Halévy, *The Era of Tyrannies* (Allen Lane, 1967), p. 196.

Suppose that in 1905, instead of a small Labour Party exerting only some sort of moral pressure upon the old parties, you had had a large Labour Party in the House of Commons, are you sure you would have had the budget of 1909 and the National Insurance Act of 1911? Suppose that in the United States there was a Labour Party worth speaking of, do you think you would have had, for good or evil, the Roosevelt experiment? I doubt it.*

A democratic socialist Government tends inevitably to be too cautious, too distrustful of the State, insufficiently confident in itself, too bereft of the habit of authority, to dare to put socialism into operation.

It is no accident that it was an authoritarian aristocrat, Bismarck, who in 1905 gave Germany its great socialist insurance acts; Roosevelt, the authoritarian American aristocrat, who gave America its radical New Deal; and Sir Oswald Mosley, the authoritarian British aristocrat, then a Labour Minister, who was prepared to solve unemployment in the 1930s along genuinely socialist lines. The paradox is that socialism is a creed suitable either for revolutionaries, like Lenin, with a confidence born of fanaticism, or for aristocratic innovators with a confidence born of being members of a ruling class.

So we come back to my central point: democratic socialism's need for a social stratum sufficiently secure to act as a firm base for a socialist political order. In a communist State this presents no problem, since the Party constitutes the firmest of all political orders. But we are considering the problems of democratic socialism operating within the context of a mixed economy. Clearly, in practice, as the last six years of Labour Government made unmistakably clear, the working class can no longer be relied on as the base for such an order. That was a utopian dream that is no longer taken seriously outside the pages of *Tribune*—a dream that would depend for its realization on the Labour Party's being committed to a kind of socialism aimed at actually getting working-class hands directly on the levers of power. But in fact, as the Wilson administration showed so clearly, democratic socialism

---

* *The Era of Tyrannies*, p. 192.

today does not mean government *by* the workers but government *for* the workers. Labour Governments conceive their role as making sure that the great transformations required to modernize British society are carried out as humanely as possible, so that the resulting increase in wealth is used in the interests of social justice. This is a laudable aim, but it will do nothing to refashion Britain in the working-class image. Indeed, as the new generation of trade-union leaders, like Mr Jones and Mr Scanlon, are coming to realize, it may well alter the balance to the detriment of working-class power. For the central fact that emerged from those six years was that the changes desired by the Labour Government, however much they might promote the cause of social justice, would certainly not strengthen the workers as a political class. Indeed, the more the Labour Party became the instrument of radical structural reform, advocating the application of enlightened reason to the organization of society, the less can it expect to command working-class loyalty. This is the dilemma that those six years made so clear: that change is the enemy of the working class.

The fact has to be faced that in the kind of flux created by technological change, the working class will find itself increasingly lost and broken up. This does not mean that the workers will necessarily suffer in terms of individual social welfare. They may well benefit. But what the trade-union movement is faced by is a new kind of middle-class Labour Party that may have bags of heart and soul but is bent on creating a society in which the strong left arm of the working class itself is rendered weak and crippled. Change, which until recently was accepted as almost synonymous with change for the better so far as the workers are concerned, is now a much less reassuring concept. All right, it may mean more jobs, higher wages, better conditions. But it also means uprooting old communities, disrupting old loyalties, introducing new patterns of work and living—in short, a period of unparallelled disorientation, and the harsh truth is that working-class people, being less educated than the middle class, are at a severe disadvantage at such periods, less able to adapt, more frightened, more vulnerable. I cannot see how any trade-union leader concerned with working-class power can be expected to welcome change at the present juncture. Whatever else it may bring in its train, however much material welfare may ensure for individual workers, the cohesion of the workers as a class is bound to suffer. The modern Labour Party stands for more economic growth through technological change and more 'civilization' through permissive legislation. It is difficult to conceive of two parallel processes more certain to create a society in which the educated middle class will be at an advantage over the educated working class. This does not mean, as I say, that the working class will be exploited. The Labour Party can be relied upon to look after their interests. But it will be a form of middle-class paternalism, of managerial *noblesse oblige* and the very opposite of working-class power. The Labour Party has a vision of a transformed Britain, a modern, humane society operated within a context of social justice. This means mobility of labour, a willingness on the part of the workers to be for ever learning new skills, moving from one part of the country to another. Individually, of course, they will stand to benefit from the resulting economic growth. But what will be the effect on the working class as a cohesive movement, on the great trade unions? Will they be able to remain in control in circumstances of permanent change? Will not this strange, restless, incomprehensible society further weight the balance of social power in favour of the middle class, precisely because they will be better able to adapt to its new mores and requirements? The combination of socialist bureaucracy and capitalist big business may operate a system based on social justice. But the resulting society will be built in the image of the middle class, not of the working class, a matter of socialist *measures*, perhaps, but certainly not of socialist men.

The Labour Party has come to terms with this vision of socialism—government, as I say, for the workers but not by them. This, its leaders have concluded, almost certainly rightly, is the only way of turning Labour into a party of government rather than of opposition. But the great Left-wing trade-union leaders, who are now the new conservatives, have not come to terms with it and propose to fight, fight and fight again. Whatever else, therefore, democratic socialism may hope to rely on in the years ahead, it will not be the organized working class. Working-class votes may get Labour back into power, but the trade-union movement will never be the base for a socialist political order.

But the managerial class presents a picture of almost comparable disintegration. Indeed, nothing is more obvious today than the insecurity of the managerial class. This is partly because of the breakdown of 'family capitalism', and the transformation to corporate capitalism, as a result of technological factors which have little to do with political preference. The same process of economic transformation is at work in all the Western countries, irrespective of their political coloration. Indeed, it is more marked in the United States than anywhere else. As Daniel Bell put it in his essay on 'The Prospects of American Capitalism':

> The new class of managers, recruited from the rag bag of middle-class life, lacks the assured sense of justification which the older class system provided.... The corporation may have an assured continuity; its administrators have not. They have no property stake in the system; nor can they pass their power on to their heirs.*

If this is true of American society, as a result of neutral technological factors, how much more true is it of British society, where the Labour Party insists on deepening, even institutionalizing this insecurity by transforming it from an economic consequence of neutral forces into a specific object of fiscal and social policy. But this insecurity of the managerial class, which socialists used to welcome as the death-watch beetle eating away the social base of the capitalist system, is equally corrosive of the social base of democratic socialism, since the Labour Party has no plans now for creating a more satisfactory social base.

What has to be recognized in the present situation is that there is no secure social stratum for a democratic socialist political class to grow out of. If Labour's plans for economic rationalization and progressive civilization offer little security, either material or psychological, to the working class, its plans

---

* Daniel Bell, 'The Prospects of American Capitalism' in *The End of Ideology* (Collier-Macmillan, 1960).

for social egalitarianism offer even less of either to the managerial class. Add to this general condition of malaise the disruptive contribution of the growingly influential intellectual community and we get a society about as unsuitable for the implementation of democratic socialism as it is possible to conceive.

Let us be quite clear about this. Democratic socialism requires a *political* economy; that is to say, depends on the existence of a political order capable of articulating, in Keynes's phrase, 'a common will embodied in the policy of the State'. It assumes a political order capable of bringing about an organized consensus (the social interest) to replace 'pure economics' or the 'natural laws' of distribution, as determined through the market by the sum total of individual decisions. But how is this consensus to be reached, and its decisions applied? Here, it seems to me, we come to the crux of the contemporary democratic socialist problem. The left-wing answer is clear enough. It is through such a moral transformation of society as to solve the problem of consensus by removing all causes of conflict. But this is a utopian escape from politics, and is certainly not the view of the modern Labour Party, whose views are taken more from Keynes than Marx. How, then, does the modern Labour Party answer the problem of consensus? The key to the answer can be found in Keynes, who simply ignored it. As Daniel Bell puts it:

> Writing in the full stream of English political thought, with its sense of homogeneity and the 'image of a common will embodied in the policy of the State', he felt such problems could be solved simply and rationally. His programme, 'moderately conservative in its implications', excluded any question of the ownership of the instruments of production; all that it required, Keynes wrote blandly, was a 'somewhat comprehensive socialization of investment' in order to assure full employment.*

But we have to ask ourselves the further question: why did Keynes ignore the key political question? The answer seems to be absolutely central to the inadequacy of democratic

* *The End of Ideology*, p. 71.

socialism today. He overlooked the problem of consensus because a consensus seemed to him part of the natural order of things; something that he took for granted. But the consensus, which Keynes took for granted, was not part of the natural order of things. It was an extraordinary, infinitely remarkable, social artefact forged by the British class system. It grew out of a social system that bred a supremely authoritative governing class and a uniquely deferential governed class; from a social system that enabled those on top to gain voluntary acquiescence for *their* interpretation of the social interest. The irony is that the modern Labour Party have accepted Keynes's economic theories, without realizing that they took for granted a social system which democratic socialism is determined to destroy. Keynes's enchanting variety of socialism operated on a snaffle, on a rein as light as gossamer, made sense in a society where the rider was a superbly authoritative equestrian and the steed an exceptionally docile beast, made sense, that is within the context of the traditional class system, but makes no sense at all once the rider has been unhorsed by punitive taxation and the steed fed on the oats of egalitarianism; once, that is, the class system has been destroyed.

Modern democratic socialism, in short, assumes the existence of the very political condition—a secure governing class capable of articulating the common will—which its disruptive social policies guarantee does not exist; assumes a consensus which is only likely to emerge from a settled society, while doing everything in its power to maximize fluidity; assumes a consensus requiring immense political skill to bring about, while promoting a social system that precludes the emergence of a political class; assumes a consensus that used to exist, while elevating the very section of society—the intellectual community—most certain to make sure that no consensus can ever be obtained again. Consensus is absolutely central to democratic socialism. Yet the Labour Party is fatally loth to recognize the implication of this necessity. It rejects the arbitrary consensus brought about by political authoritarianism. This, of course, is greatly to its credit. But it also rejects the contribution which social authority can make, indeed has to make, if political authoritarianism is to be avoided. A hierarchy based on brain-power, which is the only social system it is prepared to tolerate, is essentially unauthoritative. It produces an intellectual meritocracy cut off from the people and out of sympathy with them; a meritocracy whose social values will be inherently antagonistic to popular prejudices; a meritocracy unversed in the arts of political leadership, contemptuous of the democratic process; a meritocracy at once provocatively superior but at the same time denied the social trappings that make such superiority acceptable; a meritocracy without the internal cohesion or the external glamour of a social class; a meritocracy instinctively disruptive rather than unifying, a meritocracy, in short, tragically unsuited to shoulder the unprecedented burdens which socialism seeks to put upon its sloping shoulders.

I do not quarrel with the Labour Party's belief in the economic necessity of socialism; in the necessity for the State to assume an ever greater responsibility for the economic ordering of society. But precisely because of this, precisely because the levers of State power are going to have to be enlarged, it is going to be more important rather than less that those whose hands are on the levers should be the right kind of people. This is why it is so vital to have a social stratum out of which can grow a socialist political class— one with enough security of tenure to have developed the habit of authority, one in which brainpower is so diluted and humanized by association with wealth and rank as to have learnt the art of inspiring popular confidence; one with so distinctive and magnetic a way of life as to counteract the disruptive effects of higher education. It is because none of this is dreamt of in the Labour Party's philosophy that it presents today such a picture of arid irrelevance. Nothing is more important today than to consider how to restore the authority of the State, how to evolve a governing class whose loyalty to the national institutions is so exemplary as to rally the people behind it; how to create a way of life at the top of society which give at once fulfilment to those able to get there and inspiration to those less fortunate. By comparison with these pressing needs, the problem of poverty and social justice are the merest bagatelles. It is not the base of contemporary society that needs fortifying; it is the apex. The crisis is one not of underprivilege at the bottom but of underprivilege at the top. It is the few, not the many, who are in need of care and attention; the pediment that needs repair, not the plinth.

Such a diagnosis is anathema to democratic socialists. They would rather die than face the truth. But the truth must be faced, if democratic socialism is ever to make progress. So long as democratic socialism seeks to build the New Jerusalem on the basis of equality, it will undermine its own foundations with each new stone it lays.

8

So far I have been considering the dilemma of the Labour Party, which I have diagnosed as follows: that its ideological commitment to central planning requires an authoritative governing order which its ideological commitment to equality prevents it from creating. I have sought to show that the need for socialist leadership becomes more urgent as the likelihood of socialist partnership becomes more remote. What I should like to do now is to consider the problem of leadership in the widest sense, in the belief that the deeper we probe into it the clearer it will become that Labour's ideas are fundamentally inadequate, tragically out of touch with contemporary reality.

In one sense democracy today is at its zenith in the Western world. Every adult has the vote, in Britain even the eighteen-year-olds. But the irony is that there is nobody anybody particularly wants to vote for. Democracy has gone to great lengths to enable everybody to choose their own leaders. But at the very moment when this great ideal is realized, it is found that there are no leaders left whom anybody wants to choose.

This is the problem which I would like to consider now. Democracy has certainly done a fine job in enfranchising the people, in depriving the privileged few of a hereditary right to rule, in transferring political power from the minority to the majority. But what does it profit the many, the majority, if, just when they have won the right to choose by whom they are governed, the very democratic processes which have won them this right have also guaranteed that the candidates for power are so unattractive as not to be worth choosing?

Social democracy is a great leveller. It cuts everybody down to size. But the trouble is that it may have done the job too well; so well as to reduce political democracy to a fraud. For if as the result of social levelling the choice of leaders is reduced to a field made up of indistinguishable faceless mediocrities, what kind of choice is that?

There is a genuine problem here. Egalitarianism has much to commend it and democracy is clearly rendered inoperative in a society where great inequalities of wealth and status prevail. Such a system so entrenches the privileged in possession of power that the vote becomes a meaningless fiction. This is such a familiar point that it needs no emphasis. But there is another point that is equally relevant, although almost universally overlooked: that the vote is also reduced to a meaningless fiction if the system is so egalitarian as to preclude the emergence of men and women worth voting for. For about three hundred years all the emphasis of democratic thought has been on building up the led at the expense of the leaders. This was a job that had to be done. But it is possible that it has been done too well, and that we have reached a stage where democracy is endangered by the problem of too little leadership rather than too much.

This is obviously not a problem of too little government, and I am not trying to suggest that democratic governments today have too little power. It could very easily be demonstrated that democratic governments now have more power than ever before. The levers of control at their command are immensely—unprecedentedly—potent and numerous. Judged as a piece of machinery, modern democratic government is far better formed for the purposes of transmitting orders than it was ten, twenty or thirty years ago. What I am referring to is the absence of people skilled at using these levers in an effective manner. There are not too few rulers; there are too few *leaders*, too few men and women whom the public *want* to follow.

This is not a lament for the present lack of 'great men' around. It is perfectly true, of course, that Heath and Wilson are not Winston Churchills, Nixon is no Kennedy, Pompidou no de Gaulle, and so on. But this is not surprising or even worrying. 'Great men' are obviously few and far between, almost by definition, since it is their rarity, their extraordinary magnetism, that makes them so outstanding, head and shoulders above the generality. To rely on the presence of 'great men' as a permanent source of leadership is to rely on the exceptional which is manifestly a silly thing to do.

But the widespread distaste and dissatisfaction with the calibre of contemporary politicians is much more than a regret that they are not charismatic leaders. Charismatic leadership has always been a rarity in any political and social system, depending on historical accident, biological chance; and although some systems may be more conducive to it than others, in none can it be guaranteed, since it is essentially an uncovenanted blessing. But precisely for this reason, precisely because the emergence of 'great men' has to be left largely to chance, leadership, at any rate so far as this country is concerned, has traditionally been put on a more secure basis —the basis of a superior class rather than of a superior individual.

That Heath and Wilson are not 'great men', therefore, is normal enough. What is new about them is that not only are they not superior individually, not themselves endowed with the qualities that command confidence and respect, but they also belong to a class that enjoys these attributes as a group. They are outstanding neither individually—by virtue, that is to say, of their charismatic personalities—nor as members of a class that enjoys corporate glamour. In this respect the modern democratic politician is far worse off than the princely or aristocratic leader of old. Not all princes were great men. But because all were touched by the majesty of monarchy all enjoyed an extra pedestal that enabled them to tower above their fellow men through no intrinsic virtue of their own. So too, with members of a ruling class. Its members did not have to be outstanding to stand out, because they were part of a social order that lent them distinction, however undistinguished they might be themselves. The modern democratic politician, however, has no such extraneous aids. For him to stand out or tower above his fellow men he really has to be outstanding, a towering personality—in short a 'great man', which, in the nature of things, he is unlikely to be, except very rarely.

Of course democracy is prepared to take these risks; indeed insists upon taking them. The point was clearly made in all the furore over Alec Douglas-Home, who was thought to be unsuitable as a democratic leader because he was the 14th Earl, the very reason for which, in an aristocratic society, he would be regarded as specially suitable for leadership. No one doubted that he had certain qualities, born of his breeding and background, that commanded confidence and respect. But because they were felt to be hereditary virtues, the product of aristocratic privilege, they were regarded as unsuitable for contemporary purposes.

The fact that he was a prominent member of the former ruling class was held against him. It was thought to be more in keeping with the democratic spirit of the age to have a commoner, Ted Heath, at the head of the Conservative Party —in spite of his manifest inadequacies as a leader—than an aristocrat, however gifted he might be in this particular accomplishment.

This was a very significant decision by the Conservative Party. Nobody could pretend that Alec Douglas-Home is a great man. But he is a reasonably good exemplar of certain upper-class qualities that still carry weight with at any rate a large section of the public, not an individual leader, but a good class leader. Yet he was rejected in favour of a man who is a great leader neither in individual terms nor in class terms. This is not to argue that the Conservative Party was wrong to depose Home and replace him with Heath. The democratic spirit of the age may have brooked no other decision. But what the decision does show is that the spirit of the age puts up very serious obstacles in the way of choosing leaders, since even the Conservative Party can no longer exploit the obvious advantages of class, can no longer, in a lean personal leadership period, fall back on the built-in advantages of superior birth, even when the result of not doing so is to be saddled with a democratic leader in whom most of them have no confidence at all.

The truth is that now, for the first time in British history, we are relying on the processes of democracy alone to produce the nation's leaders, relying, that is, on the political system rather than the social system to throw up the right people fit to govern. It has taken a long time to reach this point. If one studies the composition of Parliament since the first great Reform Bill of 1832, the most striking conclusion is the extent to which upper-class and upper-middle-class dominance has been preserved, in spite of the enfranchisement of the working class. Social deference has played a formidable role in slowing down the advance of political democracy. It is possible to deplore or applaud this strange phenomenon. But what one cannot sensibly do is ignore its implications for the problem of leadership. It has meant that virtually up to the present time, British political democracy has gone hand in hand with social aristocracy, the latter providing the former with a continuing stream of leaders from which it was content to choose. Leslie Stephen,* writing in 1867 about the Reform Bill of that year, thought this arrangement could go on for ever.

In a healthy and quiet condition of society, where the lower orders are not united by any strong class prejudice against the higher, I believe that ... wealth and rank and social estimation will always produce an effect which no legislation can neutralize ... it is only by the voluntary abdication of the upper classes that the people may be led in time to choose a lower class of leaders; and there are many reasons why such an abdication is highly improbable.

For almost a hundred years after Leslie Stephens wrote these words, 'wealth and rank and social estimation' *did* continue to produce an effect which no legislation could neutralize, and to some extent they still do so today. But it has been a slowly dwindling effect. Where Leslie Stephen went wrong was in underestimating the inevitable long-term effect of political democracy *on* wealth and rank, devaluing the political magnetism of both. Not only have wealth and rank been increasingly dissociated from political power, but they have been increasingly positively associated with political impotence, becoming more a barrier than a springboard to political advance. Indeed, it is no longer sensible to talk about 'wealth and rank and social estimation' as part of the same package, since social estimation, so far as politics is con-

* Essay reprinted in W. L. Guttmann (ed.), *A Plea for Democracy* (Mac-Gibbon & Kee, 1967), p. 86.

164

cerned, tends to prefer to rest upon those without wealth or without rank. (Alec Home has both; Ted Heath, neither.) Of course wealth and rank still exist, some old but much that is new. It is only necessary to study the gossip columns, or the list of Mary Wilson's guests at Downing Street parties, to get the flavour of the new 'crème de la crème'. But the new social aristocracy, the men and women who comprise the gossip-column galaxy, whom the public like to read about, are seldom politicians. They are business tycoons, show-biz personalities, T.V. celebrities, swinging Dukes, famous journalists, artists, writers, even trade-union leaders. (Clive Jenkins and the Duke of Bedford vie for the over-exposure stakes.) But the striking aspect of all this new amalgam of wealth and rank and social estimation is that it no longer has political magnetism; the glamour from it no longer rubs off on or is associated with the political system. Indeed, the strange thing about Mr Harold Wilson's new-style hospitality was that when he wanted to give a party which might catch the popular imagination, the first thing he did was to make sure that as few members as possible of the political establishment were invited. The point I am seeking to make is that there has been a growing divorce between social magnetism and political power; between wealth and rank and social estimation, on the one hand, and Parliament on the other; between the men and women whom the public are interested in and those whom they are governed by. Whereas until recently the social glamour of wealth and rank lent the political system a polish that attracted and held the public eye, the two being indistinguishably intertwined, today they are separate, the political leadership and the social leadership operating in different worlds, scarcely even speaking a common language. When Mr Wilson invited the contemporary social stars to Downing Street it was headline news, an extraordinary event, with the host staring at the guests and the guests staring at the host as if each thought the other animals in the zoo.

This, however, is not an accident. It is part of the democratic intention, implicit in democratic theory. What has to be realized is that democratic theory applies a principle to politics that it does not apply to any other human activity. Democratic theory is based on the proposition that the people are fit to govern themselves, from which it flows that politicians should be as ordinary as possible, since if they are extraordinary this is an implicit denial of the basic democratic proposition. Nobody would seriously maintain the same proposition in relation, say, to business, the theatre, the arts, television, journalism, or any of the other spheres of life to which importance is attached. It is not maintained, for example, that ordinary people can play Hamlet as well as Sir Laurence Olivier or paint pictures like Graham Sutherland or make as much money as Charles Clore. Here the public recognizes and demands extraordinary qualities, outstanding personalities, conspicuous style, and does not for a moment pretend that it can do these things as well itself. It is not envious or suspicious of the implications of the towering superiority of the few in these respects. They do not want to cut the great artist down to size, because no one has told them that everybody can be a great artist. But this is what they have been told about politics: that everyone is equal in politics. I am not trying to suggest that this proposition is wrong. Of course it is an immensely important notion, or fiction, faith in which is crucial to the maintenance of a free society. What I am seeking to suggest, however, is that as a result of the successful propagation of this notion or fiction, a growing gap is emerging between the quality of political life and the quality of life in every other sphere, with the magnetism and glamour tolerated and encouraged everywhere except in politics.

This was bound eventually to create an acute problem of political leadership, since the cumulative effect of democratic pressure has been to create a society where those with outstanding talent tend to climb all the non-political ladders, from the summit of which they sparkle and shine, by contrast with which the political summit seems sadly unattractive. Instead of rank and wealth and social estimation being part of the political hierarchy, leading the exercise of power the magnetism of social superiority, they have become the measure by which the political hierarchy is judged and found wanting. Instead of the social sun shining and warming the political field, it is the one field left in the shadows, with the leading politicians more and more forced to fall back on the ersatz charm of public relations because they are denied the genuine appeal of social distinction. The truth is that democracy, in promoting a system of thought that levels down the inequalities of the human condition primarily in the political race, creates a situation—for the best of motives, of course—where the existence of giants in every other sphere turns politicians into pygmies.

Let me repeat; this is not something untoward. It is the natural result of the cumulative implementation of the democratic theory, at least as understood in the English-speaking democracies. Great men have no part in the Anglo-Saxon idea of democracy. Arthur Schlesinger puts the position well in his book *The Politics of Hope*: *

> The heroic leader has always constituted an anomaly in democratic theory. Since democratic theory arose historically as a protest against theses of the 'divine right' of particular personalities, its early proponents naturally put their major emphasis on the sufficiency of the people (or a majority thereof) as against the need for heroic leadership.
> Most democratic theory derives from Locke: and in Locke's account, the people assert their rightful control over the State through the process essentially of spontaneous combustion. 'The people,' he wrote, 'generally ill-treated and contrary to right, will be ready upon any occasion to ease themselves of a burden that sits heavy upon them. They will wish and seek for the opportunity, which in the change, weakness and accidents of human affairs, seldom delays long to offer itself.' This analysis of the requirements of a revolutionary situation proposes no special role for leadership; it stands in marked contrast to, for example, the writings of Blanqui or to Lenin in *What is to Be Done?* The Lockeian assumption was that the people were endowed with sufficient purpose and intelligence to produce out of themselves, so to speak, the initiative necessary for successful revolution and for effective government thereafter.
> If one defines democracy as a system in which the majority under constitutional procedures freely chooses among competing persons for limited-term control of the State, then

---

* Arthur Schlesinger, *The Politics of Hope* (Eyre & Spottiswoode, 1964), p. 40.

the inescapable drift of democratic theory is against investing too much significance in any particular competitor.

Other inherent factors have reinforced this tendency to minimize the problem of leadership. Thus democratic theory has resisted emphasis on leadership on ideological grounds—because this emphasis has seemed to imply that some men should lead and others should follow, a proposition which clashes with the traditional democratic commitment to equality and majoritarianism. It has resisted this emphasis on emotional grounds—because it irritates the populist strain in democracy which often includes an envy of superior persons.

Most important of all, it has resisted this emphasis on compelling practical grounds—because it has seemed to encourage the erosion of democracy. Since Lockeian theory assumed the omni-competence of majorities, most post-Lockeian attempts to rehabilitate the idea of leadership have begun precisely by asserting the incompetence of majorities. Rousseau, it is true, argued the case for heroic pro-democratic leadership in the instance of the Legislator, who was to constitute the State, and the Dictator, who might be called upon to save it; but these were both emergency functions, and his theory made no provision for leadership as a continuing feature of democratic society. In any event, his limited vindication of leadership seemed only further evidence of the perils of leadership theory since his whole system led so easily towards totalitarian democracy. And most ideologists of leadership have been, like Carlyle and Lenin, polemicists against democracy: they have invoked the supposed ignorance, fecklessness, and instability of the crowd as a chief reason for according special respect to leaders. Historically, the idea of leadership has thus become associated with élitist philosophies; leadership theory has seemed a weapon to be employed by reactionaries or revolutionaries against Lockeian democracy. And history seems fully to have corroborated this supposed association. The Führerprinzip, the cult of personality, the rituals of hero worship, have too often led to the suppression of freedom, the establishment of authoritarianism, and the destruction of democracy.

All these considerations have thus produced the implicit assumption in classical democratic theory that numerical majorities provide a substitute for heroic leadership and that too much speculation about the need for leadership may be subversive of democracy.

So far as the two great Anglo–American democracies are concerned this assumption has, until recently, proved reasonable enough. In neither Britain nor America has the problem of leadership presented itself in an acute form. In Britain's case, as I have already suggested, political democracy has marched forward hand in hand with social aristocracy, the latter acting as a necessary support for the former. John Locke, in adumbrating the theory of democracy for the seventeenth century, could afford to ignore the problem of leadership, since the existing landowning ruling class were more than prepared in practice to plug this theoretical gap. There was no need for him to come to grips with this problem, for the very good reason that there already existed a pre-democratic social system which had solved it before the democratic experiment ever began. Until recently the British democracy has been operated by the hangover of a feudal aristocracy. The problem for British democrats has not been to find leaders, whose existence has been guaranteed by the social system. What it did not guarantee, and what democratic theorists have understandably concentrated on hitherto, is the rights of the led. The rights of the leaders could be left to look after themselves. The great, gaping hole in democratic thought—the absence of any theory of leadership—has never been properly exposed because—so far as Britain goes—it was conveniently covered over by a thick carpet of aristocracy.

Although the American experience has been very different, the effect has been the same. Its democracy has operated under circumstances which have also minimized the problems of political leadership. Exploiting a richly endowed virgin continent with almost limitless frontiers for expansion provided a uniquely advantageous stage on which to try out the theories of democracy. The problem of political leadership was not so much solved as not posed, or posed in such a way as to make the democratic solution appear much more satisfactory than it would have been in less fortunate circumstances. The fact should be recognized that the American democracy has proved adequate largely because the tests to which it has been subjected hitherto were, compared for example to those on the European continent in the nineteenth and twentieth centuries, and to those in the under-developed world today, unusually mild. Even so, from time to time, when the going got difficult, the American democracy *has* had recourse to a style of heroic leadership which classical democratic theory did not really allow for. It is difficult, for example, to see how Teddy Roosevelt or F.D.R., still less John F. Kennedy, fit into the pattern so immortally outlined by John Locke. The American democracy did turn to those efforts, it is true, but not without deep self-questioning. It was fascinated, but also not a little appalled at the necessity to fall back on a kind of aristocratic leadership that had far too much to do with the cult of superior persons for democratic comfort. Although in practice the American democracy is no stranger to strong leadership, the theory itself has never been adapted to incorporate this need. Such has been the American experience that political leadership is still seen as an occasional necessity, a bonus that will turn up on the day, not as something that has to be consciously developed as a permanent part of the political and social system.

Both the great democracies, in short, have been able to escape the necessity of grappling seriously with the problem of leadership, Britain because of its good fortune in inheriting an existing ruling class—which blurred democracy's inadequacies in this respect—and America because, until very recently, its blessings have been such as to spare it most of the ills which only political leadership can contain or cure.

But what of the position now? It seems to me that the classical democratic assumptions about leadership are, for the first time, being put to tests that will really prove or possibly disprove their truth, tests of the same cruel harshness as have afflicted continental Europe ever since the French revolution. In Britain, the present generation of Parliamentary leadership is the first to try to govern without the advantage of social authority, to try to govern, that is, on the basis of political authority alone. Messrs Heath and Wilson, and most of their colleagues, are political leaders and nothing else. Their authority rests purely on the democratic process, on having won their way to the top through political skill. Neither can call to his aid the extra distinction of social or economic pre-eminence, the advantage of being associated with a ruling class that has acquired the habit of authority over many generations. This is nothing new, of course, for Labour leaders, many of whom have come from the working class or lower middle class all along. But the very fact that they came from non-ruling-class background, at a time when ruling-class background was the norm, gave them a certain style, all the more magnetic for being so unusual and challenging. The early Labour leaders had a touch of the exotic about them. They were extraordinary, startling, even frightening. After all, in getting to Westminster at all they had proved themselves to be major political characters, so hard was the climb that they had successfully completed. This is one of the advantages of a class system. It lends authority not only to those who are born at the top but also to those who are born at the bottom and fight their way to the top, since the battle is such as to endow those who succeed with the authority that comes from exceptional achievement. To some extent Mr Wilson still has something of this flavour about him. He manages to retain a little of the working-class-lad-made-good appeal, of the cheeky underdog who has got to the top by use of his exceptional wits. The H.P.-Sauce style of leadership is a style, so long as it is abnormal; so long as it is slightly shocking, a shade revolutionary. If high aristocratic breeding commands one kind of snobbish allegiance in a class system, low plebeian vulgarity—precisely because of the provocative contrast— commands the anti-snobbish allegiance, both styles in their different ways lending their practitioners a certain air of distinction. But without a class system there is neither an aristocratic style nor an anti-aristocratic style; neither the glamour attaching to authority exercised in the customary manner nor the glamour attaching to the exercise of authority in a novel manner. The trouble today is that increasingly both Tory and Labour leaders emerge in a social context that deprives the former of inherited traditional social authority and the latter of the authority that comes from successfully cocking a snook at traditional social authority; deprives political leadership, that is, of the charm of respectability and the charm of its opposite.

What we have to consider, therefore, is the problem of leadership in an increasingly purely political context, with authority resting on political magnetism alone—political magnetism no longer buttressed by the bulwarks of conspicuous social distinction or conspicuous social vulgarity. Theoretically this should not constitute a problem at all, since in theory the democratic process of choosing political leaders should endow them with adequate authority. That they are democratically elected should be a sufficiently legitimizing process. But is it?

Nobody questions that contemporary Parliaments are constitutionally elected or that contemporary governments are legitimate and lawful. All the democratic processes are fulfilled which should make their decisions as authoritative as those of any of their predecessors. Yet the fact remains that when members solemnly determine a great issue of state like, for example, the abolition of capital punishment, the people are much less prepared to accept the verdict of their leaders than they used to be.

Democratically speaking, Messrs Heath and Wilson, and all the rest of the present House of Commons, are our elected leaders, as much as any of their predecessors. But the authority of their predecessors rested on a social as well as a political base, was buttressed by a style of leadership which drew its strength from a pre-democratic social system. Their decisions were listened to with deference not primarily because they were democratically elected, but primarily because they came from a social class which was assumed to be specially well-suited for affairs of state.

But what happens to democracy when the authority of that class has been eroded, as is the case today? Why should a mere handful of men and women indistinguishable from the rest of us, and who do not look or sound in any way out of the ordinary, whose habits are pedestrian and manners commonplace, and whom it is difficult to tell apart so much do all merge into a common pattern of grey mediocrity—why should *they*, who are so eminently ordinary, presume to tell *us* that they are right and we are wrong?

According to democratic theory, of course, because they have been elected through democratic elections. But it is an answer which was acceptable only so long as it was not put to the test; so long, that is, as the social system guaranteed that most of those elected as leaders were already leaders before they were elected.

What we are experiencing today is the problem which democracy runs into when the social system no longer supplies a ready-made choice of leaders, when it is charged with the task not only of choosing leaders who are already there but of creating them as well.

Far too little attention has been given to this problem since, according to democratic theory, it did not exist. The theory assumes that the people are capable of deciding issues for themselves, and that they simply elect a representative assembly as a convenient method of giving effect to their common will. In practice, however, no large and complex society can be or has been governed in this way. If, for example, Britain joins the Common Market, it will not be a democratic decision in this sense at all, any more than was the decision to abolish capital punishment or, indeed, most of the social legislation of the last few years. These are decisions taken by an élite in defiance of the popular will. In reality, democracy means something very different from the myth. The people do not govern themselves, because this is an impossibility. All they decide is by whom they should be governed and, just as important, by whom they should not. The essence of democracy is that the people choose their *leaders*. Of course the leaders have to pay some attention to what the people want, since this is the way to win votes. But paying attention is a means to an end, and the end is the acquisition of power.

Democracy is not a substitute for leadership. It is primarily —as all effective political processes have to be—a method for determining *who* will lead, and only very secondarily a method of determining *how* they should lead. This, of course, is not the way in which the classical democratic theorists have presented their doctrine in the past. One can study the

173

seventeenth-century writings of John Locke, for example, without gaining the impression that democracy is about leadership at all. In the mind of that seminal propounder of Anglo-Saxon democratic thought the people were perfectly self-sufficient. But implicit in this optimistic assumption, as I say, was the existence of a governing class which at that time, and indeed until the present time, enabled democratic political theory to ignore the problem of leadership in the confident knowledge that in practice the social system would fill the gap. Aristocracy, in short, provided the raw material which democracy needed to make it work; that is to say it provided the people with a reliable supply of leaders to choose from. The great question today is whether democracy can work without a social system that fulfils this crucial function. According to the theory this is no problem. But the theory is a very misleading guide since it developed at a time when its inadequacies were never put to the test. But they are being put to the test today, and not only in Britain. The United States experience bears on this point even more significantly than Britain's.

America has long been thought of as a democracy that had flourished without the aid of aristocracy, proving that Britain could do the same when the time came, which it now has. Such optimistic complacency, however, looks rather empty today. Now that the American democracy is beginning to have to operate without the benefits of earlier blessings, which enabled its body politic to live a charmed life, it too is running up against the problem of leadership in a far more acute form than it has ever done in the past. The authority of a democratic government, unsupported by a class system, was more than sufficient to exploit a miraculously fecund continent. But the task of governing the continent once it has been developed, and using the immense national power that has been the consequence of this development, requires an authority of a different and higher order, which is tragically unforthcoming at the present time.

But the reason it is unforthcoming is highly relevant to my present theme. It is because, for the first time in its history —except for the very early years—America is being called upon to face problems which cannot be resolved either through the dynamism of popular leadership—that is to say, through whipping up mass enthusiasm—which is one way of solving problems open to an egalitarian democracy—or by ignoring them—that is to say, sending the people to sleep, which is the only alternative method. The problems are far too serious to be amenable to the traditional Republican quiescent therapy—the tranquillizing style of leadership; yet they are also—and this is the novelty—totally unamenable also to the Democratic method of harnessing public opinion to their solution, since public opinion, if it were to be aroused, would be likely to make matters worse rather than better.

Take the three great tormenting American issues, Vietnam, race and localized poverty. The stark fact has to be faced that on these three problems, none of which can any longer be ignored, the voice of the people is much more like the voice of the Devil than the voice of God, and the more it is listened to the more disastrous are the resulting policies certain to be. On the Negro problem populist leadership would mean more segregation rather than less, since there can be little doubt that releasing popular feelings means giving the green light to racialism. The same kind of considerations apply to Vietnam, just as much. The more the public is brought into the question the more difficult it becomes to pursue flexible policies, and the more necessary it becomes to veer erratically between the two extremes of too much interventionism or too little, between emotional jingoism and emotional isolationism. Solutions in both cases require progress by stealth, by subtle manoeuvring conducted, so to speak, behind the back of public opinion, since the more the public is aroused, the more it is certain to press for words and actions that preclude solutions rather than facilitating them. Nor is this true only of Vietnam and the Negro problem. It is also true of the whole problem of poverty in the U.S. at the present time. The American poor are now an underprivileged *minority*. Their needs arouse little general sympathy. Let us be clear about the implications of this. On the three great issues, Vietnam, race and poverty, harnessing popular emotions is the opposite of constructive statesmanship.

But in an egalitarian democracy populist leadership is the only *active* style of leadership, an aroused public opinion is the only available fuel to power dynamic action. Unless the people are aroused nothing much effective can be done. During normal times, of course, when nothing much needs to be done, this is harmless enough, and for the greater part of American history a quietist style of leadership has sufficed. The politicians have simply got on with the job of doing very little, since inaction has been what the public wanted. But today, for the first time, a new situation is emerging—a situation where the problems are enormous, where the need for dynamic action is very great, but where the only available source of action cannot be tapped without doing more harm than good. In an egalitarian democracy everything is possible when the problems are by their nature such as to be responsive to solutions backed by mass public opinion. But when they are not so amenable, when public opinion has become counterproductive, when what is required is an authoritative exercise of leadership, not in line with but in defiance of public opinion, then an egalitarian ship of state finds itself adrift, able to rely neither on the winds of popular passion to carry it forward—since they cannot be unleashed—nor on navigational brilliance from the bridge, since no political officer class exists to provide it.

Herein lay the tragedy of the Kennedy dynasty. Theirs was a formidable and marvellous attempt at populist leadership, at seeking to harness popular passions to great causes, alike at home and abroad. Recall, for example, the noble rhetoric of the J.F.K. inaugural address: 'Let every nation know, whether it wish us well or ill, that we shall pay any price, bear any burden, meet any hardship, support any friend or oppose any foe in order to assure the survival and success of liberty. This much we pledge, and more.' Similar fine rhetoric was poured out about the Negro problem and about all the other burning social issues. What was the result? So far as foreign policy was concerned, the limited intention of seeking to test the water of Vietnam became caught up in the great swirl of crusading passion which carried the United States far out of its depth. So, too, on the colour question. John F. Kennedy aroused wild expectations among the Negroes which could only be disappointed and cause needless frustration and disillusion among the blacks and dangerous fears among the

176

whites. Of course the Kennedy style of leadership was in the classical populist tradition—with a few sophisticated extra gimmicks thrown in for good measure. But it was bound, in present circumstances, to end in tragedy, being based on a fundamental misunderstanding. It assumed—and this, of course, is the classical American assumption—that the problems facing America today can still be solved by arousing the public, whereas the truth is both at home and abroad that they are now of a type new to the American experience; of a type that can only be solved through a deliberate exercise of authoritative leadership from the top, combined with deliberate damping down of the grass-roots at the bottom, a combination wholly alien to the American tradition.

The trouble, of course, is that the style of leadership required in America today is much more aristocratic than democratic. It is the realization of this that lies at the heart of the current liberal malaise, the realization that populist politics, far from being the ally of radicalism, are today ranged on the other side of the barricades. Two very significant American minorities, the affluent educated white young and the impoverished uneducated black young, have become conscious of a state of affairs in Vietnam and in the Negro ghettoes which, although intolerable to them, is clearly by no means intolerable to the great majority of their fellow citizens. They, numerically a minority, have been shocked to the marrow by things which the majority have been prepared to overlook. A majority of the Americans are not shocked by the Vietnam war, and would have been quite happy if the Generals had been able to win it. Nor is the majority shocked by the Negro grievances, which would be swiftly forgotten if only the Negroes would stop threatening to riot. This has raised an agonizing question which is today the cancer at the heart of the American body politic; if the majority can be so morally blind should they enjoy such overwhelming power? Is there not something morally wrong with a political, and social system that allows so fallible a majority such unlimited sway?

These questions have not been asked since the earliest days of the Republic. Take the 1930s slump, for example—America's last great moral crisis. Then, as now, there was a tremendous soul-searching, but of a fundamentally different kind. The educated minority were appalled *on behalf of* the majority. They were shocked at what seemed like the callousness of the capitalist minority exploiting the proletarian majority. Indignation was directed against the rich for the suffering they were imposing on the poor.

This was a moral problem which American political assumptions could cope with well enough. Call in the power of the people and all would be well. Let the pressure of public opinion be felt and the few would have to start behaving themselves.

Today the liberal-minded are being forced to the opposite conclusion. They are beginning to see the people as the cause of the trouble rather than its cure and to realize that it is the passions and prejudices of the many, much more than anything for which the few can be blamed, that constitute the real difficulty. It is not the plutocracy, or the aristocracy or the power of the élite which is at fault. It is the democracy itself. The liberal-minded today are not shocked on behalf of the majority; they are shocked *by* the majority.

This is what the so-called new politics is all about—an attempt by the few to save America from the many, an attempt by affluent and educated Americans, particularly those in these categories among the young, to increase their influence over national affairs at the expense of the great brute mass of ordinary voters—for the élite, if you like, to gain power over the heads of the people. Nothing was more symptomatic of this new mood among the educated American young than the man they chose in 1968 to be their standard-bearer, who, although now sunk beyond trace, for a few months illuminated the current yearning for a different style of leadership. Eugene McCarthy was the nearest thing to a true—that is to say, British—Conservative to have surfaced in American politics since the days of the founding fathers, and was certainly much nearer that ideal than any of the recent batch of British Tory leaders. That such a man should have been the favourite of the educated student young in, of all places, America, is almost unbelievable.

One aspect of the paradox is that thoughtful Americans, as well as the young, were and are deeply anxious, as I say, for a change of style, for new intimations, for something fresh, original, different; and as far as the United States is concerned, with its deep populist tradition, there could be nothing newer, fresher, more original, more different, indeed more revolutionary than a man who campaigned for the presidency in a manner quite startlingly reminiscent of the Whig aristocracy of eighteenth-century England. It was a totally different manner from the royalist glamour of the Kennedy family, all gold and glitter and high heroism, and totally different from the ponderous populism of Lyndon Johnson, all corn, sentiment and pseudo-moralism; different, too, from the Eisenhower approach of business as usual; different even—and most significantly so—from the Adlai Stevenson type of liberal idealism. It was purposefully non-heroic, non-moralistic, non-charismatic—the politics of civilized reflection rather than of purposeful action, of understated witticisms rather than heavy perorations, the politics, if you like, not of power but of the limitations of power, above all of common sense.

McCarthy's message to the American people was *'pas trop de zèle'*—'not too much enthusiasm'. This was not a counsel of complacency or of inaction or of apathy. It was the advice which any sensible man gives a hysteric: calm down first and then let's see what has to be done. McCarthy, in short, played it cool, which of course, is a profoundly undemocratic thing to do. Progressive American politics since Andrew Jackson have been based on a fundamental assumption: that there is only one fuel with which to drive the American political engine and that is the raw spirit of popular emotionalism, the spirit released by stirring the people up. McCarthy sought to quieten them down, so that educated people, like himself, could get on with the business of government quietly, undramatically, above all sensibly. For American liberals, and still more for the American young, this was such a new idea that they thought it the last word in avant-garde radicalism. McCarthy offered them Edward Burke, who came as a blinding flash of revelation, the latest fashion, and far more up-to-date than Karl Marx.

This was the crux of the McCarthy phenomenon. Vietnam had brought about a crisis in the American liberal tradition. Vietnam was a people's war. It arose out of the popular will to spread the American gospel. For the liberals and the young, who had come to hate the war and to regard it as evil, this posed a terrible dilemma. The people had been proved wrong, even dangerous. Moralistic politics had been proved wrong, even dangerous. That is why, at least for a time, they turned to McCarthy, who was neither a populist nor a moralist and was not ashamed of admitting it.

Nothing better revealed the McCarthy approach—and the gap that divided him from the other presidential candidates in 1968—than his reaction to the secret service protection which was cast around them all after the assassination of Robert Kennedy. Nixon and Rockefeller, I recall, made a brave show of determination to carry on pumping hands in spite of the police screen. Nothing, they said, would stop them meeting the people. McCarthy told me that he positively welcomed the protection since it gave him a longed-for excuse to cut down on these primitive rituals. He did not want to take his anti-Vietnam case to the people in this way, since he knew that this meant mounting a crusade, putting his opposition to the war in moral terms. In his view it was precisely an excess of moral fervour that caused the war. His opposition to the war was not moral at all. He saw the war as out of proportion, grotesquely and monstrously excessive, not so much evil as absurd. Uncivilized, yes, but not evil. That was not a point that could be got across by pumping hands and touching flesh; nor was it a heroic view. It was essentially dispassionate politics, but because dispassionate politics are so fundamentally un-American it rolled across the land like a clap of thunder, shaking the people to their very roots.

Dispassionate politics does not mean cynical politics. McCarthy was no cynic. His hero was St Thomas More, with St Thomas à Becket as runner-up. He was a deeply religious man but a political sceptic. What he hated was the kind of messianic political language which arouses passionate enthusiasm, so that enthusiasm on one side provokes enthusiasm on the other, and the two enthusiasms cancel each other out, preventing rather than accelerating progress.

At one point in his campaign McCarthy promised to pull down the walls of the White House if he was elected. But he did not mean letting the people mill around on the White House lawn, as they did in the tumultuous populist days of

Andrew Jackson. He had in mind almost the opposite: a style of presidential leadership that so reduced the monarchical aspects—which the Kennedy family dangerously enhanced—and so played down the role of superhuman hero, that the people would not need to be kept out because they would have no obsessive desire to get in. It was all very old-fashioned but to a people suffering at the time from a surfeit of passion, strangely appealing, fascinatingly fresh, like a cool hand placed on a brow racked by fever. Put your trust, he argued, in the sign of superior education; give the people a rest; try a little touch of civilized politics run by people of sensitivity.

His campaign was a portent not so much in political terms as in social. Of course he never had a chance of winning the nomination, still less of reaching the White House. It was an exercise in social seduction, a demonstration of the gentlemanly approach to public life, a teasing, titillating reminder of the inadequacies, not of democratic politics but of democratic politicians, a lament, not of course for aristocracy but for the style of aristocracy, a hint at the surprising potency of the amateur touch, of the magnetism of intellectual distinction, of the glamour, in a word, of being unapologetically, almost arrogantly *superior*. But superior in the throwaway, casual, bored, slightly contemptuous manner of a man born to govern. Nothing could have been more light years away from the traditional American approach to electioneering. Yet this anti-hero was the hero of the radical young.

I am perfectly aware that the old politics triumphed in the end. But my point, let me repeat, is not a political one. What the McCarthy phenomenon showed is that there is a yearning in America today among the young for a change of political style, prompted by the realization that the—in American terms—old-fashioned populist approach is not enough; that it is irrelevant. even harmful to the country's present needs. This, as I say, is a social phenomenon, part of a general cultural preference among the young for people who keep their 'cool', who are detached, casual, not cynical but sceptical, dry, caustic—the very opposite of folksy and sentimental. Yet the more one thinks about these characteristics the more it becomes clear that they are the virtues appreciated by and produced by aristocratic societies, the products of an upper class. McCarthy was not a 'great man'. He had none of the vulgar magnetism of the popular orator. He was not, in this sense, a leader at all. His authority with the young sprang from his being patently outside the normal tradition of egalitarian democracy, from his being—although his followers would have been staggered to hear it—an almost exact replica of a type of grandee democrat which the British class system habitually threw up, a kind of contemporary Lord Melbourne, the secret of whose success lay in a strange social amalgam of personal charm, sophistication, wit and, above all, independence of mind. These are not democratic virtues, as traditionally understood in the United States. But the fact that they aroused such staggering enthusiasm among so large a section of the educated and affluent young suggests that there is a growing constituency which respects the qualities that an egalitarian society finds it diffcult to produce, which in turn suggests the need for changes not in the political system, but in the social system, or rather in the relationship between the two.

What has to be recognized about America is that at any rate for the last hundred years there has been a basic contradiction between its egalitarian political system and its inegalitarian social structure. An upper class, based on inherited wealth, has existed, with its own economic privileges, but it has felt no need to involve itself except indirectly in politics. Its members have not, by and large, personally gone into politics. They have, of course, financed the Republican Party to fight their political battles on their behalf, and an excellent mercenary body it has proved to be. The interests of business and industry have been well served. The Republican Party has shown that it can look after the interests of capital within an egalitarian political system very satisfactorily. There have been ups and downs, of course, but by and large the rich have been content to remain an *economically* dominant class, and have never sought to become a politically dominant class.

Such a self-denying ordinance worked well enough until recently because the business of America was primarily business, and so long as politics did not interfere too disastrously with business why should business bother to interfere with politics? The point I am making is that such were America's peculiar internal and external circumstances that politics did not terribly matter. So long as the upper class was left alone enough to get on with running business, and doing well out of that, politics could be left to the people, almost as a kind of harmless, if unedifying, distraction.

But the circumstances today in America have radically changed. It is no longer a country without real political problems. It is now a country faced on all sides by challenges which call for statecraft of the highest order, for political skills that far transcend the kind of economic horse-trading which passed for politics in more fortunate times. Manifestly, for example, the integration of the Negroes cannot be left to the ordinary processes of political bargaining by which earlier immigrant groups have clawed their way to recognition. Nor can the foreign policy of the world's strongest power be left to the shifting winds of popular ignorance and emotionalism. Agonizing problems are emerging, in short, which require an exercise of political imagination, of, in short, statecraft, which machine politics, politics designed primarily around vote-catching tactics, are unable to supply, except far too rarely and spasmodically.

But the American style of politics is peculiarly discouraging to those with political imagination, and by no means an ideal training ground for statecraft. It is a style of politics that has emerged in a country where politics have been regarded by the upper class as an activity for hacks and mercenaries, and where the social system has been designed to guarantee an attitude of public irresponsibility among the economically privileged. But how long can such an attitude endure, once the political problems facing the country are seen to involve the very foundations of the State? How long can an economically privileged upper class agree to remain non-political, agree to leave politics to 'the people', once it is clear that such an abandonment of responsibility is leading to national disaster? More important, what will be the effect on the assumptions of egalitarian democracy if and when the upper class, for the first time since the earliest days of the Republic, does feel compelled to become directly involved in the political process, and most important of all, what would the effect of such a decision be on the attitudes of the upper class itself?

So far there are no clear answers to these questions; only a painful squirming of the body politic as some of their implications begin to sink in. But some points can be plainly discerned. The affluent, educated young are no longer content to remain in a cocoon of economic privilege cut off from active political involvement; are no longer content, as their fathers were, to limit their political involvement to the extent of financing a political party to look after their economic interests. But in seeking to extend their political involvement they run up against the obvious difficulty of breaking into a political system rooted in a populist tradition of the utmost vulgarity and venality, which shows no interest in politics beyond the pork-barrel level. Nor do they themselves carry any political weight, since the American social system has been such as to develop no tradition of political leadership in the class from which they spring; has been such as expressly to disassociate economic power—which they have been allowed to inherit—from political skill which they have never been allowed to acquire.

As a result, America is passing through a strange experience; one in which the younger generation of the upper class either opt out, so unsuited are they by their background to effective political involvement in circumstances so uncongenial to their tastes, or take to the streets in futile encouragement of anarchic rebellion, having despaired of the democratic process. But surely this is likely to be a transitional phase. One cannot believe that as the nature of the dilemma begins to become apparent, the truth will not dawn that America's future depends on certain modifications being made to the social and political system—modifications designed to make the *political* system more regularly responsive to the involvement in it of the socially privileged, and the *social* system more productive of an upper class specifically brought up to play a more effective role in the political life of the nation.

The Kennedy dynasty was a not very successful experiment in both directions—an attempt by an immensely economically privileged family to train itself expressly for political leadership and then to use its wealth to buy its way into a position of dominance over one of the established political machines. It was a novel experiment in grafting the principles or style of aristocratic leadership on to the existing plant of egalitarian democracy. The trouble, however, was that to make this exercise of economic and social privilege acceptable it was necessary to create an aura of such exceptional personal glory, so rich a personal myth, that the style of aristocracy was overblown into the style of monarchy, which turned out to be so heady a brew as to induce hysteria in a body politic accustomed to egalitarian democracy. The Kennedy family was too greedy for power, sought to inject too powerful a shot of high leadership into the American body politic all at once, with the result that the patient went off its head. McCarthy, in this sense, was a more significant phenomenon—an application of the aristocratic principle not to the centre of power but to the periphery, not an attempt to get to the top in one dazzling, majestic display of heroic leadership, but rather to display the charms of civilized leadership on the sidelines, to attract the affluent young into politics—a kind of dummy run which never really had a chance of being the real thing. But the response to it was very remarkable, quite sufficient to show that there is a constituency today for a style of leadership that is neither heroic nor populist, neither charismatic nor rabble-rousing, a style of leadership, that is, suitable and congenial to a *political* class, if such turned out to be what the economically privileged wish to become.

The point about McCarthy, as I say, was that he was an exemplar of how certain human qualities become politically relevant in a society when the socially privileged have become politically active, as they are now beginning to do in the United States. As an individual, he was obviously far less potent than John F. Kennedy or Robert Kennedy, both of whom were outsize personalities, natural leaders. McCarthy was not an outsize personality, not king-size at all, in fact rather ordinary, the kind of man which a gentlemanly class might be expected to throw up in abundance. The Kennedys were a hysterical attempt by American society to find a short-cut way out of the dilemma of an egalitarian democracy suddenly finding itself faced by political challenges demanding a quality of leadership that it had never expected to have to produce; a panicky attempt by an economic élite to exert its influence in a roar and rush of dazzling drama. The McCarthy phenomenon was a much more significant long-term development; the first attempt at a style of leadership suitable to an affluent élite determined to grow slowly into a political class, a style of leadership that had nothing to do with the charisma of a particular individual, but a lot to do with a representative ideal of conduct for a governing class. The point about the Kennedy family is that it was unique, a blazing meteor which nobody could be expected to follow. McCarthy was eminently imitable, a model of civilized statesmanship in whose footsteps any American gentleman could easily follow if he had the incentive to do so.

I realize that even to talk about an American 'gentleman' is to use a term that invites instant mockery, and even if the reader has followed me so far his mounting suspicions as to my seriousness will now be finally and conclusively confirmed. But this risk will have to be taken. I do not believe that American politics can be discussed without raising the subject of class. Economically speaking, America *is* a class society. Enormous differences of wealth exist and are encouraged to exist; a minority enjoy preponderant economic power. To this extent America is a plutocracy. Yet the problems it faces are more than a plutocracy can cope with, go far beyond the political skills which are natural to a plutocracy, and far beyond the skills that a plutocracy can buy, and far beyond the skills likely to emerge in a political system connected to a plutocracy on a mercenary basis. Under the shadow of the plutocracy, authoritative political leadership either wilts into inactivity or takes exaggerated almost paranoiac forms, as it did under the Kennedys, and even more so under L.B.J. One answer, of course, is to break the economic power of the plutocracy. This is the revolutionary answer. But how realistic is that? That is the most fanciful answer of all. The other answer is for the plutocracy to take its political responsibilities far more seriously than ever before, with all that this implies in terms of developing a social system geared to the task of producing statesmen, not just leaders of industry; of producing a political class—not just the occasional 'great man'—capable of supplying a quality of leadership suitable not only

186

to the creation of wealth, but to the governance of a continent, indeed of a world in the throes of crisis.

Let me illustrate this theme with regard to the most sombre failure of American leadership at the present time—in Vietnam. Here was an exercise in imperial power conducted by an egalitarian society that has given no thought to the need for producing leaders fit to conduct so vastly ambitious an endeavour of such infinite complexity, demanding political and military skills of a higher order. The man who was responsible in the crucial years, for example, was Robert Macnamara, a former head of the Ford Motor Company, whose claim to fame was that he had succeeded in introducing the principle of cost-effectiveness into the Pentagon. Imagine any other great Power in history entrusting a gigantic imperial operation to a businessman, with no experience of politics, whose gifts were not even supposed to be more than those of an outstanding Quarter-Master General. But who else was there to appoint? The American social system has not been geared to the production of such talents. This deficiency goes all down the line, from Robert Macnamara to Lieutenant Calley, the pitiful young officer involved in the Pinkville tragedy. It is not only a political class that is lacking in America: it is also an officer class.

Britain, it is said, has no further need of a public-school system, because she no longer has an empire for its products to administer. Those upright Christian gentlemen moulded by Dr Arnold's precepts and Rudyard Kipling's poetry are out of place in modern little Britain which has ceased to rule over palm and pine. But when one considers the fate of Lieutenant Calley, and studies his background, it is difficult to avoid the thought that a modern version of those upright Christian gentlemen would certainly be very far from out of place in contemporary America. Having taken over Britain's imperial burdens, perhaps America would have been well advised to take over the system which produced the necessary 'white men' fit to shoulder them. If the Battle of Waterloo was won on the playing-fields of Eton, might it not be that the war in Vietnam was lost through the absence in America of anything comparable?

Britain, on the whole, did succeed in her colonial heyday

in producing a governing cadre, both military and civilian, inspired with a sense of mission, endowed with the habit of authority and instilled with a code of conduct that largely precluded corruption, cruelty and injustice. These somewhat unsympathetic paragons did not make Britain loved. But they made Britain respected. Can America really be expected to carry on her post-war role of leader of the western world without evolving a social system which takes the problem of producing leaders a good deal more seriously than has been the case hitherto?

Leadership today is a dirty word. It has only to be mentioned to produce contemptuous laughter. Yet it was a failure of leadership that caused the terrible outrage of Pinkville. That much derided figure, the British 'officer and gentleman', would not have behaved in the way Lieutenant Calley is alleged to have behaved. The reason for that is not superior moral virtue. It is because of something much simpler, something, if you like, laughable; because that kind of behaviour simply is not done, simply is not cricket.

The gentlemanly ideal, so much traduced today, may have little relevance to the preoccupations of contemporary Britain. It is indeed difficult to show that it can contribute much to a society obsessed with the overriding need for economic growth. But for a society like America, engaged in the unprecedentedly ambitious adventure—far more ambitious than anything Britain ever attempted—of upholding the values of civilization throughout the world, such an ideal has much to commend it. It buttresses the teachings of morality with a code of conduct, turns the exercise of power into a superior kind of behaviour, lends leadership a tone and style that are truly exemplary.

The century of the common man, however, has little time for the gentlemanly ideal, because it is at war with the great unchallenged principle of equality. Modern democratic society, of which the United States is the prototype and pioneer, finds it difficult to tolerate the idea of a gentlemanly class consciously trained to regard itself as committed to special standards and values appropriate for people born to lead. Yet the century of the common man has not abolished the need for leaders, has not so transformed the reality of life that the quality of leadership is less relevant. The appalling difficulties of Lieutenant Calley's predicament were not less appalling than those facing British officers in the days of our imperial rule. The challenge is the same. All that is different is that whereas British officers sprang from a social system designed to enable them to meet it, Lieutenant Calley sprang from a social system that makes no such preparations.

The truth is that the common man cannot and should not be asked to bear responsibilities and burdens of an uncommon nature. For a country setting itself the most ambitious task ever undertaken in modern history, the common man is not enough. But how can a society dedicated to the ideal of equality and organized to give it ever more perfect expression afford to recognize this truth? This is the agonizing question which the Vietnam war is posing for the American people.

For imperial Britain there was no such problem. The traditions of a ruling class whose function was being slowly eroded at home were adapted and transmogrified for use overseas. But the United States has struggled to avoid the need for a ruling class at home; it came into existence to prove the point that such a social system was both evil and unnecessary. It has emphasized all those strands of democratic thought which decry the need for leadership. For nearly two hundred years it has done a splendid job in proving this point. The spirit of egalitarianism has helped to create the richest country on earth.

But with the riches have now come the terrible responsibilities which accompany such pre-eminence, and the open social system, ideally suited to the task of economic development, is cracking under the strain of running an empire. For the first task a ruling class which would have been an albatross around America's neck, as some would argue it is around Britain's today. But for the kind of challenge now facing America it may well be a necessity. Perhaps the social price of egalitarianism has become too high to pay.

Lieutenant Calley is part of that price. To be in command of men in a cruel colonial war many thousands of miles away from home requires more than a few years of officer training. It requires the habit of authority engendered over generations, a professional pride and ingrained self-discipline, a tradition of leadership which only an officer class is likely to be able to nurture.

But the problem is much deeper and wider than that. It is tragic to see the great American democracy floundering in a sea of irresolution, its political leaders unable to summon up the courage of their own convictions. The American 'establishment' has long since decided that the Vietnam war is lost and that withdrawal is the only answer. But such is its lack of self-confidence, so minuscule its authority, that it dare not lead decisively or effectively in this direction. It lacks the habit of authority, operates in an egalitarian tradition that allows little place for leadership, passionately opposes the idea of superior people.

In this crisis, possibly the most acute in its history, the American people look up but find nobody to lead them. This is no accident. American society has been organized so as to make sure that there should be nobody. This tradition was fine for the purpose of exploiting a largely empty continent, but is tragically inadequate for a role of world responsibility. The leadership that springs from democratic egalitarianism has proved itself capable in the past of winning wars. But it seems miserably incapable of rising to the far greater challenge of losing one.

The Vietnam tragedy raises very profound questions for American society. At every stage and at every level there have been lamentable failures of leadership, with no end to this catalogue of calamity yet in sight. But leadership is precisely the quality that is left to chance in American society. Democratic thought simply assumes that it will emerge when needed. Imperial Britain had the hangover of a feudal class system to fill this gap in democratic thought. America has no such hangover, and the gap cries out to be filled.

Democratic egalitarianism has been put on trial by the Vietnam challenge. Although Lieutenant Calley was in the dock, he was symbolic of the common man whose century this is supposed to be, symbolic of a social and political system that is today paying the price of having turned leadership into a dirty word.

Let me try to sum up the position of the United States

before returning to the broader theme which, in any case, it throws much light upon. What I am trying to suggest is that democratic theory has failed to evolve a solution to the problem of authority that stands up to the kind of tests which America is now experiencing; tests which, if they are to be met, require a governing order capable of exercising leadership at many different levels. The question that has to be asked is whether a governing order formed exclusively by the democratic process—i.e., by winning votes—is capable of providing this measure of leadership, or does it need to be buttressed by a social system that is designed to produce the right kind of leaders for the democratic process to choose from. Society can, after all, very easily rig the democratic stakes. John F. Kennedy is an obvious case in point. He was bred to win. His parents specifically brought him up to be a democratic *leader*. If society wishes to encourage such parental attitudes it is not difficult to do so. This was done with very great success in nineteenth-century England, for purposes of imperial administration. There is nothing to stop American society seeking to produce a steady stream of John F. Kennedys: a steady stream, that is, of privileged young men determined to serve their country in public life; nothing to stop America from putting the fact of economic privilege to the broad purpose of engendering an effective governing order.

That such an idea is alien to the American egalitarian tradition is, of course, all too obvious. But the tradition grew out of rather special circumstances that no longer apply. So long as the main business of America was business there was blessedly little for a governing order to do except allow business to get on with the job of developing the continent subject to the proviso that if the public felt their interests endangered they could bring pressure to bear on the governing order to step in on its behalf. But the more complicated a country's political problems become, the more necessary an authoritative governing order becomes, not only because the task of governing is infinitely more delicate and challenging but because—and this is the crucial point—it becomes increasingly necessary to ignore the popular will, to rise above it. The truth has to be faced that the authority that comes from winning votes may no longer be enough. It may be necessary to ensure that those who win elections do so because they are special, and do not become special simply as a result of winning votes; that their authority precedes and accounts for their election and does not grow out of it; that, in short, they get elected because they are leaders and do not simply become leaders by being elected.

What I am trying very tentatively to suggest is that the less likely it is that the people will choose good leaders through the political process, the more important it becomes to help them in this task by allowing the social system to tip the scales. Of course, there have always been anti-democrats who have made this allegation, and this is part of the trouble, since the critics of democracy have cried wolf too often in the past, and from brazenly suspect motives. They have been concerned at the democratic tendency to promote majority interests at the expense of minority rights. But the minority rights which they have been mostly concerned about did not really deserve such concern, since they were, in practice, the minority rights of the economically powerful who could well look after themselves. Although in theory democracy has always posed a threat to minority rights, because of the power it places in the hands of the majority, in practice the minority has been able to make up for its paucity of votes by it abundance of money.

But a new situation is emerging in America, and indeed in all the Western democracies, where fears about majority rule go beyond the crocodile tears of a plutocracy concerned about its privileges. Today, thanks to the affluent society, the majority is not only politically powerful, rich in votes, but also in wealth as well. It is not only overprivileged politically; it is overprivileged economically. In the affluent society the rich are the majority and the poor the minority. The balance of power which previously existed between the politically underprivileged but economically overprivileged rich minority and the politically overprivileged but economically underprivileged majority has been upset. The Negro problem illustrates this new development in a particularly acute way. All earlier minority ethnic groups enjoyed the political benefits of being part of the majority; that is to say, of the poor. But the Negroes today are not only a minority in terms of economic power but also a political minority in terms of votes. They cannot, like earlier ethnic groups, enjoy the advantage of being part of the political majority. What the American democracy is faced by today is the theoretical problem of minority rights—which had previously been only theoretical since the minority was protected from exploitation by economic superiority—made actual. The problem is no longer one of an economically powerful minority kept in order by a politically powerful majority. It is of a politically and economically weak minority facing a politically and economically strong majority. This is not only true of the Negroes in particular. It is true also of the poor in general. The affluent society, in short, has transformed the fears about democracy from the realm of phony special pleading on the part of the rich into a genuine problem. The voice of the people is no longer the voice of the toiling and suffering masses, crying out for social justice. It is increasingly the voice of the contented and complacent. And the voice of the minority is no longer the voice of privilege, of the beneficiaries of the status quo. It is the voice of the deprived.

It cannot be questioned that this changed internal situation, taken in conjunction with the formidable change in America's external position—the change, that is, from a position of protected isolation thanks to the Royal Navy to her present pre-eminence as the leader of the Western world —together call in question the adequacy of the egalitarian tradition. The load of responsibility placed on the shoulders of the governing order has become so great as to necessitate a retreat from egalitarianism, which must hereafter be seen as one of those childish games that an adult democracy, at the plenitude of its wealth and glory, can no longer afford to play at.

There are some indications that this retreat has already begun. It is significant, for example, that a man like Nelson Rockefeller, whose multi-millionaire status would have ruled him out of national politics a few years ago, so deeply would it have conflicted with egalitarian sentiment, today enjoys one of the country's most important elective offices, Governor of New York, and was a leading contender for the Presidency in 1968. This would have been inconceivable a few years ago, as inconceivable as it would be in Britain today—and the

Douglas-Home experiment really is the exception that proves the rule—for a hereditary aristocrat to become Prime Minister. The voters would have instinctively recoiled from the idea of economic privilege being able to buy political power, just as today the British electorate recoils from allowing social privilege to win it. What is so fascinating about America today, however, is that just at the very moment when the British aristocracy is being forced out of politics its American equivalent is being drawn in. Whereas egalitarian pressure is mounting in Britain, it is declining in America.

It is worth considering what it is about the Nelson Rockefeller, and those like him, that makes them such appealing vote-catchers. In egalitarian theory he should not be popular at all. He has himself done nothing to deserve public respect. He is the very opposite of a self-made man. His only claim to fame is to be a Rockefeller, a member of an illustrious family —a family whose somewhat murky origins as original robber barons has been lost, partly in the mist of time, and partly in a great billowing smokescreen of subsequent philanthropy and public service. The truth is that the Rockefeller appeal is unmistakably aristocratic. It is because he did *not* make the money himself, is *not* a self-made man, that he is trusted. His charm lies in his hereditary position; that he is part of American history, bears a name, belongs to a house, that strikes all sorts of echoes in the American imagination. It is not his money that counts. A first-generation Texan oil tycoon would have no comparable appeal. It is the combination of great hereditary wealth and a social pre-eminence that has grown up over generations.

It was always rather fanciful to suppose that such a combination, if allowed to continue, would not eventually make its impact on democratic politics, ineluctably diluting the egalitarian tradition. The Rockefellers have been immensely rich and socially prominent now for the best part of a century. They are part of the American legend, living a dream life, cocooned in a great network of philanthropy and conspicuous consumption—exuding an aura of power, mystery and social glamour. Of course in time these advantages were bound to be transferable into the currency of political privilege, once those who possessed them wished to do so; once, that is, politics began to attract such people, began to carry real prestige and be involved with great deeds.

That, of course, is precisely what is happening now. The nineteenth-century plutocracy is emerging into an aristocracy just at the moment when political power in America is assuming an importance that makes it an irresistible object of attraction. For the first time in American history the exercise of statecraft has become a more challenging activity than the exercise of entrepreneurial skill; to be a Senator, Congressman or Governor, a more glamorous way of life than that of the business tycoon. Two developments have to be noted. First, the magnification of the importance and glamour of politics, consequent on America's emergence as the greatest power in the world. Secondly, the emergence of an economically privileged *hereditary* upper class which is more suited to politics than business, brought up to take money for granted, to be contemptuous of the money-making skills—an upper class, moreover, with a sense of guilt for its past misdeeds, imbued with a desire to make amends, with a sense of noblesse oblige. How could the conjunction of these two developments, the magnification of the importance of politics, on the one hand, and the emergence of a hereditary upper class, on the other, not make a dramatic impact on the practice of egalitarian democracy, creating at once a need for superior statesmen, and an instinctive recognition of this need among the public, and a class bound to feel itself both well suited and obliged to respond to the challenge?

Surely the practice of egalitarian democracy in the capitalist society was only likely to last so long as the capitalists were primarily entrepreneurs fascinated with the adventure of business, living in a society artificially inoculated against the normal ills affecting a body politic. Such can be said to have been America's condition roughly up to the end of the Second World War. But once America became a country with real political problems, and with a hereditary plutocracy made up in part of a generation brought up in a style of life inducing an inclination for public life, then in practice egalitarian democracy was bound to be eroded, since the privileged few would want to erode it, and be in a position to tempt the many into wanting to see it eroded.

Added to this, however, there is, as we have seen, the third factor; the idealistic disillusion with majoritarian democracy, because of its manifest unsuitability in an affluent society to cope with some of its most pressing problems. But this disillusion is largely to be found among the student young, who themselves are mostly the products of economic privilege, the offspring of the affluent. So the interest in politics among the economically privileged comes from two levels, from the top —from the Nelson Rockefeller fathers who seek to make the impact in a spirit of noblesse oblige, and from their sons who seek to make the impact in a spirit of rebellion or noblesse disoblige—both interventions, however, being part of a process designed to weaken the country's commitment to egalitarian democracy, the former by bringing the weight of social distinction into the scales of political power and the latter by introducing the weight of educational superiority.

In Britain, by contrast, the claims of egalitarian democracy have never been so strong. It is not altogether surprising that the two great Anglo-Saxon democracies should be experiencing this reversal of attitudes, since they are also experiencing a reversal of national roles. Britain, as a declining power with no further imperial responsibilities, protected by the American thermonuclear umbrella, thinks it can afford—as America in the nineteenth century could afford—to do without a governing class, on the ground that the particular qualities associated with one are no longer necessary. A society that does not feel it has any longer any very important role to play, or one that sees its problems as primarily technical— balancing the trade account, for example—obviously has no time for the aristocratic virtues which are designed for societies with a rather grander idea of the purpose of politics. No democrat would argue that social inequality, a class system, is an absolute virtue, a good in itself. Its virtues only become apparent as part of a discussion of the wider problem of creating an effective governing order, a governing order capable of meeting major challenges. What is so interesting about the respective experiences of Britain and America in the last few years is that while theirs have been such as to encourage at least an unconscious awareness of how inadequate political democracy is by itself as a source of leadership, ours have had the reverse effect of encouraging the belief that it is perfectly safe to destroy the traditional buttress of social class, since it is no longer needed. As America more and more turns to its privileged class for leadership, and its privileged class more and more shows itself willing and eager to respond, Britain is ever more eager to discard hers, and the ruling class is ever more willing to be discarded. The roles, as I say, are dramatically reversed, with America's Nelson Rockefellers moving on to the political stage just as Britain's Douglas-Homes move out. The British mood is: Let us throw off the shackles of an out-of-date class system, of statesmen who lack expert training, since they serve no purpose in a society dedicated to carrying through a technological revolution; while the American mood seems to be: Let us make use of the products of inequality; since, like it or not, rightly or wrongly, they seem to have certain qualities, a particular style, that is relevant to political leadership in times that transcend the relatively limited problems of economic management.

What I am saying is that an economically orientated democratic society, one that gives top priority to the maximization of wealth—such as America in the nineteenth century and Britain today—can afford to forget about or ignore some of the deeper dilemmas that affect more troubled societies, can afford to forget or ignore the specific problems of authority and leadership which an inegalitarian social system is designed to answer. The most obvious example of this, of course, is the ability to ignore the problem of war. A society that does not expect to have to take the strains of war can afford to ignore the need to evolve a social system capable of producing an officer class; can afford to ignore association between privilege and patriotism—the role, that is to say, which the privileged class, with a great deal to lose, plays in setting a patriotic example; just as a democratic society without world responsibilities can afford to ignore the need to evolve a social system capable of producing a political class trained from birth in the skills of statecraft and able to exercise authority in a manner that elicits a voluntary response without recourse to compulsion. It surely stands to reason that societies will organize their social systems differently in accordance with how they assess their destinies, attaching different priorities to different desiderata depending on their national aspirations. Clearly a democratic society like contemporary Britain which believes its days of greatness are over, or a democratic country like America in the nineteenth century which believed that its days of greatness had not yet arrived, will have different social priorities to one like Britain a century ago or America today. Nor do these considerations apply only to a society's role on the world stage. They apply equally to its assessment of its internal dilemmas. If it is assumed, for example, that the class war is over, or that the end of ideology has arrived, and that the responsibility of government is limited to the relatively simple task of sharing out a national treasure of which there is more than enough to go round, then clearly conditions will be thought to exist wherein society can function without an authoritative governing order, without the social discipline that comes from hierarchy and status, without, in short, a ruling class. A society that takes order and discipline for granted, or one that deems its main political problems to have been permanently solved, will be much less appreciative of the strengths and virtues of an inegalitarian social system, for the very good reason that these strengths and virtues will seem increasingly irrelevant. It is nonsense to suppose that questions of political democracy and social inequality can be considered in a vacuum, as if they had nothing to do with the kind of problems facing a society at any particular period. My contention is that America is passing through a period that tends to highlight the dangers of egalitarianism, and to induce a respect for the strength and virtue of aristocracy, since it is becoming hauntingly aware that political democracy alone, unfortified by the buttress of a class system, cannot take the strains to which it is at present subjected. One reaction in America is to call political democracy in question and to move towards a more authoritarian *political* order. But another reaction, and obviously a far more encouraging one, is to move towards a more authoritative *social* order, to fortify a failing political democracy with the reviving impact of social aristocracy. Britain, on the other hand, sees no such necessity. She is passing through a period when the advantages of egalitarianism seem overwhelmingly obvious. But how long will this period last? Is it not already beginning to come to a close? I believe, for reasons that I have tried to suggest in earlier chapters, that it certainly should be, that Britain's problems are also increasingly of such a nature as to require certain qualities of leadership, and a certain relationship between leaders and led, that political democracy alone cannot supply, unless it is buttressed by a social system which takes the problem of leadership far more seriously than has been the case in recent years.

We have been living, it seems to me, in a fool's paradise about the problems of democratic government in an affluent society, assuming that they would become less onerous and delicate as the progress of material well-being reduced the great historic sources of social tension and dissent. In one obvious sense these assumptions have been proved right. The clash of material interests has become much less fierce as the size of the national cake has grown large enough to allow everybody a tolerable slice; not of course as much as everybody wants, but enough to prevent passionate dissatisfaction among the great body of the voters. This does not mean that economic arguments about how wealth should be produced and distributed, and who should control its production and distribution, are not still what politics are about. Of course they are. But the arguments are no longer of so fierce a kind as to be worth coming to blows over; are no longer so divisive as to cause basic social disunity. This is a very remarkable achievement. It would seem reasonable to assume that barring unforeseeable economic disaster affluent societies have reached a stage where material problems can be resolved relatively easily through democratic bargaining.* This has certainly been the case in Britain in recent years. It is difficult to point to a single issue in the field of *economics* which has aroused intense *popular* passion. Incomes policy, nationalization, welfare, trade-union reform and so on—the various interest groups certainly disagree on these questions, but in a manner that poses no real threat to the democratic process. The disagreements are manifestly resolvable through democratic bargaining. Doubtless the compromises hammered out are far

* America is different because of the Negro problem.

from ideal. No one would pretend, for example, that the problem of inflation had been satisfactorily solved. But it is a problem, like all the other economic problems, that society has come to be able to live with. None of the interest groups regard the solution as ideal and each continues to manoeuvre to win advantages as the occasion arises. But none feels aggrieved to the point of despair. Clearly it is possible to argue that the ideal of social justice requires this reform and the ideal of economic efficiency requires that change, but the arguments tend to be more about detail than principle. In this sense, therefore, it is perfectly possible to talk about the end of ideology. The emotional steam has gone out of the class war.*

It is not at all surprising, therefore, that we should have come to take an optimistic and complacent view about the possibility of ordering society in a manner that minimizes the problem of authority. Our habits of mind are rooted in a context which gave economic issues pre-eminent priority, and having reduced these problems to manageable proportions we are inclined to suppose that henceforth political leadership can be a comparatively low-key business. And so in this sense it can. So long as people are prepared to bargain, to negotiate, politics is a form of brokerage. One does not wish to denigrate the kind of conciliatory skills required for such a function, since they are obviously very considerable. But they are a different and lower kind of skill from that required to govern a society riven by violent ideological passions. It surely stands to reason that Britain is easier to govern today, in so far as *material* issues are concerned, than it was even twenty-five years ago because the issues that divide it are less explosive, provoke less intensity of feeling. So why bother about an authoritative governing order in a society where economic divisiveness is so manifestly on the wane?

To some extent, however, this question is already beginning to answer itself in this country, as it is in a much more acute form in America: because, in an affluent society, where the majority are materially content, minority material needs can only be protected by a governing order that enjoys an authority

* The Conservatives' Industrial Relations Bill looks as though it may be putting some of the steam back.

which draws its strength from sources other than popular approval expressed in the ballot-box. It was possible to believe that popular election constituted a firm enough base for a governing order seeking to curb minority selfishness. But is it a firm enough base, by itself, for a governing order seeking to curb majority selfishness? If politicians do not start with the advantage of a certain social authority—as was the case when they were drawn from a traditional governing class—and have to rely for this position in society exclusively on their vote-catching skills, how can they stand for social justice when its needs are ceasing to be so obviously in the majority interest? After six years of Labour Government the scale of this dilemma is becoming more and more obvious. The Labour Government certainly showed itself loyal to the working-class interests in the material field. But working-class interests in the material field are no longer synonymous with the interests of the poor and underprivileged, since most workers are no longer poor and underprivileged. The interests of the poor and under-privileged, in short, are no longer the interests of the majority. Social justice, in other words, can no longer be guaranteed by majority rule; can no longer be guaranteed by a governing order whose authority rests solely on the electoral process. For a governing order in an affluent society to be able to safeguard the interests of the poor, who are now a minority, it must enjoy a prestige which is aristocratic as well as democratic, paternalistic as well as fraternal, which impresses the people by a status other than that conferred *by* the people.

What has to be understood is that in an affluent democracy, precisely because the popular passion for social reform is so relatively weak, the governing order needs to be able to exert far more moral authority from the top than in a non-affluent one which can rely on effective popular passion from the bottom. In this sense the very success of an affluent society deepens the problems of democracy by removing or profoundly diluting the main impulse behind reform and improvement —majority dissatisfaction. The quality of leadership, in short, becomes all the more crucial.

But how to get a governing order with moral authority in an egalitarian society which cannot tolerate the idea of superior persons? In practice, of course, modern Britain offers a revealing answer; by evolving an élite based on superior brainpower, in short, a meritocracy. This is precisely what Britain has been doing for the last twenty years or so, with results that are already marked in the composition of the Labour Party, which is increasingly made up of dons, school-teachers, journalists; made up, that is, of members of what used to be called the intelligentsia. So far as the material problems of an affluent society are concerned, such a meritocracy can be said to have many advantages since, being itself propertyless, it will have a built-in bias towards economic social justice. But in an affluent society the search for economic social justice ceases to be the only or even the principal challenge for democracy.

What has to be realized is that economic divisiveness is by no means the most serious problem to challenge an affluent democracy, and that in some ways economic issues are much easier to resolve than those which arise once affluence is taken for granted. Release from pressing and overwhelming material preoccupations sets a society free, as it does an individual, to chase after goals that are much less easy to realize, and the pursuit of which provokes far more uncontrollably divisive passions. We can already see this process at work. What are the issues that have really stirred the blood of the body politic in the last few years? Not unemployment but immigration, not poverty but permissiveness, not corporation tax but capital punishment, not S.E.T. but SEX, not the cost of living but the crime rate. It is the moral issues, not the material ones, that increasingly arouse the deepest passions. I do not mean by this that it is the moral issues that determine elections. The majority are still concerned with material matters in the sense that these are what they vote about. But the sources of minority dissent in society, of deep dissatisfaction, of alienation are no longer primary material. They are increasingly moral. In so far as democratic processes are threatened by forces that seem unable or unwilling to work through them, by forces that threaten the democratic framework, it is over the moral order-ing of society rather than the material. These are the elements of deepest friction, the real dividing barriers in the contem-porary society, and the more the uneducated majority refuse to take them seriously the more the educated minority comes to despair of democracy, and to operate outside it. Alternatively, the more the minority insist on their being taken seriously, and succeed in imposing their will, the less the majority come to have faith in democracy, and the less willing are they to accept its legitimacy.

The significance of this change for democratic politics has not begun to be properly considered. The awkward truth is that whereas the tensions and problems arising from material arguments are essentially amenable to solution by the democratic process—given a relatively stable and cohesive society which has passed beyond the initial agony of capital accumulation—those arising from questions of conscience are not. This is really very obvious. Arguments within a democratic society in which everybody has the vote about who should own what, about which group should have this and which group that, about, that is, the share-out of the national cake, can be settled by compromise. Economic issues are essentially compromisable, because material matters lend themselves perfectly to those small adjustments which are the essence of compromise. If Group X wants a little larger slice of the national cake than Group Y, or Group A wants to improve its share in respect of Group B, these changes can be relatively easily brought about by democratic give-and-take. No doubt, in the course of the bargaining, there will be much thumping of the table, much anger and recrimination, with vested interests digging their toes in and radical reformers asking for the impossible. But behind all this froth there will always lie the possibility of compromise, as our history shows so clearly. The class war might have been devised to demonstrate the practicality of democratic politics. Conflicts over matters of material concern are eminently negotiable, ideally suited to be solved by consensus politics; that is to say by the democratic process. When people are worked up about money a bargain can be struck. It is when they are worked up about morals that they are in danger of coming to blows.

It was, I think, the great mistake of the Marxists to overlook the inherently negotiable nature of economic issues, given a condition of universal franchise; given, that is, universal access to the negotiating process. Of course those in positions of economic privilege were bound to struggle like hell to hang on to what they had got. But in any mature society it was not a very demanding task for the governing order to reconcile the various interests in a manner that avoided undue social tension. My contention, in short, is that democracy in this country, by coinciding with a period when society has been primarily concerned with the production and distribution of wealth, with a period when social divisiveness has largely followed the lines of economic class, has avoided being put to any impossibly difficult challenge. So long as material deprivation guaranteed that the politically active forces in society concenrated on arguing about questions of economic organization and power, it was always relatively easy to get a democratic consensus, since the subjects under debate were essentially adjustable, at any rate in a country like Britain with a long history of national cohesion. One could almost say that lack of affluence, by forcing economic debate into the position of overwhelming prominence which it has enjoyed now for well over a hundred years, has been crucial in the success of the democratic experiment, by guaranteeing that democratic authority should only be challenged by dilemmas well within its capacity to solve. Nobody on either side of the economic barricades felt the necessity of coming to blows, because the democratic process constituted an adequate method of arbitration for what were essentially arbitratable issues.

Moral issues, however, are profoundly different. Moral issues are non-negotiable. Yet it seems that these are the issues which come to the surface as soon as the pressure of economic deprivation is lifted. Nor is this surprising. Material want concentrates the mind on what is a fairly narrow front of human aspirations. We know this as individuals. If we are hungry or thirsty we cannot consider much else beside satisfying these compelling physical needs. The great imponderable questions of truth and beauty, of right and wrong, of God and the Devil, tend to be pushed into the background. Material want tends to simplify life for the individual, to reduce it to essentials. So it does for society. The really difficult questions are not asked. But once affluence is achieved, a society, like an individual, starts tormenting itself with moral conundrums. This is what is happening in the affluent democracies today, forcing them to realize that although counting heads into a consensus was a good enough method to solve divisiveness born of economic strife—because in the final analysis material disputes are by definition negotiable—it is a far less satisfactory method of resolving the problems of democratic politics; far from reducing their temperature, affluence has the reverse effect. In releasing the body politic from a single-minded preoccupation with an area of life that is peculiarly susceptible to compromise and consensus, it helps to open up a range of moral aspiration which is peculiarly unsuitable to those processes.

For as soon as society moves from a preoccupation with material matters to a preoccupation with moral issues, it moves into infinitely deeper waters where the democratic body politic finds itself badly out of its depth. How can a democratic bargain be struck about the morality of nuclear weapons or about the rights and wrongs of playing cricket with South Africa or even about such moral issues as capital punishment, divorce, homosexuality? That society should be free to determine its material dispositions according to the will of the majority would appear irrefutable in theory and acceptable in practice, since in practice the will of the majority, in a mature society, takes minority interests into consideration. It is difficult to see how the moral disposition of a society can be reached so satisfactorily by the same method. If Group A thinks that nuclear weapons are the instruments of the Devil, or Group B thinks that playing cricket with South Africa is morally inexcusable, they are unlikely to change their views because the majority of their fellow countrymen do not share them. Or alternatively, if Groups X, Y and Z are repelled by the idea of living next to people of different race, while Groups A and B think that God ordains such mingling, it is difficult to see how a satisfactory consensus can emerge from such mutually imcompatible moral standpoints.

The dispute over the South African cricket tour is a very significant and alarming example of this difficulty. Those who opposed the tour refused to allow the majority view to prevail and, by threatening violence, compelled the Government of the day to give way to their objections. It was a profoundly undemocratic process, the true nature of which was largely disguised by the moral nature of the issues involved. Translate what happened into a field that has nothing to do with morals. Say a trade union had threatened an industrial concern with large-scale violence unless it withdrew certain plans for moving factories from one area to another—plans which were perfectly lawful. If the Government gave way to the threat, would it not have to be clearly admitted that democratic parliamentary government had collapsed? Power would be seen to have passed from the democratically elected representatives of the people to a violent minority. The same would be true if an industrial organization threatened violence to impose its will on a trade union exercising its lawful rights, and the Government refused to protect those lawful rights. Such a situation has never arisen in this country because the class war has always been fought within the democratic rules. At no point has the working class or the owning class felt it necessary to challenge the laws of the land as determined by Parliament. Each side has been prepared to allow the other the protection of the law; has been prepared, that is, to respect the enemy's rights. This is a vitally important issue to be clear about. Material disputes have often been very bitter, arousing strong passions on either side. But in the final analysis they have always proved resolvable through compromise. Nor, as I say, is this difficult to understand. Such disputes obviously are susceptible of compromise, by their very nature. Public opinion insists that they should be. No minority would be allowed to press a selfish material interest beyond a certain point, and if it tried to do so the Government of the day would have overwhelming support in refusing such a claim. One can go further and say that no minority would conceive of challenging the majority in this way for a material interest. So deeply embedded is the respect for the democratic process in this country, and so successful has it proved in the past in reaching compromise in the material field, that it is as inconceivable for the threat to be made as that it would be conceded.

But in the moral field it has been made and has been conceded. It is essential to ponder this development very carefully, and to be clear about its implications. They are two-fold. First, it is clear that when a minority feels itself possessed of an issue of conscience it is prepared to go outside the democratic process, and when the majority is faced by a minority threatening to use violence for a moral purpose it lacks the will to resist. That was the lesson of the South Africa cricket tour; that moral issues strengthen the will of minorities, who feel justified in challenging majority rule, and weaken the will of the majority, which does not feel justified in defending its rights against claims of conscience.

This is a very formidable new development, with acute relevance to the theme of this chapter. For what we are witnessing in this country is the emergence of a new challenge to democratic order—a challenge that comes from a novel claim to privilege which is challenging democracy more brazenly than any aristocracy or plutocracy of old. It is a privileged minority that rests its claim to power not on property or lineage but on a qualification far more formidable and overwhelming: moral superiority. It does not demand that the wealth of the country should be organized to suit its interests. It demands that its will should prevail in matters of morals, that the quality of society should be determined by its values and according to its tastes.

But in an affluent society more and more of the burning political issues are matters of morals. Nuclear weapons, race, permissiveness, and so on—these are the genuinely divisive issues. How can the majority will prevail in these fields against a minority that claims divine sanction for its views? Democracy is faced today by a new version of the divine right of kings and of the prescriptive right of aristocracies. It is the divine and prescriptive right of the progressive establishment to impose its moral patterns regardless of the majority will. And because this claim is essentially moral it is infinitely less open to democratic compromise than earlier disputes centring on the class struggle.

The class struggle was about wealth, about the distribution of property, about the share-out of the national cake. By its very nature it was susceptible to democratic compromise, since the argument was essentially quantitative not qualitative, about good rather than the Good, about money not morals. The class war, therefore, by its very nature was susceptible to arbitration to the democratic process of give and take.

But moral issues are obviously much less so. A minority armoured in moral self-righteousness is a far more serious threat to democracy than one buttressed by material or social power, because of its claim to have God on its side. The House of Commons made no secret of representing this minority in its vote to abolish capital punishment. Not a single member who voted for abolition pretended that this was what the majority of the people wanted. They boasted, however, that on questions of conscience this did not matter; that it was their duty to consult their individual consciences rather than the voice of the people. Can one imagine present-day M.P.s making a comparable claim on a burning issue in the material field? Or if they did, can one imagine it being so passively accepted? The truth is that the claim to moral rectitude disarms democracy; not only does the claim give the minority an arrogance which no minority furthering its material interest would dare to demonstrate, but it also weakens the resistance of the majority, which is overawed by such a vigorous display of moral passion. Nobody really believes that the voice of the people is the voice of God. The voice of Mammon, yes. But not the voice of God. What has to be recognized is that as the emphasis of politics switches more and more from the material dispositions of society to the moral, majority rule will in practice become more and more difficult to practise. Whereas the contention that everybody should have equal say in determining the physical side of life, the bread and butter issues, has now won universal acceptance—with the corollary that no group should be in a position to challenge this principle through a monopoly of material power—the contention that everybody should have an equal say in the spiritual side of life, with the corollary that no group should be allowed to challenge this principle through a monopoly of moral power, has not won anything like the same universal acceptance.

Yet in the Britain of today the challenge is increasingly coming from a minority not only claiming but actually enjoying a monopoly of moral power. Other minorities at earlier periods have often sought to challenge majority views on certain moral issues of the day, sometimes with glorious success. This, of course, is how the slave trade was abolished, the Catholics emancipated, the Factory Laws introduced. But those earlier crusading minorities were in a profoundly different position from the minority we are talking about today. They were minorities, not only numerically in respect of the population as a whole, but also in respect of the prevailing establishment of the day. Against them were massed not only the prejudices of the masses but the conventional wisdom of the ruling class. The new crusading minority, however, *is* the contemporary establishment, and instead of being opposed by all the institutions of Church and State it is supported by them.

It is not difficult to see how this has happened. The very success in Britain of democratic thought in recognizing the social and economic system so as to dilute the influence of inherited wealth and social position has had the result of elevating educational ability into the primary determinant of political advance. Money-power and land-power have been curtailed. But brain-power has been exalted. The old ladders of social and economic privilege have been blocked with the result that the educational ladder has become increasingly crucial. Economic and social egalitarianism mean in practice that brains, rather than wealth or class, becomes the primary means of political and social advancement. The inevitable trend is toward a governing élite increasingly drawn from the highly educated—government, that is, by the very minority whose claim to moral superiority constitutes today the main threat to democracy.

The Labour Party perfectly illustrates this trend. With each new Parliament its ranks are more and more solidly filled with university teachers, schoolmasters, journalists, intellectuals of one kind or another. To a lesser extent the same trend can be noticed in the Conservative Party. I do not see how this can be avoided, given an egalitarian commitment which insists on either eliminating inherited wealth and social advantage or so disapproving of them as to render their beneficiaries electorally unacceptable. What has to be recognized is that if self-made men are to be the staple raw material from which politicians are chosen, they will have to come increasingly from the ranks of the intelligentsia, since those who are making their own way in business or commerce will—if they are to be successful—be too busy for politics. In an egalitarian system, where there is no traditional ruling class to draw upon, the politicians will increasingly be drawn from those who are successful in activities that can easily be combined with politics, that overlap with politics. The communications media, notably Press and television, obviously come within this category. So, par excellence, do the university arts departments, particularly the sociological faculties. The communications industry generally and the teaching profession—these are the obvious sources of political talent in a society where few other activities allow the successful to have time for politics, or inculcate an aptitude for them. Lawyers will also always be fairly well represented in Parliament, since their training also fits them for Parliamentary life. But in so far as the legal profession is turned into a career genuinely open to talent, with the old-boy network counting for less and less, the lawyers will also tend to be part of the new élite of brainpower. Nor will the trade-union movement guarantee an effective representation of working-class culture, since the brighter working-class boys will also be creamed off into the intelligentsia and put through the indoctrination process of higher education. The Ernest Bevins and Frank Cousinses will be more and more turned into Clive Jenkinses—indistinguishable in their cultural attitudes from all the other members of the new élite drawn primarily from the echelons of higher education.

So long as the divisive issues of politics were overwhelmingly material it could be argued that a propertyless political meritocracy that had reached the top via the educational ladder was in the interests of democracy, since it could be relied upon to protect the majority against capitalist economic exploitation. Its likely anti-capitalist bias could be seen as a useful corrective, in the public interest, to the weight of private economic power. But now that the divisive issues of politics are increasingly in the moral field such an élite must be seen as a threat to democracy, since in these areas, far from being on the side of the majority against the minority, it is on the side of the minority against the majority.

The importance of this point is still woefully misunderstood. Materialism still dominates democratic thought, and it is difficult for us to conceive of minority selfishness in terms other than economic. In fact, however, moral power can be just as selfish, can be used in such a way as to disregard popular needs just as much as material power. Immigration constitutes a perfect example of minority moral power being used in precisely such a way. Until the middle of the 1960s the new élite in all the three political parties pledged this country in principle to the ideal of creating a multi-racial society—an ideal which they sought to implement in practice by allowing unrestricted Commonwealth immigration. A multiracial society was regarded by the new élite as a moral imperative, something which they felt themselves pledged to work towards as a matter of moral obligation. Their peace of mind depended on progress being made as fast as possible in this direction. So they went ahead and allowed unrestricted immigration.

The great mass of the public, however, do not want a multiracial society. The prospect fills them with disquiet. An influx of black and brown faces into their neighbourhood is found unsettling and jarring. Of course it is. Poor and uneducated people are conservative in their habits and tastes, since the immediate world around them, the sights and sounds and smells off the street in which they live, the atmosphere of the pub on the corner, the general tone of the locality, means a great deal to them, since they lack the money and the imagination to inhabit a wider world. Education and wealth open up broader horizons, allow those who possess them to escape both physically and mentally from the constraints that encompass their less fortunate citizens. For the poorer and less well educated, therefore, a multiracial society, translated into the practical terms of living cheek by jowl with people who are strange and different, raises all sorts of acute problems of adaptation. They lack the imagination to enjoy what is exotic and unfamiliar and the means to dilute the physical impact by moving further away. Nor can they be expected to understand the moral obligation which this country is supposed to feel towards the black and brown Commonwealth, since they have not experienced the guilt-inducing experience of contemporary higher education.

The immigration issue, however, is just one of many where the peace of mind of the élite is in direct conflict with the peace of mind of the great mass of the people. What has to be recognized is that the moral patterns of a society which suit the highly educated are not the same as those which suit the less-educated. Take, for example, the key issue of nationalism versus internationalism. For the well-educated internationalism is a tempting option, since they are at home in several cultures and languages. It is not difficult for them to lift their eyes above national frontiers. But for the less well educated linguistic differences represent real barriers. They cling to a national culture and a national domain with a primitive passion, realizing in their bones what it means to ordinary people to have lived together on a certain tract of land and in a certain language for many generations. For the highly educated cosmopolitan élite, patriotism is a bit of an extra which they can do without. But for the uneducated it is a necessity, all they have got. Pride in country is the vicarious satisfaction which they enjoy to make up for all the other inadequacies of humdrum individual lives.

What the liberal progressive establishment has grossly overlooked in recent years is the cruel inequality of sacrifice which a decline in national prestige imposes on different sections of the community, with the heaviest weight falling on those least well equipped to bear the burden. Although the rich, well-educated, powerful and successful enjoy belonging to a powerful State, and may even draw material benefits from doing so, it is a marginal boon which they can be deprived of without any grievous loss of confidence or identity. They have, in their personal lives, much to fall back on: many alternative private sources of satisfaction and status. Their own success and good luck more than make up for the frustrations of national decline.

But for a great many other less fortunate citizens, whose individual lives supply them with little renown, achievement, still less excitement, sense of pride in being British played as crucial a part in their well-being as full employment or social security. The well-educated and successful can afford to dismiss the simple satisfactions of patriotism, and the reassurance to be gained from national greatness, since they can think of themselves as citizens of the world. But for many working people the spectacle of Britain being pushed around, dishonoured and turned into a laughing-stock is a deeply disturbing and distressing experience, since devaluation of their national identity is a deprivation affecting the very quality of life itself.

Yet for at least a decade, under both Tory and Labour Governments, this country has been subjected to a slow but steady diet of setback, insult and humiliation abroad, and an equally steady diet of cynicism, satire, and national denigration at home, both processes combining to give an impression that not only is Britain despised by the rest of the world but that this adverse judgment is more than justified, since the educated élite obviously share it. Masochism, however, is a very sophisticated taste. Only a tiny minority appreciate it. For the great majority it has been a decade of mounting unease made all the more frightening by the refusal of the liberal establishment to recognize and react to the depth of popular concern.

Neither party is wholly to blame. Events have moved with such unprecedented rapidity that our national style and language, bland, generous, tolerant, imperturbable, high-minded, as became a great centre of empire, so confident and complacent about its own superiority as to be able to enjoy jibes and insults from within and without, have not had time to adjust to our new position of weakness. We go on behaving with gentlemanly courtesy, turning the other cheek, dishing out aid to countries that insult us, playing the international game by the rules when others are cheating, pretending that we are still Prefects who have to set an example to the Lower Fourth and kidding ourselves that satire and national denigration are really signs of strength; and are oblivious to the fact that such a national style, while admirable and impressive in Britain's heyday, is now not only absurd but deeply irresponsible, even cruel and heartless, since although a tiny élite may enjoy playing this role of noblesse oblige, and may not notice what fools they are making of themselves, it is the ordinary people who are being called upon to pay the price of their rulers' refusal to develop a tougher, more cussed, less high-minded and more realistic style of politics suitable for a small country with its back against the wall.

What so many people are beginning to sense is that Britain

today is enjoying neither the warm glow of virtue rewarded nor the heady delights of kicking over the traces; it is functioning with all the solemn airs of a major power without enjoying any of its satisfactions, and suffering all the indignities of weakness without any of the attendant freedoms from restraint. It is a national posture quite peculiarly well designed to cut off the pleasures of patriotism from those who need them most.*

The same considerations apply to traditional morality. It is easy enough for a sophisticated intelligentsia to adapt to a period of rapid moral flux. They enjoy the excitement and drama of change. Shocking the masses is a positive pleasure. But for the less well educated the process of adaptation is agonizingly painful. They lack the moral resources to be able to live their lives outside a framework of rules and regulations, without the landmarks which have made the moral landscape familiar for centuries.

The point I am trying to make is that the kind of Britain which an élite determined by educational superiority is likely to create may well serve the cause of social justice in the material sense, may well guarantee a fair distribution of wealth, may well save the people from economic exploitation, may well, in all these respects, be a striking improvement on the former hereditary ruling class based on social and economic privilege. But in the non-material fields it could be a far less satisfactory guarantor of the general interest because its needs, its preoccupations, perhaps even its ideals, are not only profoundly different from those of the masses, but in many ways actually in direct conflict with them.

There have, of course, always been minorities who have sought to give the majority a lead in matters of morals, which is absolutely as it should be—for example, the slave trade and so on. But the situation then was quite different from what it is today. Those were examples of minority groups arguing their case, preaching their cause, with such conviction that the establishment of the day conceded them victory. But the new moral minority *is* the establishment. It is both advocate and judge; it is in a position both to press for reforms

---

* It is greatly to Mr Heath's credit that he is trying to change this.

that suit its taste and to concede them; its foot is on the accelerator of change and nobody else's is on the brake.

The point that needs to be grasped is that as we have gradually adjusted the social system so as to deny social rank and property a disproportionate influence on the political process—with results that have led to a marked improvement in social justice conceived in material terms—we have accorded brainpower a comparable hegemony which is leading to a new kind of social injustice—the injustice that comes from allowing society to be shaped according to moral and cultural patterns which cruelly overlook the needs and concerns, fears and even prejudices of the great mass of ordinary people.

In this respect there is not a great deal of difference between at least the leaderships of the two political parties. Both are increasingly dominated by men and women who, however much they disagree about the organization of industry, about nationalization, the social services, and so on, share a progressive, liberal point of view on matters of morals—believe, that is, in multiracialism, in sexual permissiveness, in internationalism, in the abolition of capital punishment, in short, in creating what Mr Roy Jenkins, to cries of approval from the then Sir Edward Boyle, called 'the civilized society'. What is so disturbing, however, is that what they call a 'civilized' society is one which the great majority of ordinary people find unrecognizably alien and unlovable.

This point cannot be emphasized too strongly: a 'civilized' Britain means a country which the reigning minority approves of, finds congenial to its predispositions—a country made in their image. It is a Britain with a guilt complex about her imperial past, and therefore disposed to believe in her duty to open her shores to coloured immigration, and to romanticize the underdeveloped world. It is a Britain with little concern for preserving the national identity, nationalism being deemed old-fashioned and primitive, and therefore, disposed to romanticize the potentialities of federal Europe. It is a Britain which, because she is fascinated with moral permissiveness—authoritarian regulation being regarded as unnecessary if not harmful—is peculiarly susceptible and sympathetic to student agitation. It is a Britain soft on law and order, because the retribution side of punishment is seen as a hangover of barbarism. It is a Britain with a contempt for tradition and continuity, since the need for both is ignored. In a word, it is a Britain fit for intellectuals to live in.

One would not wish to argue that such a Britain is wholly undesirable. Many of the ideals of civilization which it would embody have much to commend them. But the fact cannot be gainsaid that such a Britain is socially unjust in a far deeper sense than it ever was as a result of the maldistribution of wealth and property; far more likely to disintegrate through lack of moral cohesion than it ever was through lack of economic cohesion; far more two nations, in the sense of being divided on moral issues, than it ever was when the divisions were basically material. The truth which has to be recognized is that the new political élite yearns for a kind of Britain— multiracial, internationalist, permissive, youth-dominated, without tradition or continuity—which simple people find hell on earth to live in; against which they react with sullen apathy, feeling neither able to understand what is happening nor able to do anything effective to stop it.

Yet such a political élite is bound to result from the present egalitarian social system, where success on the educational ladder is increasingly the crucial passport to political power and influence. It is perfectly true, of course, that in the British kind of mixed economy large tracts of social life are immune from the control of the political élite. So far as consumption is concerned market forces still very largely prevail. But this tends to make the problem worse rather than better. It is impossible to overlook the extent to which all the institutions of Church and State are falling under the influence of an unrepresentative minority whose tastes and values are not those of the majority, while those in the economic field that are still unaffected by this minority—notably in the field of consumption—are in the hands of an economic élite which is not allowed to be socially responsible, which, out of deference to the egalitarian principle, is expressly denied the economic security of tenure out of which social responsibility springs. In other words, the shape of society is being increasingly determined in part by a political élite dominated by the values of the intelligentsia, and in part by an economic élite deminated by the lack of values of the huckster—a combination that means in practice that the public is at the mercy of politicians who aim above their heads and businessmen who aim below their navels.

What has this to do with the problem of leadership, with which this chapter is concerned? The point I am seeking to establish is that the new political and economic élites, born of an egalitarian social system, constitute a peculiarly unsatisfactory governing order, the former being provocatively and intolerably superior and the latter corruptingly and cynically inferior, the political élite seeking to create a society that demands too much of ordinary people, and the economic élite seeking to create one that demands too little. This is an absurd and impossible situation, since the political élite tends all the time to work towards a society which would only be viable if all its members were very superior persons—a society, that is, cast in its own mould—while the economic élite militates in the opposite direction—towards a society organized around the principle of appealing to the lowest common denominator of popular taste which would only be tolerable if all its members were very inferior persons. Such a governing order is at once superhuman and subhuman; at once too good and too bad, too good for ordinary people to identify with and too bad for them to be able to respect.

Let us take two representative examples of what egalitarianism has produced, Roy Jenkins for the political élite, and Lew Grade for the economic. What a combination! I do not believe that a governing order so constituted can survive. Yet before it can be improved and strengthened a conscious decision has to be taken: to re-create a social system that can render the political élite more vulgar and the economic élite less so—a social system which humanizes the one and civilizes the other, which, in a word, produces a style of leadership in all fields that is impressive without being alien, and popular without being populist.

These used to be the characteristics of Britain's governing class, which the pressures of democracy have done so much to destroy. The question today is whether this process may not have gone too far. America, which adopted egalitarianism far earlier than us, is busily rowing back, just as we are rowing forward, regardless of the American experience. But in both countries, as much in America which is splashing around in an effort to create a class structure as in Britain which is splashing around to destroy one, there is a refusal to bring the matter of class back into the calm water of dispassionate analysis. Yet this is what is most urgently needed in both countries, since it is absolutely clear that neither capitalism nor socialism, or the present combination of a bit of both, can produce a governing order that is at once sufficiently popular and authoritative to preside over the problems of a free and affluent society.

9

The question which we are considering is whether contemporary democratic affluent societies can be successfully governed without some form of a ruling class; whether, that is, an egalitarian social system, a classless society can adequately grapple with its problem of authority. I do not believe that an affirmative answer is at all obvious. In all fields of activity there has been a breakdown of authority, in the sense that those who give the orders are not at all certain by what right they do so, and those who receive them do so with mounting reluctance, the former feeling apologetic and uncomfortable, and the latter resentful and ill used. How could it be otherwise in a society where Jack has been expressly taught to feel as good as his master, and where society has been increasingly organized with the express intention of blurring class distinctions? Just as for hundreds of years society was expressly organized to inculcate habits of authority among the few and habits of deference among the many, in recent years pressure has been applied in the opposite direction: to break the habit of authority at the top and the habit of deference at the bottom. I am not saying for a moment that this was not a necessary switch of emphasis at the time it was first applied, because society had manifestly become too rigid. The question is whether it is a desirable emphasis for all time, and in particular for the present time.

The question, it may be objected, is at best academic. For do not the forces of democracy demand and insist on an egalitarian society? Certainly it used to be assumed that they did. But the assumption today strikes me as increasingly dubious. What has to be realized is that the forces of democracy, *in practice*, compel society towards a shape that is highly inegalitarian, since if the popular insistence on high material living standards is to be met, it is necessary to reorganize industry and commerce, local and central government, the administrative structure, all in a manner which, like it or not, concentrates power in the hands of the few more than ever before.

Doubtless great efforts will be made to minimize the disagreeable consequences of technological progress. We shall hear a lot about consultation and participation in industry and devolution in government and so on. But none of these measures can possibly alter the fact that the business of working in ever larger combines, of living in ever larger conurbations, of being governed by ever larger federal structures, is increasing the extent to which the many are pushed around by the few. This then is the first point to be clear about. The structure of modern technological society is such as to place a great deal of power into relatively few hands —to demand from them a very active role—and to demand from the majority an unprecedented degree of voluntary acquiescence. This trend, moreover, is not running against the democratic grain; it is running with it. It is impossible to conceive of a modern democratic society—that is to say one in which the masses have the political power to insist on a high standard of living—which does not necessitate a great deal of rationalization, the consequence of which in reality is that the many have to be willing to do what the few decide. And the more democratic the society is the more inevitable this trend becomes, precisely because the material well-being which the people demand—and insist on getting—will accelerate all the technological processes which have the effect of concentrating power in the hands of the few.

The point that has to be realized is that political democracy, in this sense, is compelling society to organize itself in a manner that requires authoritative leaders and acquiescent followers, since without such ingredients the national cake will never be large enough to meet the democratic appetite. What is equally apparent is that this process of reorganization is taking place very rapidly. Giant industrial combines—not to mention giant trade unions—are being formed which require fomidable qualities of leadership in those who lead them and enlarge the gap in power between management and men (or leaders and the led). The bureaucracy, too, grows ever larger —despite the best Tory efforts to reverse the trend—since the more people expect from the State the more authoritative must be the instrument which meets the demand. The same goes for the governance of the great conurbations. Unless anarchy is to prevail, the authorities will need to be vastly strengthened in their powers. In other words, there is going to be no diminution of the need for a minority to give orders and for the many to receive them. Far from having found a way of so organizing society that everybody is his own boss and all decisions are taken jointly, we are in fact moving steadily away from this utopian ideal, and we are moving away from it, not in spite of democratic pressure but very largely because of it.

During the period of the first postwar Labour Government this trend was easy enough to disguise. It was possible to pretend that democratic socialism was in process of creating a society that genuinely corresponded to the egalitarian ideal. It seemed as if there really was an affirmative answer to the question posed some eighty-five years earlier by Alfred Marshall at the Cambridge Reform Club: 'The question,' he said, 'is not whether all men will ultimately be equal—that they certainly will not be—but whether progress may not go on steadily, if slowly, till, by occupation at least, every man is a gentleman?' One could point in those early Attlee days to a number of hopeful signs. Not only were modern technological developments sharply diminishing the need for degrading manual work, so that there was a tendency—which automation and computerization have subsequently done much to encourage—for the whole population to develop into one vast white-collar class. The machine also promised, by making possible the mass production of good-quality products at cheap prices and by the mass dissemination of popular culture through radio and television, largely to destroy the contrasts in life styles that used to mark off one class from another. This process has been carried far further in the United States than it has been here in England. But even in this country it is becoming increasingly difficult to tell the difference between, for example, the businessman's wife and his typist by the clothes they wear, the food they buy, the way they spend their evenings. In the U.S. it has even been found necessary to erect artificial consumer distinctions to divide one social grade from another. Managing directors, for example, drive Cadillacs, vice-presidents Buicks, and so on down the scale to foremen with De Sotos and wage hands with Chevrolets and Plymouths. But to the uninitiated the difference between one powerful and luxurious limousine and another is more formal than real, just as the differences in privilege at the Court of Versailles between a Duke, who was allowed to put on the King's slippers, and a Vicomte, who only handed the vest, were quite without any real content.

Class distinctions in this country are also increasingly blurred by shared welfare facilities that were made available to all. I do not mean by this simply that these services involve taxing the rich and subsidizing the poor. This aspect of the equalizing effect of the social services was always less important in the long run than the equality of experience which they imposed on all classes. Nearly everyone, it was thought, would become a panel patient; all would learn what it was to have an insurance card stamped, or to collect a pension or children's allowance from the post office. The doctor's waiting-room would join the confessional, the polling-booth and the law court as places where class distinctions counted for nothing. And as more and better council houses and more and better state schools became available, the drawing-room and the schoolroom would be added to the list.

It is not surprising that this prospect should have gripped the imagination of some political leaders—in all parties—who in the 1950s were already talking as if the classless society was just around the corner. What however was overlooked then, and is now so dismally apparent, was that the industrial methods needed to produce this social cornucopia would also necessitate the organization of industry into larger and larger units, which in turn would widen the gap between the *power* of those at the top of the hierarchy and that of those at the bottom. In the giant combines that today dominate the industrial scene, the chief executive, the managerial staff, and above all the small group of technicians and engineers who design and maintain the crucial machines on which everything now depends—this industrial élite enjoys a degree of potentially unfettered power to which the nineteenth-century entrepreneur could never aspire. Although the workers are better organized than they have ever been before, the pivotal processes of industry depend less and less on their services. The steady draining away of the workers' fundamental bargaining power has been disguised by the fact that keeping wages down is no longer the principal concern of corporations; it is less important now to keep wages down than to use the new machines in increasing productivity per man-hour. And it is less important to be near a supply of cheap labour than to have control of a patent pool. This shift in the competitive strategy of corporations, although it has seemed to augment the workers' bargaining power by leading to a free-and-easy attitude to wage demands, will in the long run have precisely the reverse effect.

The bargaining power of labour is also likely to be affected by another development which, strange as it may seem, the workers are welcoming with open arms: the extension of wages into the field of social rights. Every discussion of wage rates and indeed professional salaries is now dominated by the notion of status. What *ought* an engine-driver to earn? Would twice as much as a plate-layer be fair? The claim is not merely for a basic living wage with such variations above that level as can be extracted from the conditions in the market at the moment. The claims of status are to a hierarchical wage structure, each level of which represents a social right and not merely a market value. Every British citizen now regards himself as having the right, inherent in his particular status, to a particular wage or salary. Since it is the prime duty of governments to guarantee each citizen his rights, it follows that wages cannot be left to labour–management haggling, any more than a man's right to vote can be left to a bargain struck with the polling officer. The responsibility of determining what constitutes a just wage rests, therefore, in the last resort on the State. This shift from contract to status as a means of determining wage differentials has, to date, vastly benefited labour. But by invoking this right, labour has un-corked a genie that may be something less than benevolent. The State is obliged to accord each citizen his rights; but each citizen is precluded from demanding more than his rights. If wages are not the result of a bargain or contract, but are rather the reflection of what society considers to be a particular group's status rights, then for anyone to insist on higher wages may be comparable to his demanding more than one vote. Moreover, if the wages are to be determined like tax exemptions, on the ground of social value, the corresponding duties (in this case efficiency, productivity, regularity of attendance, and so on) will need to become as obligatory as tax payments. This is indeed the direction in which we are moving.

I emphasize the increasing disparity between, on the one hand, the practical power of management and technicians in industry today, combined with the new authority over wages which the State is so eager to assume, and, on the other hand, the real declining power of labour's bargaining position, because this is something which the new equality in consumer patterns has tended to camouflage. Because the chief executive (and the trade-union leader) wear the same suit as the packaging clerk, chuckle at the same comic strip, even consult the same doctor, it is dangerously easy to overlook the significant fact that in terms of power they are probably more widely separated than the feudal baron and the serf.

In all fields of human activity, in politics, administration, commerce, and even the mass media, the power to take meaningful decisions is concentrated in fewer and fewer hands. Today, for example, instead of the countless small shops serving particular neighbourhoods, with innumerable individual merchants deciding how best to attract and influence local custom, we increasingly have giant chain-stores, controlled by one central board of management, with mass centrally directed advertising replacing the personal interplay between individual customer and tradesman. Again, instead of innumerable independent entrepreneurs exercising absolute control over the private concerns, we have massive state and private corporations whose broad policies are laid down by central directing boards. The power of management in a massive firm like, for example, Courtaulds, although limited by counter-balancing trade-union strength in the field of wages and working conditions, is truly dazzling in other directions. A decision taken perhaps by two or three senior executives in London can transform in a few months—as nylon actually did—the clothing habits of millions of women in every continent. To an extent that would have seemed incredible a few decades ago, modern management can, through centralized administration and marketing methods, revolutionize the habits, tastes and even environment of whole populations. If the old-fashioned aristocracies had the power to force people to conform unwillingly to their wishes, the modern industrial élites enjoy unique instruments for psychic manipulation that make people willingly behave as they want them to.

The same concentration of authority can be seen in the trade unions, with negotiations at the factory level largely replaced by decisions reached at the national level. In the armed forces the army commander of today can exert such detailed authority over subordinate formations that all intermediate chains of command have been vastly reduced in effective independence. In any future atomic war only the small group deciding where and when to drop the bombs will have any significant part to play in the conduct of affairs.

It may well be true, of course, that in a society made up of a few concentrated centres of power some kind of balance is struck. Concentrated labour strength, for example, balances concentrated capital; the chain-stores, with their monopoly over distribution, curb industrial corporations with their monopoly over production. But this, it seems to me, does not alter the fact that in all the main activities in which human beings are engaged the ratio between those who make the meaningful decisions and those who carry them out, between those whose lives are active and those whose lives are passive, between those who form opinions and those who receive them, gets steadily wider.

My point is that it is highly unwise to allow the increasing similarity—or apparent similarity—between patterns of consumption at all levels in society to obscure this trend. Because the democratic five-star general, for example, wears a very similar uniform to the private and lives in very similar quarters, we all too easily forget that his actual control over the men under his command is far greater than that exerted by the aristocratic Duke of Wellington over the press-ganged recruit. Modern technology has thrown up a smokescreen of consumer equality which obscures the growing abyss that cuts off the power élites in the political, bureaucratic, industrial and military fields from the masses.

Current talk about an egalitarian and classless society, therefore, strikes me as either irrelevant nonsense or mischievous deception—propaganda put out by the new élites to distract attention from the true developments. Equality, in fact, is replacing religion as the new opiate of the people. Just as medieval society asserted that equality at the altar rail excused inequality everywhere else, so today our new masters pretend that consumer equality in the chain-store is the only equality that matters. I fear that the relative extension of material equality in this century will afford the strong just as good excuse to exploit their power as did the idea of equality before God in the Middle Ages. The old strata of society are being destroyed, but they are being replaced by strata no less unequal for the fact that their inequality is less obvious.

This is the point. It is idle to continue pretending that we are moving towards an egalitarian society. Given the pattern of modern industrial society, the choice facing us is not between an inegalitarian class structure and an egalitarian classless society. It is between various forms of inegalitarian stratification. British democratic socialists consistently evade this issue from fear of antagonizing their working-class allies and going against the egalitarian sentiment historically bound up with the Labour movement. But few others now deny that a modern economy requires a high degree of social stratification. Managers and technicians must be given encouragement similar to that enjoyed by the entrepreneurs in the heyday of capitalism (nowhere, of course, is this better recognized than in Russia). Because in the last few years all the emphasis in this country has been on depriving the old upper and middle classes of their privileges it has been easy to ignore the fact that new élites with new privileges are growing up to take their place. This has enabled democratic socialists to advocate the abolition of class without having to defend the creation of élites. They can pretend that the classless society has all the virtues of bringing sections of the community closer together without admitting that a society divided into élites and non-élites also cuts off the many from the few, although on a different principle. But if we are honest and realistic, the choice we must make in the next few years is not between equality and inequality but between two different systems of stratification. What I am trying to suggest is that a class structure has, as against an élite structure, certain virtues which a liberal society would be foolish to discard; certain virtues which may well be more popular with the masses than those attaching to élites.

For a class system does not come to terms with the problem of authority, in that it makes its exercise seem *natural*, as much to those who give the orders as to those who receive them. Each section of society behaves as to the manner born. To all of us brought up on egalitarian assumptions such a thought will seem profoundly repugnant, since for half a century the best minds have been seeking to break the habits of both authority and deference. And they have been highly successful. Jack now does feel himself as good as his master, and his master feels himself no better than Jack. But the trouble is that although socialism has created this climate of egalitarianism it has failed—and now even abandoned the attempt to carry on the attempt—to create a real world that corresponds to this utopian dream. The real world of power and organization is increasingly one in which the few are called upon to shoulder unprecedented burdens of responsibility and the many to accept on trust the dictates of those who are deemed to know best—more than ever before in history. This is not a real world that is coming into existence in defiance of socialism; still less in defiance of democracy. It is the real world conjured up by democratic socialism, the real world that is bound to arise from applying the use of human reason to the mass demands of an enfranchised industrial population. The facts are absolutely clear. The more we seek to plan the productive resources of the country to meet the rising material aspirations of all the people, the more necessary it becomes to build up the authority of the planners and the compliance of those who are planned for. I do not mean the dictatorial *power* or the *enslaved* compliance. I mean the ability of the planners to exert a form of authority that inspires voluntary compliance.

But the trouble about egalitarianism is that it does precisely the opposite. It creates a social climate in which the exercise of authority is made as difficult as possible; in which the unequal lives which people are called upon to experience in reality bear no relation to the values with which they are imbued. It produces a social system, in short, at war with its organizational structure, a social relationship between the élites and the masses that induces the maximum guilt among the former and the maximum frustration among the latter. What I am pleading for is a reassessment of this unhealthy situation; a reassessment that starts from the acceptance of stratification as an unavoidable necessity and goes on to consider how the social system can best make this necessity acceptable and civilized. Once it is recognized that democratic socialism cannot create a society where authority is genuinely shared, and must in reality create a society where power is more unequally shared than ever before, it is the height of irresponsibility to insist on promoting a social system that conflicts with reality. The brutal truth is that if Jack is not as good as his master, nothing but harm accrues from telling him that he is, educating him as if he is, just as nothing but harm accrues from insisting that his master lives a social lie based on disguising his superiority. Élites are a functional answer to the problem of inequality, a recognition of the reality, but one which strips it of all the consoling magic that makes a class system so much more human and acceptable. Under democratic socialism élites are allowed to exercise power, but denied all the social trappings that makes its exercise seem natural, just as those over whom they exercise power are allowed to be bossed, but without being brought up in a manner that makes compliance seem natural. This is to have the worst of both worlds: inequality in fact, but a form of inequality that refuses to allow the experience to be tempered by all the classical methods by which a class system makes the best of a bad job, by inducing authority and responsibility at the top, born of security, and voluntary compliance at the bottom born of a natural respect which is expressly promoted instead of being, as at present, consistently undermined.

At the moment, of course, the scales are heavily weighted against the concept of class, not only by orthodox egalitarian sentiment, but also by the failure of the British ruling and owning class in recent years to come to terms with the technological revolution. The great triumph of the British upper class, and the source of its continuing strength in the nineteenth century, was the way in which the landed interests blended with, and tamed, the aspiring capitalist élites thrown up by the industrial revolution. Its great failing in the post-war years was its inability to absorb and civilize the élites produced by the technological revolution. Not only was the ruling class miserably slow in approaching the industrial significance of technology and modern managerial skills; it also, as a result of this blindness, failed to appreciate the need for winning the loyalty of the new social groups which this revolution has thrown up. Politicians, like generals, always fight their campaigns with weapons and strategy of previous wars. Because the post-war Tory Party was conscious of its prewar failure to command the confidence of the working class, it concentrated in the fifties primarily on making good this defect, while making no attempt, except in words, to enlist the loyalty and energies of the new crucial sector—the technologists, engineers, managers, whose skills held the key to the country's future. Lord Woolton, it is true, made a valiant effort in this direction in the 1950 and 1951 election campaigns, but the subsequent Conservative Governments failed, once elected, to fulfil his implicit electoral promises. (Whether Mr Heath will do any better remains to be seen.) Society, with a capital S, which was once only too prone to embrace new wealth-producing élites, showed little or no interest in their modern counterparts. The social frustration of these Lucky Jims in the 1950s was a revealing condemnation of the class structure. Self-made dons—so long as they studied the humanities—barristers, journalists, politicians, could all be found dining and wining at the Establishment tables, but the new industrial élites were kept at a distance. Much more important, of course, their moment of functional breakthrough saw no comparable breakthrough in their capacity to earn and save. For the first time a new élite was allowed to feel that its utility did not guarantee it a place in the ruling class. This failure of the traditional ruling class to attract into its ranks the contemporary élite was the result not so much of rigidity as of anaemia; fiscal bloodlettings had drained away not only class wealth but also class responsibility. It was not so much a case of the upper-class embrace failing to work; it was not attempted, with the result that the class system came to be seen as an obstacle standing in the way of ambition rather than the coveted goal on which ambitions are pinned.

I am the first to admit, therefore, that the 1950s were a period when it was right for an aspiring élite to seek, through the Labour Party, to expel a previous governing class. History is full of such examples; and such élites, once they have achieved power, have usually themselves formed a governing class, modelling themselves on the style of their predecessors so as to maintain the continuity. But it is one thing to believe that the social hierarchy requires reshuffling, for a particular purpose, at a particular stage in a country's development, as was the case in Britain after the war. It is quite another to argue that this process should be raised from a temporary expedient into a permanent principle. At the moment we are in danger of assuming that because egalitarianism was a useful instrument for reshuffling society at a given moment it is also suitable as a guiding principle for its long-term ordering.

The doctrine of equality can fulfil a vital role in breaking down an over-rigid class structure and in maintaining the necessary degree of social mobility. But a society that raises this secondary virtue to its principal objective—as the Labour Party would still have us do—is likely to defeat its own purpose. Surely it is now clear that the exercise of power in a modern industrial state is far too comprehensive, far too easy, far too irresistible to be left to professional élites whose authority is undiluted by the human weaknesses and failings of a hereditary ruling class. Moreover, resistance to State power today can only be effective in a society where the lower strata contain men of independence and ability who, in a classless society stratified on a strict basis of merit, are increasingly creamed off at birth. I do not believe that, if Britain had been a classless society in the nineteenth century, the temptations to misuse the new sources of wealth would have been resisted by the governing élite any more than they were resisted by the governing class of the day. The only difference would have been that the workers, with their potential leaders creamed off into management, would never have organized the Labour movement.

We are now passing through a new technological revolution, quite as far-reaching socially as the industrial revolution, which is not only providing those in command with oppor-tunities for exercising unprecedented power but also depriving most of those underneath of the stimuli of material want. I can think of no worse moment to create a social system that both disguises the exercise of power—by separating it from obvious and recognizable social privilege—and makes resistance doubly hard by depriving the workers of both potential leadership and moral justification for opposing the State.

Let me admit at once that social class has two obvious disadvantages as a principle of dividing society. First it allows a great many individuals of no social value to enjoy privileges which they have done nothing to deserve; secondly, it arouses resentments among those who would themselves enjoy these positions, if ability rather than birth was the determining factor in social stratification. Class divisions, therefore, tend to be both socially inefficient and individually unjust, making for a badly run and discontented society. Thus runs the familiar argument. But on the evidence of the last few years it is very arguable that élites have far more serious faults. The first thing that opponents of class must offer is some alternative system by which those most fitted by individual merit to wield power in the various fields—political, administrative, cultural, economic, religious, scientific—are picked and appointed. This can be done by the State bureaucracy or by local councils on a strict basis of competitive examinations, or it can be done by the governing élites themselves on a basis of personal choice. In each case, however, some groups in society will have the power to decide which qualities justify promotion. Government and administration by élites chosen on merit can only mean that those at the top at any given moment decide whom they will recruit to join them in their lofty eminence. It will be their decision, rather than birth or money, that determines whether a man makes good. They will set the examinations and correct the results. They will preside over the interviewing boards that separate the sheep from the goats. They will determine the qualities that justify

231

recruitment into the élites. Promotion, in fact, will depend entirely on a man's ability and willingness to conform with the tastes, standards and manners of his superiors. To be compatible with the men at the top it would be necessary to act like them, to think like them, to look like them or at least to display oneself to them in such a way as to create this impression. If everyone is dependent absolutely on impressing his superiors —and in a society where everyone starts from scratch this is the case—then right from his earliest days each child will concentrate on fitting in with the prevailing patterns. Up to a certain point in the hierarchy, professional merit—formally determined by objective criteria and based on skilful performance of professional duties—might prevail. But the higher reaches of the hierarchy will always be kept for those who embody the political views and social mores of those on top. Conformity, in short, becomes the one safe road to success.

Up to a point, of course, this is also how an upper class operates. We are all conscious of old-school-tie exclusiveness and class nepotism. But the very element of *hereditary* privilege which egalitarians criticize most fiercely guarantees that an upper class always includes a minority who can afford— to put it no higher—the luxury of independence. Leaving aside the political benefits of a class strong enough and independent enough to stand up to the State power—what a massive debt, incidentally, British liberty owes to the Whig aristocracy—it does seem to me of prime importance to preserve some elements in society from the need to make their own way in the world. A class system ensures that at least a sizeable minority without personal ambition reach positions of power and influence. The very irrationality of a class structure based on birth, the fact that the top levels contain individuals both wise and foolish, able and inept, useful and useless, a cross-section in short of all the human virtues and vices, avoids that total lack of common understanding that cuts off an élite, based exclusively on merit, from the rest of society that has not made the grade.

An upper class may feel superior and a lower class may feel inferior; but how much more rigid and unfraternal is a society in which those at the top not only feel but *are* superior and those at the bottom not only feel but *are* inferior—and know it. The very evils of a society stratified by money and birth at least avoid the worst danger of all—a society dominated by men whose privileges are invulnerable because entirely deserved.

A few years ago these objections might have seemed fanciful. But we are already beginning to experience their relevance? Was the old governing class ever so remote from the experience of ordinary people as the new élites are today? Has there ever been such a wide gap in cultural attitudes between the top and bottom of society as there is today? Has the problem of two nations ever been so marked? The Labour Party is a microcosm of this trend, which it perfectly embodies. Its members in the House of Commons are admirable representatives of the new meritocracy. But they are less representative of ordinary people than was the Tory Party in its most exclusive days. But this is true of all the new élites who all share a common distinction, superior brainpower, in one form or another, which is the most absolute and provocative distinction of all.

But let us assume, for the sake of confounding the argument, that a society stratified on a strict basis of merit is a desirable goal. The next problem facing the egalitarian is how to prevent the élites at any given moment from solidifying their position at the top. Historically, social classes began as élites whose initial privileges resulted from some function which they fulfilled for the visible advantage of society. The members of the original élites spread their privileges to their relations and children who, in turn, passed them down to their relations and children until, like a tree, each member of the élite had produced a lush foliage of privilege casting its protective shadow down the centuries. In other words, a ruling class is an élite or a collection of élites which has grown over the generations into an organic body quite transcending the original purpose—military, administrative, entrepreneurial—for which it was formed. If generations were like stratified rocks, superimposed one on another but not interconnected, then it would be easy enough to organize society with exclusive reference to the individual merit of those who make up each new generation. But men are not born orphans and do not die bachelors. Each individual, being both child and parent, grandchild and grandparent, has interests that bridge many generations. So long, therefore, as the family remains the basic social unit any recognition of individual merit will inevitably set up a chain reaction leading to the formation of social class.

One way, of course, for the egalitarian to escape this result is to make sure that every member of society enjoys more or less similar means. But this is to assume that potential élite members will exert their talents without any special rewards, for the pleasure of patriotism and public service. It is, of course, just possible to imagine a political élite governing for the sheer pleasure of power, or a military élite risking their lives for the glory of it, or artists producing great works because they feel the urge. But the creation of wealth, which is the crucial role of the bourgeois, is another question. Business, commerce, industry—none of these occupations is vocational. They attract simply as means of making money. For a country like Britain that depends so absolutely on trade and industry, it is essential that capable men enter these fields, which means that they must hold out prospects of profit. It is only reasonable to assume, therefore, that in any social system suitable for this country, whether it be socialist or capitalist, there will be a sizeable section of the population with a great deal more money, or more of the advantages money can buy, than the remainder. The Labour Party has, as we know, reluctantly but unmistakably now reached this conclusion.

There are only two ways of preventing this section from forming itself into a social class. Either the State allows the wealth-producing élite to accumulate and spend fortunes during their lifetimes, but confiscates this capital on the death of every individual member of the élite through a death duty; or it allows the individual élite member to live a luxurious life himself, while actually on the job, so to speak, but makes sure that his family are rigorously excluded from these benefits. Death duties sufficiently steep to be effective in preventing the carry-over of privilege from one generation to the next are clearly self-defeating: it is simply no incentive to allow a man to lavish money on his family during his lifetime if he knows that, on his death, his children will be deprived of the means to maintain anything like the same standards. The modern Labour Party, therefore, prefers the system that precludes the family as far as possible right from the beginning. But this system has its own follies, as an examination of the system of business expenses reveals.*

Whatever may be the economic justification of business expenses, their social consequence is to enable individuals presumed to be fulfilling socially useful functions to escape from the dreariness of their home lives. Take a typical day in the life of a business executive or professional man, supposing that he has inherited no capital. Living in a small house without servants, he probably cooks his own breakfast, while his wife dresses the children for school. But from the moment he steps on the accelerator of the office-financed motor-car, he speeds into a different world. In his office he is served by a bevy of secretaries who have no objection to 'sirring' him, whereas the 'char' at home—supposing he can afford one— would never think of calling his wife 'madam'; he entertains a client to luncheon at an expensive restaurant, choosing dishes and wines that he would never consider if the bill were his personal responsibility, while his wife back home is sitting down to scrambled eggs in the kitchen. If he is a member of the professional élite, he will probably lunch at his club, savouring a glass of Tio Pepe before the meal—at home it would more likely be something cheaper, possibly South African, although that is not likely—while breathing in the plush comfort, the old silver, good claret, deferential and dexterous butling, oil paintings on the walls of Edwardian upper-middle-class life which he is utterly incapable of reproducing in his own home. A whole generation has grown up since the war who know of the amenities of life only through their business and public lives. Just as the universities, monasteries, and cathedral closes maintained a tradition of civilized living during the Dark Ages, so today it is left almost entirely to corporate institutions to preserve style and manners in daily living. By day the élite member is a man of substance, with the prestige, tastes, habits of a privileged being, dispensing tips to grateful attendants, hailing taxis with seigneurial

* Although the Labour Government altered the tax concessions on these, they are still a major part of the new social order.

command, cut off from the common run by his expense account immunity. In the evening, with the office-financed magic carpet garaged for the night, he is just another suburban father, for whom the cellar means not wine for the dining-room table but coke for the boiler. His day will end, as it probably began, at the sink.

It is now relatively easy for a young man with ability, through grants, scholarships, and so on, to raise himself from a low social origin to positions high in the hierarchy. But, at least in the professional élites, however high he climbs his monetary rewards (after taxation) will not enable him to lead a life conspicuously different from the conditions of his origin. He himself, in his role as a successful barrister or journalist, will enjoy a vastly superior existence, but his wife and children—unless they are fiddled into the business structure—will be only marginally better off than they would have been if the husband had never made good. A society that encourages a man to beautify his flat and mistress—if they are for purposes of business prestige—everything in fact except his home, wife and children, clearly regards the family more as a biological necessity than as the basis of the social order.

In business, of course, the socialists still allow salaries high enough even after taxation to enable their recipients to buy houses, educate their children, and generally enjoy a distinctive and superior family life. But this is a loophole that they are still determined to close. At the moment, private industry offers high salaries so as to tempt able men into its service and the nationalized industries, unless they are to make do with the second best, have to follow suit. But one of the recurring socialist arguments for further nationalization—the only one that is now heard—is that only when the State can determine the salary scale for the majority of industry will present inequalities of income be ironed out. The intention is that although élite members themselves must inevitably be allowed high incomes, the taxation system must be such as to prevent them from benefiting their families; prevent them, that is, from developing a distinctive and superior way of life.

It seems to me that the price socialists are prepared to pay to prevent élites spreading their privileges to their families, thereby forming themselves into a social class, can now be seen to be far too high. The vast majority of mankind are willing to forego satisfaction of present desires in the name of future benefits for one reason only—their children. There are always a few exceptional people who will act selflessly in the long term in the interest of their country or community, but they are a declining minority. In times of national emergency perhaps a majority will act in this way. But only family pride canalizes individual selfishness into social channels consistently and comprehensively through the length and breadth of society. The fundamental error of socialism is the belief that human beings will be willing, as citizens, to sacrifice the same amount of time, money, effort and loving care on communal objects as they will sacrifice, as parents, on their own families. In a democracy, where the expenditure of public money must be dependent on popular agreement, public bodies—whether in housing, education, or anything else—will never be free to choose the 'best'. This is not only, or even principally, because they will want to please as many electors as possible, or because of the pressure to economize, but because men, in their capacity as councillors or M.P.s or borough engineers, do not *want* the best. It is only as parents that they have a sufficiently profound and personal interest in the future to justify the sacrifice of present satisfactions for future blessings, which is what the best requires. Local councils, State agencies, civil groups will more often than not plump for what is adequate rather than for what is excellent. In town planning, for example, they will inevitably consider how best to meet present housing needs rather than how to build squares and crescents of lasting beauty. Only in a society a proportion of whose citizens can earn enough and save enough to spend money themselves on their own families, where the driving force of family pride is allowed a considerable measure of freedom, will spending voluntarily rise above the drab level of meeting day-to-day needs.

Yet the egalitarian ideal is profoundly opposed to the institution of the family. It depends for its realization on extracting élites from their family circles, so that they should neither be affected by the success or failure of their parents nor, in their turn, affect their own children by their success or failure. The egalitarian society has to be graded on the basis not of the family but of the individual extracted from his family. The ideal of a graded hierarchy of individuals during working hours being reduced, on returning home in the evening, to a common social status, sounds attractive. It seems to hold out the prospect of a society that is both hierarchical—which is necessary for its efficient ordering—but also fraternal, in that those at the bottom will not feel cut off from those at the top. But except in small, homogeneous societies, such a prospect is illusory. In a highly complex, industrialized nation, class distinctions do not divide society; they reflect the fact that society is bound to be divided and make the best of those impulses towards combination and community that do exist.

People combine into social groups on a basis of shared distinctions. If we do away with these distinctions, if we reduce all social backgrounds to one approximate level, with the overwhelming majority living in roughly the same kind of house, wearing the same quality clothes, this will not bring people closer together but drive them farther apart. If we do away with what makes people different, we do away with the very thing that makes them wish to combine most—the pleasure of finding others as different as they are themselves. Social groups must always be exclusive. They are held together by a shared sense of being different, even if it is the shared sense of being oppressed. The egalitarian must realize, therefore, that the more you make people the same, the less they will have in common—or rather the less they will have in common that they are proud of or aware of. An egalitarian society will therefore tend to be one in which the social bonds have been so stretched, in an effort to enclose everyone within the same circle, that no one will feel bound to anyone else. A class society, it is true, imposes arbitrary *segregation*. But a classless society does something far worse: it precludes natural *integration*.

This is already tragically apparent in contemporary Britain and even more so in the United States. The outstanding individuals who are now fighting their way to the top of the hierarchy have little in common except their shared functional skills. Their inter-relationship is of the same impersonal kind that connects the various members of a committee who have come together for some particular purpose and will separate when their objective has been achieved. And the more egalitarian Britain becomes the worse this will be. Depending on how far egalitarianism is carried, élite members will either all come from different backgrounds—and have nothing in common except their professional pre-eminence—or what they have in common, since it is shared by everyone else, will constitute no more of a bond than common citizenship does at present. Such an atomized élite, or combination of élites, as we are now discovering, is quite unsuited to fulfil the role of social leadership which society requires. The function of an upper class is not only to provide material from which perhaps a majority of the élites are drawn—it naturally never includes all the available ability—but rather to provide the framework within which the various élites can communicate and mingle, thereby exercising a continuous, corporate influence over society in general. The specialist regards the public good as beyond his technical competence. The great shortcoming of rule by constantly changing élites is that although only men of ability will occupy positions of influence, there is no body of men who, generation after generation, accept the obligation of determining the use to which élite skills are put.

All the problems of social leadership in a classless society are very much on view, as we have seen, in contemporary America. Élites exist there in profusion, but appear to be prevented from exercising any general function by the absence of any corporate cohesion. The politician, soldier, scientist, manager, technocrat, all wield great power within their own fields, but are socially neutral. That is to say, they accept no social responsibility beyond their particular functions. Not only do those at the top of the hierarchy evade the social responsibility which should properly accompany power, but their very failure in this respect is the necessary condition of their continuance in power. An egalitarian democracy will tolerate the reality of privilege, but what it will not tolerate is privilege which feels itself so secure as to produce paternalism. It insists on maintaining the notion of equality, with the result that those at the top feel threatened—and therefore insecure and defensive—and those at the bottom unfulfilled, and therefore resentful and aggressive. A mobile society—

or one where the notion of mobility is built into the national psyche—is therefore bound to lead to an irresponsible governing order, because those at the top are compelled to believe in the impermanence of their position—or to pretend to believe in it—since to do otherwise would be to develop the attitudes of a ruling class, which would be an unforgivable presumption. We have already seen in an earlier chapter some of the pressures in contemporary America which are challenging these traditional egalitarian assumptions; pressures which are promoting, in effect, aristocratic or paternalistic attitudes, particularly among the affluent young. But what has to be recognized is that these new attitudes are a logical consequence of a society that is experiencing the failure of egalitarianism; of a society, that is, which has passed through the experiment and is beginning to see its inadequacies.

This is the crux of my contention. A classless society stratified by achievement, measured either in wealth, as in the United States, or in professional, bureaucratic or corporate seniority, as is increasingly the case in Britain, faces an inexorable dilemma. Either those who compose the élites eschew broad social responsibility beyond their specialist fields because their superior position in the hierarchy is essentially temporary, insecure and conditional on continued popular approval—or the élite members, because they are consciously chosen for their particular qualities of leadership, feel justified in ruthlessly imposing their acknowledgedly superior tastes on their fellow citizens.

Perhaps I could illustrate both these tendencies in contemporary Britain by reference to that most essentially representative development commercial television, which seems to me to show the workings of élitism in a particularly revealing way. If the B.B.C. was a characteristic creation of Britain's prewar class system—perhaps its last great achievement—commercial television is surely the first creation of that strange new amalgam of élites by which we are ruled at the present time. In so far as it is influenced by its commercial backers it embodies all the vices of hucksterdom in a more impure form than we have ever seen in this country before—capitalist irresponsibility at its most disgusting—and in so far as it is influenced by its professional operators—producers, and so on—it embodies all the reigning intellectual fashions which are propagated with total disregard for the public good—intellectual irresponsibility at its most odious. (The B.B.C., subjected to this competition, has been reduced to the same level.) But the point to notice about commercial television is that it is the product of Britain's new men, of the class system as broken down by egalitarianism, and we see in its operations the characteristic behaviour of a capitalist élite uncivilized by the influence of a buoyant governing class—a lot of old money went into the new companies but it is the new men who have control—and the characteristic behaviour of a radical intellectual élite without any instinctive understanding of what public affairs are all about. Irresponsibility seems to me the hallmark of commercial television, the irresponsibility of people interested only in doing 'their thing'—the backers in making money and the operators in making 'good' programmes—with neither accepting any responsibility for social stability.

Why is it, we have to ask ourselves, that when in the prewar days the challenge of radio hit these shores it was possible to evolve an institution—the B.B.C.—which was authoritative and popular without being authoritarian and populist, which engendered both popular affection *and* respect. One cannot avoid the conclusion that something of the answer lay in the nature of the class structure of the period, the availability of men and women who were more than brilliant administrators or brilliant producers, men and women who saw themselves as custodians of a national heritage, members of a governing order. It seems to me that the Lew Grades of the contemporary society, and the bright young producers, have no such attitude, for the very good reason that they see their specialist success as an end in itself, not as a means of joining a ruling class, since one no longer exists, except on sufferance, under sentence of death.

This is not a surprising development. The self-made businessmen and self-made intellectuals are both types which have a useful role to play, but before they can be regarded as suitable members of a governing order, with an instinct for the public good, it is necessary to fit them into a class where specialist skills are put into the perspective of a superior responsibility and loyalty. The trouble about the pivotal figures in commercial television, as much on the financial as on the 'ideas' side, is that they have reached the top of their particular ladders, but the pinnacles on which they uneasily sit are, so to speak, lonely eminences, without the rich foliage of the old class system which, in the old days, would have absorbed and shaped them into respected members of a governing order.

The point I am trying to make is that the new men who made it in the old class structure saw success in their particular fields not as an end in itself, but as an opportunity to gain access to a governing class, with its own rules of behaviour, its own values and disciplines, all of which the new arrivals were prepared to accept. Today we have innumerable élites—those of industry and commerce, of the bureaucracy and politics, of the universities and culture—all with special skills and virtues, different styles, contradictory values, the Lew Grades and Arnold Weinstocks, the Aubrey Joneses, Alf Robenses, Kenneth Clarks, Kenneth Tynans, the life peers and the hereditary ones, a cluster, that is, of isolated élites, with no common social thread connecting one with another, no common accent, no agreed idea of authority; and because of this no stamp of authority that can be recognized and respected throughout society as a whole.

The commercial and industrial élites, dedicated to profit and efficiency, are wholly out of sympathy with the intellectual and cultural élites, dedicated to ideas and experimentation, just as the bureaucratic élites, committed to order and planning, are out of sympathy with the political élites dependent on popular approval. The top of society, in short, is fractured into a hundred pieces, with the result that the poor public underneath is confused and bewildered, living under the guidance of governing élites at war with each other. But this is bound to be the result if the élites are discouraged from forming themselves into a social class, in the bosom of which they can be gathered together, through intermarriage, through special schools, through a shared interest in preserving a special identity, into a body whose social unity transcends its professional diversity.

242

Egalitarianism, therefore, is the enemy of authority, since it prevents those at the top developing a general style arising from shared experience. But, as we have seen, it is not the enemy of power, since élites exercise great power in their special fields. But because their exercise of power is fractured and vertical, descending from the top of each ladder down to its base, and never stitched together into a fabric of social authority spreading over society as a whole, it lacks national cohesion and credibility. The public is pushed around and manipulated this way and that, as consumers by one élite with one set of values, as urban dwellers by another élite with contradictory values, as producers by yet a third, and so on and so on, but never as citizens in the round by a ruling class in the round.

What we miss today is a thread to bind the élites together, to give them a common stamp of social authority, so that what they have in common, as members of a ruling class, is more important than what divides them as members of different hierarchies. But without such a common thread élites will never enjoy enough confidence in each other, and inspire enough confidence in others, to govern effectively in a free society. In a political dictatorship, social authority is unnecessary, because political power fills the gap. But in a free society it is a problem, *the* problem, as we are beginning to realize since it is of the essence of free societies to prevent the concentration of political power. No need, presumably, to argue about that. But precisely because in a free society political power must never be concentrated, social authority must never be muddled since, if it is, political power inevitably begins to fill the vacuum. But it is of the essence of élites to muddle social authority, since if they are prevented from coalescing, prevented from forming themselves into a social class, they are bound to constitute a fractured governing order at war within itself. Stratification by élites, in short, is the guarantee of social chaos, whereas the supreme virtue of stratification by class is that it blends élites, brings about a compromise between the qualities and values of each, the intellectual and the commercial, the industrial and the bureaucratic, the political and the cultural, out of which evolves an authoritative style which, because it is a mixture, made up of a wide variety of human facets and skills, and is lived privately as well as practised publicly, appears human and acceptable, a magnet for the strong and a guide for the weak.

So we come back to the central choice, which is not between equality and inequality, but between different forms of inequality. The Labour Party position is to recognize the need for functional hierarchy—that is to say, differences of reward and status for different jobs—but to refuse to recognize the need for allowing those with superior status and higher rewards to coalesce into a superior social class. My own view, which I would hope is still the view of the Tory Party, is that this is a very narrow and arid approach to the problem of stratification, since it dehumanizes the exercise of power, fails to allow for the fact that professional success in the rat-race is not a sufficient basis for social authority.

A cluster of élites at the top of society, whose personnel, by definition, are continually changing, who have very little in common since they have all climbed different ladders, who do not know each other socially, who only meet for purposes of professional co-ordination, who have no security of tenure —such a power structure is so lacking in social magnetism and appeal, in confidence in itself and mutual trust, so divided and confused in purpose, as to be totally unable to elicit that degree of voluntary respect and affection which a free society requires if it is to be governed with a sure touch.

A meritocracy, in short, is not the answer which it was assumed to be, since the measures needed to prevent it from solidifying itself into an aristocracy involve denying it that broad social experience which induces natural authority; involve limiting its privileges to those needed for strictly specialist purposes—that is, financial incentives for businessmen sufficient to induce them to do their jobs well but not sufficient to allow them to bring up their families in a distinctively superior manner—involve a turnover at the top that precludes continuity, involve, in short, a ruling order which is neither agreeable to belong to nor impressive to be governed by— one expressly intended to be strictly utilitarian, without any of the charm and attraction that transforms the exercise of power from a mechanical function into a social art.

The central challenge in contemporary democratic industrial societies is how to humanize and civilize the exercise of power. Utopian dreams of creating a voluntarily co-operative society in which its exercise is rendered obsolete are now seen to be totally unrealistic; dreams moreover that could only have been dreamt in a world where the pressures of democracy were fundamentally misconceived. The actual structure of society, responding to democratic demands, becomes more and more hierarchical. Yet the egalitarian Labour Party answer is still meritocracy, the system by which the hierarchy is determined by victory in the rat-race, with faceless élites operating in a social vacuum.

Is this really the best answer? Are we so deeply rooted in egalitarian orthodoxy as to be unable to recognize that a class system is a more human arrangement, theoretically less satisfactory possibly, since the resulting hierarchy contains incongruities—fools and mediocrities at the top and wise and talented men at the bottom—but in practice far more likely to induce social satisfaction at all levels, since the human ingredients making up each grade will, for this very reason, be far more variegated, far more naturally blended, because unplanned and accidental, than grades stratified by merit only. The corollary of faceless power élites is faceless powerless masses; of a meritocracy, a meritless mass. The corollary of a ruling class may be a ruled class, but a class is an organic group, a human association, with a distinctive life of its own, made up of all types, which has had time to develop historical loyalties and traditions, even a distinctive culture. Of course it is more difficult to move up and down a class structure than up and down a hierarchy determined by merit, because when a man moves from one class to another his whole being is involved. The journey is deeply significant, almost as much so as a change of nationality. But far from this being an argument against class it is a marvellous justification for it, since it suggests that class is a system of stratification which allows for real roots to grow, for men and women and, most important, their families, to develop distinctive styles of living in which they feel naturally at home. Class certainly slows down social mobility, whereas egalitarianism promotes it. But the price of accelerating social mobility and maintaining the

245

hierarchy in a state of permanent social flux is to dissolve the intricate bonds of solidarity at all the various social levels, with the result that in a classless society nobody knows who he is except by looking at his position in the firm, his job or salary.

Can we not realize that egalitarianism has the effect of creating a nation of faceless men, as much at the top as at the bottom of society, a nation socially undifferentiated except by function, a nation with increasingly one style of life so loose and broad that it suits nobody, with one type of school so loose and broad that it educates nobody, with one style of manners so loose and broad that it falls flat on every ear! This is its social consequence. But, as we have seen, the organization of contemporary society is no less hierarchical than before. Orders are given and received, men push and are pushed around, even more than they used to be. But instead of taking place in a natural manner, against a social background designed to humanize and civilize the experience, against a social background which accepts its inevitability, this process occurs against the social background which, in deference to the unrealizable ideal of equality, makes it cold and mechanical, as unsatisfactory and unsatisfying for those at the top of society as for those at the bottom.

At any time, therefore, a classless society is not a good but an evil. But the dangers are particularly acute at just such a period as this country is now passing through, when the temptations for those at the top to impose their will, and the means at their disposal to do so, have seldom been as great. The prosperity and consumer equality made possible in modern industrial societies provide those at the top with far more popular diversions than the classical tyrant's bread and circuses. So profound is the present popular absorption with consumer pleasures, so persuasive the powers of modern publicity, and so blurred the obvious distinctions that once divided rulers from ruled that those who actually obey can all too easily be made to believe that they are really giving the orders.

In such a situation, it is highly unrealistic to go on talking of abolishing privilege, which has never been so inaccessible to effective popular control. The prime aim of a liberal society today should be to temper privilege with responsibility.

Egalitarianism, however, does precisely the opposite. On the one hand it so frustrates the status and material aspirations of those new men rising to the top as to create a dissatisfied and resentful meritocracy with the power eventually to take what society refuses to bestow; while on the other, in an effort to guard against this danger, it offers incentives of the most anti-social kind which encourage an orgy of valueless spending and vulgar consumption and preclude social responsibility by denying any security of tenure. A recognizable and secure upper class, accepting public responsibility in return for un-disguised privilege, represents a far lesser danger than do the élites in an egalitarian society, whose privileges are hidden and therefore uncontrolled and/or socially barren.

Epilogue

The purpose of this essay has been to consider not so much why one particular Labour Government failed as why no Labour Government is ever likely to succeed. Having approached the question from a variety of angles, let me conclude by summarizing what seems to me the fundamental point. It is, very simply, that democratic socialism is a contradictory combination of a political theory that needs giants to operate it and a social theory that produces only pigmies; of a political theory that requires rulers of unprecedented authority and a social theory that produces rulers of unparallelled lack of authority; of a political theory which, because it elevates the power of the State, requires a ready supply of statesmen and a social theory which refuses to tolerate conditions in which statesmen are likely to emerge.

It is easy enough to understand how this contradiction arose: from the socialist belief that the problems of government spring from the evils of capitalism and will largely disappear once these are remedied. In the resulting millennium, the people would find it relatively easy to govern themselves. Hierarchy, therefore, the whole purpose of which is to facilitate the exercise of power, would become less and less necessary. Equality was not only morally desirable; it was also logical and practical, since rank and privilege, previously defended as the twin buttresses of authority, would plainly no longer serve any necessary purpose.

What is now beginning to become clear is that far from socialism simplifying the problems of Government, it enormously complicates them: far from being a system in which rulers could safely be cut down to size, it is a system that desperately needs them to be built up to size; far from being a political system whereby the need for social hierarchy vanishes, it is a political system where the need for social hierarchy is vastly augmented. Far, therefore, from rendering inequality increasingly unnecessary, socialism renders such an ideal increasingly illusory.

This, in my view, is the central conclusion that emerges from any realistic study of the Wilson years: that the post-capitalist society presents political problems for which 'the people' supply no answer, problems which cannot be solved by reference to the 'general will', since none exists. In no field was this so obviously apparent as in economic management. Instead of supporting the Socialist Government in the measures it deemed essential, 'the people' barred its freedom of action at every turn. It was not, as we have seen, primarily capitalist vested interests that made socialist economic management so difficult. The primary opposition came from the workers themselves; from the very element, that is, on which socialism had hoped to be able to rely.

I do not believe that anyone, realistically examining the experience of the Wilson years, can conclude that the problems facing the Government were due primarily to the evils of capitalism. What has to be recognized is that they were due primarily to what it was hoped would be the virtues of socialism, to the increased power socialism accords to the working class. Doctrinaire socialists may like to hoodwink themselves that all would have been different in a purely socialist economy, and that the recalcitrance of the workers was due not to the dawn of socialism but to the dusk of capitalism. But ministers, who experienced the difficulties, know what nonsense this is. Their difficulties were, in a true sense, socialist difficulties; difficulties which are likely to get worse rather than better the more socialist Britain becomes.

It is time that socialists recognized this truth; that operating a rationally planned economy, aimed at social justice for all, is going to involve measures that the working class are likely to oppose, and that this necessity is not just a passing phase, due to the remaining sins of capitalism, but a permanent condition that has got to be lived with. Socialism, in other words, is not going to prove a form of society that minimizes the problem of politics by creating a clear 'general will', based on a cohesive and loyal working class, which government can simply follow. It is going to prove a form of society that maximizes the problems of politics, since by enlarging the power of the working class it enlarges the power of precisely that element which is most certain to oppose rational planning. Governmental *authority*, in short, does not become less important under socialism, as it was supposed to do, but immensely more important, since having weakened the disciplines of the market, without winning the voluntary acquiescence of the workers, more and more depends on the skilful exercise of political power.

What cannot be emphasized too strongly, however, is that democratic socialism made no allowance in its thinking for this development. It assumed that it would be possible to weaken the authority of the top of society precisely because the bottom would have become so much more amenable; it assumed that the rulers could be undermined because the ruled would no longer need to be ruled; assumed, in short, that the traditional Tory idea of consensus percolating downwards, from the top to the bottom, could be reversed, with the working class making its will manifest from the base of society upwards. These assumptions are absolutely crucial to the theory of democratic socialism, since they form the foundation for its faith in the practicality of egalitarianism. The necessity for a governing order was seen to rest on the evils of capitalist exploitation. Remedy that defect, and the working class would govern itself, with the assistance of expert administrators who would simply have the specialist skills necessary to give effect to popular desires.

Surely the Wilson years have shown that this picture bears no relation to reality. Far from diminishing the need for political leadership, socialism vastly accentuates it. It has had the effect of firing the passion for social justice, without supplying the fuel which was meant to feed the furnace. The fuel was meant to be working-class enthusiasm. A forced consensus based on the greed and selfishness of a ruling class was to be replaced by a voluntary consensus based on the public-spirited patriotism of the working class. It is clear today, however, after the experience of the Wilson years, that social justice cannot be built on this mythical base. It is clear that if the ideal is to be realized a very much more authoritative governing order will be required than anything dreamt of in the philosophy of democratic socialism. It is clear that the driving force of democratic socialism, absolutely contrary to what was assumed, will have to come from the top of society rather than from the bottom.

This, I believe, is the inescapable lesson of the Wilson years. Socialism is too important a crusade to be left to the socialists, social justice too grandiose an ideal to be left to the egalitarians. The paradox at the heart of contemporary politics is that rational planning in the interests of social justice will require that the utmost attention be given to *Tory* rather than to socialist political insights; to Tory insights which have to do with the maintenance of conditions conducive of an authoritative governing order rather than socialist insights which have to do with their elimination. The battle for socialism will be won, not on the playing-fields of comprehensive schools, but on the playing-fields of Eton, not by undermining the confidence of the ruling class, but by harnessing its political skills to the socialist cause, not by depriving the successful of the hallmarks of distinctive superiority, but in facilitating their re-emergence; not by reducing differentials in wealth and property but by putting them to the prime social purpose of developing a responsible and impressive governing class.

None of this, of course, is acceptable to the Labour Party, the origins of which are so deeply rooted in attitudes which take working-class benevolence for granted. But this benevolence is what the Wilson years suggest cannot be taken for granted. Herein lies the Labour Party's tragedy. It banked on a vast credit balance in the bank of public opinion as the working class grew in power and influence, but when Mr Wilson tried to draw on the balance he found it was in the red. The working class proved itself no more willing to co-operate with rational socialist planning, determined by a Labour Government, than with rational capitalist planning determined by the market. Indeed, there were more strikes under Labour than under the Tories. The trade-union movement moved further into opposition under Labour than it did under the Tories.

What the Labour Party finds so difficult to understand is

that industrial bloody-mindedness is not a consequence of capitalism, but a consequence of *industrialism* itself. Heaping coal into a blast furnace day after day, or pressing a button or pulling a lever or servicing a conveyer belt, are not activities that provide much excitement or satisfaction. Socialism does not transform them; it merely guarantees that the resulting frustration is increasingly blamed on government rather than on the employers. Factory-floor agitation, after all, is one of the few active pleasures which an industrial society provides for its less well-endowed members, and it is by no means certain that any amount of material affluence can altogether compensate for the thrills and tension of a really major industrial stoppage; all the more thrilling and tense for those concerned, obviously, if it is unofficial, with the decisions being taken not in some remote union head office but actually on the shop floor.

Professional people get their kicks and uplift in a host of different ways. The barrister enjoys his moment of high drama in court; the journalist when on to a big story; the financier when about to close a big deal, and so on. Their working lives offer moments rich in drama and fulfilment. When an official strike leader comes out of the negotiating room and gives the thumbs-down sign to his followers, he sees himself as the hero in a great tradition, marching in the footsteps of Keir Hardie and Ben Tillett; rather as the young barrister, for example, scoring a legalistic point over opposing counsel, sees himself in the great tradition of F. E. Smith or Norman Birkett. No wonder he looks happy. For once in his life he is doing something that makes him feel six feet high. It is not every day that working people hit the headlines, enjoy the heady experience of being in the news, see themselves on television, get singled out for *Daily Mirror* attention.

Being a responsible worker or a responsible trade unionist is exceedingly tedious and soul-destroying, and no less so under socialism than under capitalism. Responsibility means little more than being a willing cog in increasingly large and impersonal machines, whether they be industrial combines or massive trade unions. For the middle class, as much under socialism as under capitalism, responsibility is the path leading to power and glory. For working people it is a polite euphemism for compliance and subjection. It always seemed to me one of the more idiotic socialist assumptions that, given British working-class traditions, the increased affluence of the working class would lead to a more co-operative approach. It was bound to lead to the opposite, since for the first time the working class can afford to be irresponsible. In so far as socialism has played a part in bringing security into working-class lives, to that extent it has guaranteed greater opportunity for bloody-mindedness. Entrepreneurial enterprise on the part of management may have been stamped out—or bribed out—by the encroachments of socialism. But the socialists have been far less successful in killing off its equivalent among the more enterprising members of the working class. And the irony is that the more progress is made towards improving the material conditions of the workers, the more bloody-minded they can afford to be. In this sense, bless it, the Labour Party is fashioning for itself less a cushion on which to lie than a stick for its back to be beaten with.

And it is a stick, as I say, which will become thicker and heavier the more socialism succeeds. I do not deplore this. An irresponsible working class is essential to a healthy industrial democracy. Paradoxically enough, irresponsibility among the workers is a sign of their *embourgeoisement*, because it is a sign of vitality and independence. But for democratic socialism it is a sign of much else besides. It is a sign of the impracticability of relying on the working class as the firm base on which to build democratic socialism. Yet the Labour Party does so rely. The result is weak and tentative government that dare not stamp its foot, so conscious is it that nothing solid lies below.

Nor, as I have sought to show, are the new power élites, the meritocracy based on brain power, much more helpful. Fashioned in the mould of an ideology deeply unsympathetic to the problems of democratic government, they compound the malaise rather than curing it. Not only, therefore, is the cause of democratic socialism unable to rely on a consensus rooted in working-class loyalty, on a firm base at the bottom of society, but neither is there a reliable consensus percolating down from the top. Indeed the effect of socialism is to provoke both the top *and* the bottom of society, the working class *and*

253

the meritocracy, brainpower *and* brawnpower. I see no way out of this dilemma, except for the Labour Party to change its fundamental character. To some extent, under the pressure of office, this is what the Labour Government actually did, becoming in many ways more Tory than the Tories. But this raises the fundamental question: is it desirable for Britain in present circumstances to have two Tory Parties, two natural governing parties?

This brings me, in conclusion, to a final point. The Wilson years proved two things. They proved how difficult it is for Labour to govern effectively, which has been the subject of this book. But they also proved something else: how difficult it is for the Tory Party to oppose effectively. They taught us the disadvantage of having Labour *in* office. But they also taught us the dangers of having Labour *out* of Opposition. It always seemed to me that the strongest argument for getting the Tories back to power was not so much to get Mr Heath and his colleagues into Downing Street—beneficial as that may still prove to be—as to get Mr Wilson and his colleagues back into the job of giving a proper political outlet to all the discontents at present erupting in non-political forms.

This is the job of an Opposition party: to draw disaffection into its orbit, to articulate dissent, to give expression in an orderly manner to all those aspirations, fears and suspicions which, unless constitutionally canalized, run riot on the streets, or on the shop floor and campuses. It should be like a flame whose burning brightness attracts troublesome moths and midges, wasps and hornets, gathers them around it, so as to spare the body politic from their separate depredations.

Throughout this century the Labour Party has beautifully fulfilled this essential role, has been the focus and inspiration of discontent, never in office long enough for the flame to lose its brightness, or the moths and midges, wasps and hornets to scatter and annoy at random. Until Mr Wilson. For during the years 1964–70 Mr Wilson was at pains to play down this historic Labour role, to dim the flame. He sought to present Labour as staid and solid, more reassuring than rumbustious, turning it—or such was the intention—from a party of protest to a party of government. The result was that those who used to place their trust in Labour have turned elsewhere for succour, outside Parliament, outside the constitutional order.

This was bound to happen. For when Labour is in office, and behaving as if it felt at home there, discontent is deprived of any proper outlet. In name, of course, the Tories become the Opposition, go through the constitutional motions of being 'agin the Government'. But in a mass democracy this is far from being enough. It was enough in the eighteenth and nineteenth centuries, when politics were intended to reflect the limited differences of view of a ruling class. In those days the governing party were the ruling 'ins' and the opposition party were the ruling 'outs'. But today the role of opposition is infinitely more complex. It has to be able to embrace a radical disaffection that yearns for changes that go far beyond swapping the reins of power from one set of similar hands to another. During the Wilson Government, in this deeper sense, Britain lacked an Opposition. Disaffection, therefore, lacked a political focus.

In 1964, when this process began—the direction, of course, had been set by Hugh Gaitskell and was only carried through by Harold Wilson—certain optimistic assumptions were being made about the state of industrial or post-industrial society. The end of ideology had been proclaimed. The class war was thought to be over. Henceforth social peace would reign, and what would be the point of a militant Labour Party in an era of tranquillity? Such prognostications have proved tragically false.

True, some of the old tensions have passed away, but others have come flooding in to take their place. Industrial strife is taking new forms, a new kind of radicalism in the shape of student power has risen, social troubles have been introduced —whole fresh areas of potential disaffection have begun to unfold, just at the very moment when the Party which historically existed to embrace and articulate such pressures decided to change its role, wrongly believing that a party of protest was no longer needed. But of course it is needed, desperately needed. Take, for example, the problem of trade-union disorder. So long as working-class militants saw the Labour Party as a sharp instrument whose cutting-edge was intended to carve them a bigger slice of the capitalist cake, they were prepared to agitate within and through the Labour

Party. But Mr Wilson sought to blunt that edge, even to turn it against the unions. He did not succeed, but not for want of trying. Nothing would have pleased him more than to be able to rid the Labour Party of its notorious pro-trade-union bias, which so puts off the middle-class voter. Can we wonder, therefore, that militant trade unionism, seeing its traditional outlet for political radicalism blocked, increasingly turned to industrial disruption on the shop floor?

The same phenomenon is seen in the whole protest industry. Out of office, while in Opposition, the Labour Party used to take the lead in expressing indignation about all the subjects which in the Wilson years provoked violent protest. The effect of office, however, was to mute the voice of the Labour Party, and as its voice was muted so did the stridency of nonpolitical protest increase in volume, responsibility for protests passing out of the hands of the elected representatives into those of agitators and demagogues.

That is why the return of Labour to Opposition could prove so significant. A Tory Government bent on emphasizing law and order, and Labour Opposition back in its proper role of articulating dissent—such a combination could restore relevance to the political battlefield, so that these great new issues can be fought out in Parliament, where they belong, instead of running riot in the streets. Of course, the country needs the smack of firm government. But it also needs, just as badly, the uplift of passionate opposition. The hope at least is that the last election will now lead to both.